658 KEN

707

This book is due for return on or before the last date shown below.

-7. NOV. 1995

11. JUN. 1996

14. NOV. 1996

-5. DEC. 1996

10. JAN 1997

18. APR. 1997

17. DEC. 1997

27. MAY 1998

-8. OCT. 1999

14. MAY 2000

31. MAY 2002

-4. OCT. 2002

2 5 NOV 2002

3 0 JAN 2003

0 9 NOV 2004

3 0 NOV 2004

1 4 JAN 2005

1 3 JAN 2006

24 DEC 2012

709 15

MANAGING
WITH THE
GURUS

MANAGING
WITH THE
GURUS

TOP LEVEL GUIDANCE
ON 20 MANAGEMENT
TECHNIQUES

CAROL KENNEDY

C
CENTURY
BUSINESS
BOOKS

First published 1994

© Carol Kennedy 1994

Carol Kennedy has asserted her rights under the Copyright, Designs
and Patents Act, 1988, to be identified as the author of this work.
First published by Century Ltd
Random House, 20 Vauxhall Bridge Road, London SW1V 2SA

Random House Australia (Pty) Limited
20 Alfred Street, Milsons Point, Sydney
New South Wales 2061, Australia

Random House New Zealand Limited
18 Poland Road, Glenfield
Auckland 10, New Zealand

Random House South Africa (Pty) Limited
PO Box 337, Bergvlei, South Africa

Random House UK Limited Reg. No. 954009

ISBN 0 7126 6017 8

Typeset by SX Composing Ltd, Rayleigh, Essex
Printed in Great Britain by Clays Ltd, St Ives plc

CONTENTS

PERMISSIONS ACKNOWLEDGMENTS

Grateful acknowledgment is made to the following for permission to quote from their works. Every effort has been made to ascertain copyright and seek permission: any omissions will be rectified in a future edition.

Excerpts from *A General Theory of Bureaucracy*, by Elliott Jaques, and the following works by Peter F. Drucker; *The Practice of Management, The Age of Discontinuity, Management: Tasks, Responsibilities, Practices, Managing for Results* and *Managing for the Future*, all reproduced by kind permission of Butterworth-Heinemann Ltd., Oxford.

Excerpts from *Making It Happen* and *Managing to Survive*, by kind permission of Sir John Harvey-Jones, MBE

Excerpts from *The New Rational Manager* reproduced by kind permission of Kepner-Tregoe Inc. © 1981. All rights reserved.

Excerpt from *Implanting Strategic Management* reproduced by kind permission of Dr. H. I. Ansoff.

Excerpts from *The Business Value of Computers* reproduced by kind permission of Professor Paul A. Strassmann and The Information Economics Press, New Canaan, Connecticut, USA.

Excerpts from *On Motivation* and *Great Leaders* reproduced by kind permission of John Adair.

Reprinted by permission of *Harvard Business Review*: excerpts from 'Marketing Myopia' by Theodore Levitt and 'One More Time: How Do You Motivate Employees?' by Frederick Herzberg. Copyright © 1960 and © 1968 by the President and Fellows of Harvard College. All rights reserved.

W. Deming's 'Fourteen Points' reproduced from *The Deming Dimension* by Henry Neave, by kind permission of SPC Press Inc., Knoxville, Tennessee, USA.

Chart, *Principles of Management 1954*, reproduced by kind permission of The Conference Board, New York.

Excerpts from *Back-to-Basics Management* by Matthew Culligan. Copyright © 1983 Matthew Culligan. Reprinted by permission of Facts-on-File, Inc., New York.

Excerpts from *Managing Talent* by Philip Sadler and *A Sense of Mission* by Andrew Campbell, Marion Devine and David Young, reproduced by permission of Pitman Publishing, London.

Excerpts from *Reengineering the Corporation*, by Michael Hammer and James Champy, and *The Frontiers of Excellence*, by Robert H. Waterman, Jr., reproduced by permission of Nicholas Brealey Publishing, London.

Excerpts from *On Becoming a Leader*, by Warren Bennis; *The Art of the Long View*, by Peter Schwartz; *Building a Chain of Customers*, by Richard J. Schonberger; *The Customer-Driven Company*, by Richard Whiteley; *Managing Across Borders*, by Christopher Bartlett and Sumantra Ghoshal, all reproduced by permission of Random House UK Ltd.

Excerpts from *The Renewal Factor* reproduced by kind permission of Robert H. Waterman Jr. and Bantam Doubleday Dell, New York.

PREFACE

It must be more than 250 years since any individual could claim to know all there was to know through reading. The information explosion of the last twenty years alone may have caused as much frustration as enlightenment, even with the rapid search-and-find techniques afforded by computers. How does one keep up with all the reading needed to run a business or to master a business subject in the 1990s? It's a cry every manager and student of management utters at some stage: there is just too much information, too many hectares of print and print-out.

Business literature, if one broadens that to include economics and technical works, has been at the forefront of the publishing boom since the early 1980s: it is now the largest non-fiction category in Britain, and Britain is a long way behind the United States in business publishing. What in this tidal wave of words and ideas will stay on the beach, gleaming like washed pebbles in the sun, as practical markers for people working in real management functions?

While I was gathering material for *Guide to the Management Gurus*, this question began to emerge. Clearly many of the seminal management theories of the century continue to work on and influence today's thinking; they are rocks on which others have built, but still significant in their own right. Other ideas have been washed away – influential in their time but overtaken by the turbulent currents we now have to navigate. I began to look at the gurus' wisdom in terms of practical management function. Some passages continue to resonate on the manager's desk, but they are buried in thousands of pages. A beam of light is needed to find them, and to point to further reading. There are some books no manager or student of management should be without, and I hope the extracts selected here will impel readers to bookshop or library to search them out.

What I have tried to do in this book is to provide those torch-beams, to select passages that will inspire and aid people struggling with the disciplines of management, whether at the top of an organization or in one of the many functions that make them work – marketing, customer care, strategic planning, motivation programmes.

Each chapter deals with a different issue of management, and consists of an introduction to the development of key ideas on its subject, followed by extracts from the most influential writers, past and present. Because it is intended as a practical guide, rather more emphasis is given to contemporary gurus than to those of the past, though the polymathic Peter Drucker outlined so much forward thinking as early as 1954 that he dominates almost every sector. The work of Douglas McGregor (Theory X and Theory Y) also continues to throw up fresh insights thirty years after his death as we enter the era of self-directed team management.

Max Weber's theory of bureaucracy and Henri Fayol's definition of management, both dating from the 1900s, still have a great deal of resonance as we approach the twenty-first century (so, even more, do the worker-as-machine theories of F.W. Taylor, politically incorrect though they may be), but life is no longer as it was in their day. New, harsh conditions require new thinking, and gurus like Tom Peters now challenge their readers to meet those conditions rather than prescribe comforting solutions as they did ten years ago.

In 1982, Peters set himself on the road to fame and fortune with his and Bob Waterman's eight prescriptives to attain corporate excellence. In *Liberation Management*, published just ten years later, Peters offers only the bleak advice that nothing stays still; that competition gets tougher by the week, and that everyone in business today has to find his or her own ways of getting ahead, doing more with less, understanding the bewildering world of technology, thinking global and the rest.

Today, there are no simple prescriptions – probably there never will be again. But certain eternal truths endure, and return from time to time in different guises, and management theory is no exception. That is why it is still worth understanding 'Taylorism', if only to figure out why it continues to form a subconscious bedrock in many managers' minds.

Other eternal verities, like Deming's and Juran's precepts for quality control, remain essentially unchallenged, though they can be and are being constantly refined, redirected, and absorbed into new management techniques. And some new disciplines, like business re-engineering, are none the less valid for being a skilful rethinking and recombination of older techniques, though the flashy new packaging has an element of hype about it.

Management fads, it has been calculated by a British consultant called Hugh Macdonald, have a typical life span of eleven or twelve years from their inception in academic lecture halls through first exposure in the management journals to full-blown fame on bookstalls and in boardrooms.

The ideas whose development is traced here and illuminated by selected extracts are overwhelmingly in a different league. To take just one example: the essentials of staff motivation, of understanding 'the hierarchy of needs' and what makes people committed to their jobs, are as pertinent in the mid-1990s as they were fifty years ago. Some of today's fashionable theories, such as re-engineering or outsourcing, may not outlive Macdonald's fad span, though one suspects that the drive to 'do more with less' – which both these management tools deliver – will not go away, and that a return to the old multi-layered corporate pyramid is as unlikely as a return to that once-sacred political grail, full employment.

Each of the following chapters deals with a key management function and is designed for easy reference. The extracts, by their nature, can only be a 'taster' of the theories explored by their authors in books and articles, and full references are therefore added for those who want to pursue the topics in depth. It cannot be emphasized too strongly that, although individual passages are capable of inspiring and stimulating thought and action, the supporting text will enrich the process immeasurably. In some cases, such as Kepner

3

and Tregoe's 'Decision Analysis' procedure, it is essential to read the full text; the extracts are only a pathfinder.

It has been a personal choice and others might have chosen differently. One can only say, again: read the books. If my selection leads business managers and students to wells they might have passed by in the rush of events, it will have met and fulfilled its purpose.

Carol Kennedy
London, May 1994

WHO'S WHO AMONG THE GURUS

ADAIR, John (b. 1934). Britain's first professor of leadership studies (University of Surrey, 1979-83), now a management consultant and author of more than twenty-five books on leadership and management development. Claims to have been the first to demonstrate that leadership is a transferable, trainable skill. His teaching method, Action–Centred Leadership, defines leadership in terms of three overlapping and interdependent circles: Task, Team and Individual.

ANSOFF, H. Igor (b. 1918). Russian-born academic and thinker who pioneered the business understanding of strategic planning and management with his 1965 book *Corporate Strategy*. Has since refined his approach to take account of a more unpredictable business environment. Ansoff is now Distinguished Professor of Strategic Management at US International University and a consultant in San Diego, California.

BARTLETT, Christopher A. (b. 1943). Professor of Business Administration at Harvard Business School. Co-author with Sumantra Ghoshal (q.v.) of *Managing Across Borders* (1989).

BENNIS, Warren (b. 1925). America's best-known guru of leadership and adviser to four US presidents. Trained as an industrial psychologist and after a string of international academic posts is now professor of management at the University of Southern California. Like Britain's John Adair, he believes leadership can be taught. His key book,

5

Leaders: Strategies for Taking Charge (1985), written with Burt Nanus, analysed the leadership qualities in 96 prominent US figures.

CAMPBELL, Andrew (b. 1950). A founding director of Ashridge Strategic Management Centre, previously with London Business School and McKinsey's. Prolific author of books on mission and strategy, co-authored with other Ashridge academics.

CROSBY, Philip B. (b. 1926). US quality guru famous for the dictum 'Quality is Free', also the title of his best-known book. Former director of quality for ITT. Philip Crosby Associates in Florida run a Quality College.

DEMING, W. Edwards (1900-93). US statistician who became godfather of the worldwide quality movement. His mentor Walter Shewhart taught him in the 1920s that reducing variability is the key to improved quality and productivity. Along with his contemporary Joseph M. Juran, he took the message to postwar Japan, finding a more receptive response there than in US industry. His towering reputation emerged only in 1980, in the wake of a TV documentary on Japanese industrial success.

DRUCKER, Peter F. (b. 1909). Vienna-born doyen of management gurus, who has pioneered almost every management theory and industrial trend decades ahead of the pack; among them, the rise of the knowledge industry, management by objectives, customer care, marketing, mission, 'sticking to the knitting' (the core business), and even privatization, for which a Conservative policy document credited him in 1970. In his mid-eighties, Drucker still travels and lectures extensively, and produces a book almost every year. He is Clarke Professor of Social Science at Claremont Graduate School, Claremont, California.

ECCLES, Robert G. (b. 1951). Professor and chairman of the department of organizational behaviour/human resource management at Harvard Business School. *Beyond the Hype* (1992) was written in collaboration with Nitin Nohria, Assistant Professor of Business Administration at Harvard Business School.

FAYOL, Henri (1841–1925). French mine manager who was the first to formulate the tasks and responsibilities of management (the five basics were: to plan, to organize, to command, to coordinate and to control), but his book was not published in English (as *General and Industrial Management*) until 1949.

GHOSHAL, Sumantra (b. 1948). Associate Professor of Business Policy at the European Institute of Business Administration (INSEAD) in Fontainebleau, France.

GROVE, Andrew s. (b. 1936). Budapest-born US chemical engineer who helped to found the Intel Corporation in 1968. He has been Intel's president since 1979 and is currently a lecturer at the Stanford School of Business, teaching strategy and action in the information-processing industry. His best-known book, *High Output Management* (1983), has been translated into eleven languages.

HAMMER, Michael (b. 1948). Former MIT mathematician and computer science professor who popularized the concept and terminology of business re-engineering in a 1990 article in *Harvard Business Review*. Has since become a barnstorming performer on the subject at seminars and workshops. His book *Reengineering the Corporation*, written with James Champy, was a bestseller on both sides of the Atlantic.

HANDY, Charles (b. 1932). Britain's only world-class business guru, whose writings can be compared with those of Peter Drucker on economic and social change. The son of a southern Irish archdeacon, Handy established himself as an authority on organizational culture (*Understanding Organizations*, 1976). Recent books such as *The Age of Unreason* and *The Empty Raincoat* (published in the US as *The Age of Paradox*) have been bestsellers. Among his original concepts are 'portfolio' careers (to replace the corporate ladder) and the 'shamrock organization' (with non-core activities contracted out). Formerly a visiting professor with London Business School, he now concentrates chiefly on writing and broadcasting.

HARVEY-JONES, Sir John (b. 1924). Britain's best-known and most charismatic business leader; chairman of ICI 1982-87 and subsequently an author, lecturer and media celebrity as the 'Troubleshooter', a roving company doctor of pungent views, expressed in two TV series. He now runs his own company, Parallax Enterprises, and sits on many boards.

HERZBERG, Frederick (b. 1923). One of the 'Big Three' US motivation gurus - the others being Douglas McGregor and Abraham Maslow – Herzberg differentiated between true 'motivators' and mere 'hygiene' factors such as salary and working conditions, and invented the concept of 'job enrichment'. He is now Professor of Management at the University of Utah.

HOFSTEDE, Geert (b. 1928). Professor of Organizational Anthropology and International Management at the University of Limburg, Maastricht, the Netherlands, where he heads the Institute for Research on Intercultural Cooperation. He has worked in multinational companies as well as holding a variety of academic appointments from Hawaii to Hong Kong.

HOUT, Thomas M. (b. 1942). Vice-president and director of the Boston Consulting Group in Boston, Massachusetts.

JAQUES, Elliott (b. 1917). Canadian psychologist and physician who helped found London's famous Tavistock Institute of Human Relations. Best known for his work on group behaviour at London's Glacier Metal Company between 1948 and 1965, which discovered the need of workpeople to have their role and status defined in a peer-group context. He also invented the time span of discretion theory, a method of measuring the responsibilities of management in a hierarchy (how long the effects of a decision run before evaluation by a higher authority). After many years with Brunel University, Uxbridge, Middlesex, he is Visiting Professor of Management Science at George Washington University, Washington, DC.

JURAN, Joseph M. (b. 1904). Romanian-born US quality guru, contemporary and fellow-pioneer of quality in Japan with W.E. Deming. Both men worked at Western Electric in the 1920s and imbibed the discoveries of Walter Shewhart in reducing variability. Juran's method stresses 'company-wide quality' and the responsibility of management throughout the process: he has criticized Deming for being statistics-driven. His 'Management of Quality' courses have been attended by tens of thousands in over thirty countries.

KANTER, Rosabeth M. (b. 1943). Professor of Business Administration at Harvard, former editor of the *Harvard Business Review* and a leading authority on the management of change, including what she calls the 'post- entrepreneurial organization' – flatter, more flexible and faster to respond to changing global markets, but presenting career challenges to its people. She is a pioneer of 'empowerment' and the switch from 'boss' to 'partner' mentality.

KEPNER AND TREGOE. Charles H. Kepner (b. 1922) and Benjamin B. Tregoe (b. 1926) were co-founders in 1958 of Kepner-Tregoe Inc., the Princeton-based multinational consultancy specializing in organizational development and research. The firm became a leader in methods of analysing problems, decisions and performance.

KOTTER, John P. (b. 1947). Professor of Organizational Behavior at Harvard Business School and an international authority on leadership, culture and change management.

LEVITT, Theodore (b. 1925). A former editor of *Harvard Business Review* who almost single-handedly awakened US management to the importance of marketing strategy at a time (1960) when industry was geared to production and happily selling everything it made, including Detroit cars. Now

Edward W. Carter Professor of Business Administration Emeritus at Harvard Business School.

McGREGOR, Douglas (1906–64). Professor of Management at MIT from 1954 to 1964 and renowned as the inventor of 'Theory X' and 'Theory Y' (authoritarian vs participative styles of management, based on opposing views of human nature at work). *The Human Side of Enterprise* (1960) remains perhaps the most influential of all books on motivation.

McCORMACK, Mark H. (b. 1930). Agent to stars of sport, entertainment and the media through his International Management Group, who began by representing the then unknown golfer Arnold Palmer. He never attended Harvard Business School, which figures in the title of his most famous book, but a case study on his company is taught there.

MASLOW, Abraham (1908–70). US behavioural scientist who invented the 'hierarchy of needs' in workplace motivation, progressing upwards from basic physical necessities to those of esteem and self-development.

MINTZBERG, Henry (b. 1939). Canada's leading business guru and Professor of Management at McGill University, Montreal. Mintzberg has been hugely influential in defining the real nature of managerial work (mainly 'firefighting' problems and interruptions); in the design of organizations; and in the ways strategy and decisions are formed through 'right brain, left brain' (intuitive vs analytical) interaction. He was among the first to identify the 'adhocracy' – flexible project teams – as a future organizational model.

OHMAE, Kenichi (b. 1943). Head of McKinsey's Tokyo office and now the leading mid-Pacific guru. Ohmae taught Western managers how the Japanese strategic approach works with *The Mind of the Strategist* (1982). He is now a leading authority on globalization with his books *Triad Power* and *The Borderless World*.

PASCALE, Richard T. (b. 1938). One of the brilliant,

late-1970s McKinsey team that invented the 'Seven-S' framework to assess business performance, the others being Anthony Athos, Tom Peters and Robert H. Waterman. His 1981 book with Athos, *The Art of Japanese Management*, anticipated Peters and Waterman's *In Search of Excellence* by applying Seven-S criteria to contrasting Japanese and US companies and their management styles. The message of *Managing on the Edge* (1990) – that successful companies carry within them the seeds of failure unless they break old habits – is still not fully understood in industry.

PETERS, Tom (b. 1942). The world's leading example of management guru as star platform performer, commanding international fees to match. Former McKinsey consultant who teamed up with Bob Waterman for *In Search of Excellence* (1982), the world's best-selling business book. Peters now heads the Tom Peters Group and writes his own distinctively frenetic bestsellers about managing in a chaotic business environment (*Thriving on Chaos*, 1987, and *Liberation Management*, 1992).

PORTER, Michael (b. 1947). Professor of General Management at Harvard Business School, a charismatic platform speaker and a world authority on competitive strategy and advantage. *The Competitive Advantage of Nations* (1990), analysing why countries succeed in certain industries and not others, has been required reading for international politicians. Two influential Porter themes are the 'value chain' within a production process and the 'clustering' of industries that mutually support each other and strengthen a country's global competitiveness through its domestic base.

SADLER, Philip, CBE (b. 1930). Vice-president and former principal of Ashridge Management College (1969-90) who started his career in advertising and spent ten years with the RAF as a civilian consultant on leadership, organization and morale.

SCHONBERGER, Richard J. (b. 1937). Former industrial engineer who pioneered Just-in-Time and other Japanese production techniques in the US. A crusader for 'customer-driven performance', he now heads a consultancy called World Class International. His books argue that the links in a production process should be a continuous 'chain of customers', all demanding excellence. Within the chain, cellular manufacturing is a key to working with the process flow rather than across departments – a key factor in re-engineering.

SCHWARTZ, Peter (b. 1946). A leading authority on strategy and scenario-playing and a former senior management planner with Royal Dutch/Shell. Now president of Global Business Network, an international think-tank and consulting firm based in Emeryville, California.

SENGE, Peter M. (b. 1947). Director of the Systems Thinking and Organizational Learning Program at Sloan School of Management, Massachusetts Institute of Technology. His 1990 book *The Fifth Discipline* is regarded as a classic text on 'the learning organization'.

STALK, George Jr. (b. 1951). Vice-president and director of the Boston Consulting Group in Chicago. Author of 'Time – the Next Source of Competitive Advantage', which won the 1989 McKinsey Award for the best *Harvard Business Review* article of the year.

STRASSMANN, Paul A. (b. 1929). Veteran authority on information systems and management who has been involved with computers since 1954 and has published more than sixty articles and books on information management and productivity. Former vice-president of strategic planning for the Information Products Group of Xerox Corporation, he serves on the US Department of Defense Federal Advisory Board for Information Management and is a professor at both Imperial College, London, and the Graduate School of Business, University of Connecticut. Publishes his own influential books under the imprint of the Information Economics Press, New Canaan, Connecticut, USA.

TAYLOR, F.W. (1856-1917). The Pittsburgh Quaker

engineer who invented 'scientific management', forerunner of 'time and motion' and 'work study'. Taylor's approach, seeking maximum efficiency by breaking down tasks into separate movements and finding the one best way of performing each, was the basis for Henry Ford's mass-production revolution. It has long been outmoded as over-mechanistic, but Robert Waterman believes many managers remain Taylorists at heart.

TROMPENAARS, Fons (b. 1952). Managing director of the Centre for International Business Studies in the Netherlands, a consultancy and training organization for international management. His books *Riding the Waves of Culture* (1993) and *The Seven Cultures of Capitalism* (1994, with Charles Hampden-Turner) are establishing him as a leading authority on cultural diversity.

WATERMAN, Robert H. Jr. (b. 1936). Since his best-selling partnership with Tom Peters on *In Search of Excellence*, Waterman has published three thoughtful, respected books of his own; *The Renewal Factor* (1987), *Adhocracy* (1990) and *The Frontiers of Excellence* (1994), the latter focusing strongly on developing people in an organization and on fostering self-directed performance. Waterman runs his own consultancy business in California.

WEBER, Max (1864–1920). German economist who helped to draft the ill-fated Weimar Republic's constitution after World War I and the first writer on organizations to analyse the structure of authority and leadership in a hierarchy.

WENDT, Henry. (b. 1933). Chairman of SmithKline Beecham 1989–April 1994, following a career in pharmaceuticals that began in SmithKline and French laboratories in 1955.

Chapter 1

The Changing Organization

The nature of organizations, the framework within which managers expect to operate, has changed radically since the late 1980s and continues to shift underfoot like tectonic plates caught in an earthquake. From corporate icons like IBM, confident in their culture and power structures, we are suddenly bidden to admire lean, freewheeling 'disorganizations' like CNN (Cable News Network), the news network Ted Turner created in 374 days flat, or EDS (Electronic Data Systems), the data systems giant founded by H. Ross Perot which operates as a vast collection of project teams.

It all adds up to a massive culture shock. Even Big Blue itself is in the painful throes of change and renewal. The Swedish–Swiss industrial multinational ABB (Asea Brown Boveri) under its dynamic chief executive Percy Barnevik has demonstrated on a global scale that no organization today is too big or too entrenched in its culture to undergo wholesale change.

The change catalysts have been partly economic – big companies restructuring or 'downsizing' in an attempt to reverse damage done by recession or competition – but also, irreversibly, the product of deep social shifts towards the empowerment of the individual, of both sexes, and away from 'bossism'.

The tightly structured bureaucratic organization familiar from the 1900s to the 1980s, with its rigid hierarchies and reporting lines of responsibility, is on the way out, giving way to the flatter, more participative management that Tom Peters and other leading-edge gurus decree will be the way to compete successfully in the 1990s.

Yet the old dinosaur satirized in Robert Townsend's *Up the Organization* and Billy Wilder's classic comedy of office hierarchies, *The Apartment*, is a resilient beast, not entirely without its protectors in the management jungle. It has the advantages of familiarity and security in a harshly unpredictable business environment. Managers, understandably, prefer the devil they know to the devil they don't, and reporting structures comfortingly limit the possibilities of failure.

When Ciba Geigy (now known as plain Ciba), the Swiss chemicals and pharmaceuticals giant, embarked on a managerial cultural revolution in 1991, designed to liberate decision-making processes and encourage more autonomy and entrepreneurship in a devolved structure of business units, its chief executive Heini Lippuner observed that many of Ciba's line managers felt insecure at the prospect. Avoiding mistakes had become part of the culture, and being able to pass decisions up the line meant you were unlikely to make a serious mistake.

Today we are only at the beginning of the New Age organization, and time will reveal how managers respond to its exposed challenge. In some industries, dependent upon fast and flexible responses to volatile markets – high-street fashion chains, for example, or the information media – a lean central organization and devolved decision-making, made possible by advanced technology, is virtually imperative. Tom Peters in *Liberation Management* cites CNN as a prime exemplar for the 1990s; Benetton could be another.

Even in traditional areas of manufacturing, head offices are being pared to the bone and centralized controls kept to a minimum. Percy Barnevik, ABB's awesome chief executive, decrees that all head office staff can (and should) be cut by 90 per cent. America's currently most-admired CEO, Jack Welch, has radically transformed the structure of General Electric, the only corporate monolith to survive as a leader of US industry from 1900 to the present day.

Along the way from Max Weber's early twentieth-century concept of bureaucracy as the most efficient system of administration (because it worked on an accepted principle of hierarchy, with the office rather than the office-holder commanding authority), to Peters' liberated, entrepreneurial

16

company of the future, there have been several key developments in the organization as reflected in management theory
and practice.

These can be summarized broadly as:

- Weber's bureaucracy (early 1920s)
- Alfred Sloan's pioneering work in decentralizing General
  Motors (early 1920s, gained wide currency in early 1960s)
- Alfred D. Chandler's 'structure follows strategy' (1962)
- Elliott Jaques' invention of the 'time–discretion' principle,
  tying the levels of management responsibility to the span
  of time affected by each level of decision-making in the
  organization (1976)
- The first moves away from hierarchy to flatter manage-
  ment, signalled by Drucker, Handy and others in the 1970s
- Charles Handy's 'shamrock organization' with its tripar-
  tite division into core staff, contracted-out or fee-paid
  work, and part-timers (1989)
- The 'learning organization', described by MIT's Peter
  Senge and others (in Britain, notably, Bob Garratt), dedicated to continuous improvement and evolution.

The Weberian hierarchy continued its hold on organizational
thinking well into the 1970s, as can be seen in the twelve
'Organizational Principles' published by the American
National Industrial Conference Board in 1954, thirty years
after Weber's *Theory of Social and Economic Organization* and
widely endorsed in management books for another twenty
years.

Around 1981 there was also the discovery, led by a number
of McKinsey consultants who became noted gurus in their
own right, of the virtues of Japanese organizational characteristics which appeared to lie at the heart of Japan's growing
competitiveness in international trade. Richard Pascale and
Anthony B. Athos, in *The Art of Japanese Management*, identified the key difference between US and Japanese
organizational practice as Japan's mastery of the 'soft S'
values in McKinsey's 'Seven S' model. Where the most successful US firms, such as ITT, were adept at the 'hard S'
factors – strategy, structure, systems – the best Japanese companies, such as Matsushita, combined power in these with

'soft S' attributes – style, shared or superordinate goals, skills and staff.

In the same year as Pascale and Athos published their findings, 1981, William Ouchi's *Theory Z*, borrowing its title from an undeveloped theory of Douglas McGregor's in the 1960s, postulated that US firms had seven major characteristics which fostered individualism to the detriment of social values such as trust, involvement, cooperation and loyalty. All of the latter were nurtured in the Japanese industrial 'clan' or family, where collective values were emphasized and the line between work and social life was blurred. Ouchi believed that some of America's most successful companies shared 'Theory Z' characteristics, adapted to suit American culture.

Where the management writers mentioned above identified evolutionary shifts in the organization itself, others advanced that process by analysing the inner workings and dynamics of large corporations. The first deep study in the field was Peter Drucker's 1946 classic *Concept of the Corporation*, which analysed the structure and managerial characteristics of General Motors (for which Drucker had been working), General Electric, IBM and Sears Roebuck.

Broadly in the same genre was Alfred D. Chandler's *Strategy and Structure* of 1962, which also studied General Motors and Sears Roebuck, along with Standard Oil and Du Pont. Chandler's work, however, was set in an historical perspective which traced the development of the American industrial organization from its beginnings in the railroads of the mid–nineteenth century. His thesis was that the structure of an organization follows its managerial strategy, which in turn responds to and is shaped by external market forces. Chandler, since 1971 Straus Professor of Business History at Harvard University, was the first management theorist to advocate decentralization in large corporations, and *Strategy and Structure* is said to have been a key text for AT&T when that public service monolith was forced in 1984 to switch to becoming a competitive, market–oriented business.

Chandler, however, remained a believer in managerial hierarchies, arguing that a system of official gradations of authority helped managers to become more professional.

Hierarchies, of course, breed cultures in organizations, while cultures in turn entrench and enhance hierarchies. A key book deconstructing this complex interaction was Charles Handy's *Understanding Organizations* (1976). Another was Henry Mintzberg's *The Structuring of Organizations* (1979), distilled into the chapter on organizations in *Mintzberg on Management* (1989), in which the Canadian guru identified the following five basic categories of organizational structure:

- Simple or entrepreneurial, typified by a small hierarchy with the power focused on the chief executive, often the founder;
- Machine, typified by central bureaucracy, formal procedures, sharp divisions of labour, a large number of routine operations;
- Divisionalized: market-based divisions loosely held together under a central HQ and appearing to be self-standing;
- Professional: bureaucratic yet decentralized and dependent on the skills of its operating professionals, e.g. a university or hospital;
- Innovative, sometimes called an adhocracy: flexible, organic, solves problems directly on behalf of its clients, e.g., advertising agency, consultancy.

Of the last category, Mintzberg observes that 'almost every major industry established since World War II relies on the innovative configuration', with the exception of the airline industry. This analysis clearly points the way to the deformalized, team-based organization of the 1990s. Interestingly, the 'excellent' companies identified by Tom Peters and Robert Waterman in 1982 were overwhelmingly characterized by their use of small teams or groups, to the extent that these were described as 'the basic organizational building blocks'.

Charles Handy's *Understanding Organizations* identified four main types of organizational culture, some overlapping with Mintzberg's. Three out of the four were given characteristics associated with the ancient Greek deities, a fancy Handy extended in a later book, *Gods of Management*. The four cultures were:

- The power culture, ruled by one individual's whim and impulse (usually the founding entrepreneur);
- The role culture, sometimes derided as bureaucratic because its strength rests on functions, job descriptions and definitions of authority;
- The task culture, mainly project–oriented and dependent on individual expertise working in teams;
- The person culture, where the organization 'exists only to serve and assist the individuals within it'.

Cultural studies of the organization, embracing the management of cultural change and the leadership qualities this demands, have grown in importance since Handy's pioneering work. A leading US academic in this field, Edgar Schein, was a formative influence on Handy at MIT's Sloan School of Management in the early 1970s. This area will be explored in Chapter 11.

As the 1980s progressed, and the business environment became more turbulent with the rise of global trading competition and recessions that destroyed traditional manufacturing bases in the advanced countries, management gurus like Tom Peters, his erstwhile co–author Robert Waterman, and Richard Pascale responded with a new iconoclasm.

Managing was now associated with chaos (*Thriving on Chaos*), even danger (*Managing on the Edge*), and the constant need to challenge existing assumptions in order to reinvigorate the business (*The Renewal Factor*). From this deconstructed view of management came a new style of prescriptives, or exhortations: listen to the customers, cultivate suppliers, make innovations a way of life, break habits, foster creative tensions.

Towards the end of the 1980s, Peter Drucker, who remains a pathfinder after sixty years of writing and thinking about management, began to talk of 'flatter management structures' and the concept of the organization as orchestra, with the CEO as conductor. In *Thriving on Chaos* (1987), Tom Peters listed the characteristics of the past/present organizational structure as 'hierarchical, functional/integrity maintained', and those of the structure it must become as 'flat, functional barriers broken, first–line supervisors give way to self-managed teams, middle managers as facilitators rather than turf guardians'.

In Peters' *Liberation Management* (1992), the term 'organizational structure' in the index is followed by the reference 'see also necessary disorganization', and the book is subtitled 'Necessary Disorganization for the Nanosecond Nineties'. Peters' first use of the word 'organization' is immediately followed by advice to put it in quotation marks. 'To use the word without the quotes,' he writes halfway through his 834-page book, 'is to suggest the thing is real and has a discrete location.'

Old-style pyramid companies may survive, for reasons of habit and security, in less competitive sectors, but on the whole we are entering a world loud with the sound of moulds breaking. In place of prescriptives, Peters currently looses a kind of joyous anarchy upon the business world.

One thing is certain: the new order, or disorder, will be far more challenging to manage than its predecessors, and will demand a new breed of confident, independent managers not afraid to take decisions and make mistakes.

KEY TEXTS

MAX WEBER
The Structure of Authority. From *The Theory of Social and Economic Organization* (1924, translated 1947). Extract from *Organizational Theory*, ed. D.S. Pugh (1990).

1. A continuous organization of official functions bound by rules.
2. A specified sphere of competence. This involves (a) a sphere of obligations to perform functions which has been marked off as part of a systematic division of labour. (b) The provision of the incumbent with the necessary authority to carry out these functions. (c) That the necessary means of compulsion are clearly defined and their use is subject to definite conditions. . . .
3. The organization of offices follows the principle of hierarchy; that is, each lower office is under the control and

supervision of a higher one. There is a right of appeal and of statement of grievances from the lower to the higher. Hierarchies differ in respect to whether and in what cases complaints can lead to a ruling from an authority at various points higher in the scale, and as to whether changes are imposed from higher up or the responsibility for such changes is left to the lower office, the conduct of which was the subject of complaint.

4. The rules which regulate the conduct of an office may be technical rules or norms. In both cases, if their application is to be fully rational, specialized training is necessary. It is thus normally true that only a person who has demonstrated an adequate technical training is qualified to be a member of the administrative staff of such an organized group, and hence only such persons are eligible for appointment to official positions. The administrative staff of a rational corporate group thus typically consists of 'officials', whether the organization be devoted to political, religious, economic – in particular, capitalistic – or other ends.

5. In the rational type it is a matter of principle that the members of the administrative staff should be completely separated from the ownership of the means of production or administration. . . .

6. In the rational type case, there is also a complete absence of appropriation of his official position by the incumbent. Where 'rights' to an office exist, as in the case of judges, and recently of an increasing proportion of officials and even of workers, they do not normally serve the purpose of appropriation by the official, but of securing the purely objective and independent character of the conduct of the office so that it is oriented only to the relevant norms.

7. Administrative acts, decisions and rules are formulated and recorded in writing, even in cases where oral discussion is the rule or is even mandatory. This applies at least to preliminary discussions and proposals, to final decisions and to all sorts of orders and rules. The combination of written documents and a continuous organization of official functions constitutes the 'office' which is the central focus of all types of modern corporate action.

CHESTER BARNARD
From *Functions of the Executive* (1938).

Organizations are a system of cooperative activities – and their coordination requires something intangible and personal that is largely a matter of relationships.

ORGANIZATION PRINCIPLES 1954
From *Company Organization Charts* (National Industrial Conference Board, New York, 1954). Reproduced in *Controversies in Management*, by Alan Berkeley Thomas (1993).

1. There must be clear lines of authority running from the top to the bottom of the organization.
2. No one in the organization should report to more than one line supervisor. Everyone in the organization should know to whom he reports, and who reports to him.
3. The responsibility and authority of each supervisor should be clearly defined in writing.
4. Responsibility should always be coupled with corresponding authority.
5. The responsibility of higher authority for the acts of its subordinates is absolute.
6. Authority should be delegated as far down the line as possible.
7. The number of levels of authority should be kept to a minimum.
8. The work of every person in the organization should be confined as far as possible to the performance of a single leading function.
9. Whenever possible, line functions should be separated from staff functions, and adequate emphasis should be placed on important staff activities.
10. There is a limit to the number of positions that can be co-ordinated by a single executive.
11. The organization should be flexible, so that it can be adjusted to changing conditions.
12. The organization should be kept as simple as possible.

PETER DRUCKER
From *The Practice of Management* (1954).

There are five areas in which practices are required to ensure the right spirit throughout management organization.

1. There must be high performance requirements; no condoning of poor or mediocre performance; and rewards must be based on performance.
2. Each management job must be a rewarding job in itself rather than just a step on the promotion ladder.
3. There must be a rational and just promotion system.
4. Management needs a 'charter' spelling out clearly who has the power to make 'life-and-death' decisions affecting a manager; and there should be some way for a manager to appeal to a higher court.
5. In its appointments, management must demonstrate that it realizes that integrity is the one absolute requirement of a manager, the one quality that he has to bring with him and cannot be expected to acquire later on. . . .

Organization is not an end in itself, but a means to the end of business performance and business results. Organization structure is an indispensable means; and the wrong structure will seriously impair business performance and may even destroy it. . . . The first question in discussing organization structure must be: What is our business and what should it be? Organization structure must be designed so as to make possible the attainment of the objectives of the business for five, ten, fifteen years hence.

Drucker also stresses the requirement – and this in 1954 – that 'the organization structure contain the least possible number of management levels, and forge the shortest possible chain of command.'

ELLIOTT JAQUES
From *A General Theory of Bureaucracy* (1976). Extract from *Organization Theory*, ed. D.S. Pugh (1990).

Time-span boundaries and managerial strata

The manifest picture of bureaucratic organization is a confusing one. There appears to be no rhyme or reason for the structures that are developed, in number of levels, in titling, or even in the meaning to be attached to

the ⟝○ Mgr manager–subordinate linkage. That there may
    ⟝○ Sub

be more reasons than meet the eye, however, in the underlying or depth-structure of bureaucratic hierarchies became apparent from an accidental series of observations, hit upon quite separately and independently in Holland and in England during 1957 and 1958. . . . The same findings have since been obtained in many other countries and in all types of bureaucratic system including civil service, industry and commerce, local government, social services, and education.

The findings may perhaps best be described as follows. The figure shows a series of lines of command in which time-spans have been measured for each role. The diagram is schematized to show the time-span bands within which each role falls. It will be noted that as one moves higher up the hierarchy there is a fanning out of the time-spans, a phenomenon which occurs universally. The arrows from each role denote the occupant's feeling of where his real manager is situated as against his manifest manager.

What might at first sight appear to be a rather messy diagram reveals on closer examination the following interesting regularities: everyone in a role below 3-month time-span feels the occupant of the first role above 3-month time-span to be his real manager; between 3-month and 1-year time-span the occupant of the first role above 1-year time-span is felt to be the real manager; between 1- and 2-year time-span, the occupant of the first role above the 2-year time-span is felt to be the real manager; between 2- and 5-year time-span, the occupant of the first role above the 5-year time-span is felt to be the real manager; between 5- and 10-year time-span, the occupant of the first role above the 10-year time-span is felt to

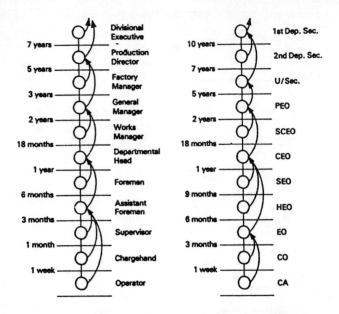

be the real manager. Sufficient data have not been obtained to show where the cut-off points are above 10-year time-span, but preliminary findings suggest a boundary at the 20-year level. . . .

The data suggest that this apparently general depth-structure of bureaucratic stratification is universally applicable, and that it gives a formula for the design of bureaucratic organization. The formula is easily applied. Measure the level of work in time-span of any role, managerial or not, and that time-span will give the stratum in which that role should be placed. For example, if the time-span is 18 months, that makes it a Str-3 role; or 9 months, a Str-2 role.

If the role is a managerial role, not only can the stratum of the role be ascertained, but also how many strata of organization there should requisitely be, including shop- or office-floor Str-1 roles if any. Measure the level of work in time-span of the top role of the bureaucratic hierarchy – say, chief executive of the hierarchy, or departmental head of a department within the hierarchy – and that time-span

Time-span	Stratum
	Str-7
(?) 20 yrs	
10 yrs	Str-6
5 yrs	Str-5
2 yrs	Str-4
1 yr	Str-3
3 mths	Str-2
	Str-1

will give the stratum in which that role will fall, and therefore the number of organizational strata required below that role. For example, if the role time-spans at 3 years, it makes the bureaucracy a Str-4 institution, and calls for four levels of work organization including the top role and the shop- or office-floor if the work roles go down to that level. If the bottom work role, however, is above the 3-month time-span – say, for example, 6 months, as may be the case in some types of professional institution – then the institution will require only three levels of work organization, namely, Str-4, an intermediate Str-3, and the bottom professional Str-2.

TOM PETERS
From *Thriving On Chaos* (1987).

Peter Drucker in his classic book *The Practice of Management* recommends seven layers as the maximum necessary for any organization. But that was in 1954, a more placid era. I insist on five layers as the maximum. Incidentally, that's the number of layers with which the Catholic church makes do to oversee 800 million members. . . . In fact, even the five-layer limit should apply only to very complex organizations such as multi-division firms. Three layers – supervisor (with the job redefined to deal with a span of control no smaller than one supervisor for 25 to 75 people), department head and unit boss – should be tops for any single facility, such as a plant or operations or distribution centre.

CHARLES HANDY
The Shamrock Organization. From *The Age of Unreason* (1989).

The first leaf of the shamrock represents the core workers, what I prefer to call the professional core because it is increasingly made up of qualified professionals, technicians and managers. These are the people who are essential to the organization. Between them they own the organizational knowledge which distinguishes that organization from its counterparts. . . . Organizations increasingly bind them to themselves with hoops of gold, with high salaries, fringe benefits and German cars. In return the organization demands of them hard work and long hours, commitment and flexibility. . . .

All non-essential work, work which could be done by someone else, is therefore, sensibly contracted out to people who make a speciality of it and who should, in theory, be able to do it better for less cost. . . .

The third leaf of the shamrock is the flexible labour force, all those part-time workers and temporary workers who are the fastest-growing part of the employment scene. . . . It is cheaper by far, though more trouble, to bring in occasional extra labour part-time, to cope with extra hours, or temporary, to cope with peak periods. Convenience for the management has been weighed against economy and economy has won.

The temptation is to exploit the monopoly power of the organization, to pay minimal fees for maximum output. The challenge is to resist that temptation and to pay good fees for good work. The shamrock organization has to remember that . . . there is no longer a residual loyalty to be relied on, no longer any implied promise of security in return for obedient labour. Good work must, in the long run, receive good rewards or it will cease to be good work. The contract is now more explicit, and in many cases more healthy for that.

ROSABETH MOSS KANTER
The Post-Entrepreneurial Corporation. From *When Giants Learn to Dance* (1989).

The model for the post-entrepreneurial corporation is a leaner organization, one that has fewer 'extraneous' staff and is thus more focused on doing only those things in which it has competence. In the post-entrepreneurial company ... more responsibilities are delegated to the business units, and more services are provided by outside suppliers. And fewer layers of management mean that the hierarchy itself is flatter. Thus, the 'vertical' dimension of the corporation is much less important. At the same time, the 'horizontal' dimension – the process by which all the divisions and departments and business units communicate and cooperate – is the key to getting the benefits of collaboration.

The post-entrepreneurial corporation represents a triumph of process over structure. That is, relationships and communication and the flexibility to temporarily combine resources are more important than the 'formal' channels and reporting relationships represented on an organizational chart. . . .

The post-entrepreneurial organization is created by a three-part mix: by the context set at the top, the values and goals emanating from top management; by the channels, forums, programmes and relationships designed in the middle to support those values and goals; and by the project ideas bubbling up from below – ideas for new ventures or technological innovations or better ways to serve customers.

HENRY MINTZBERG
From *Mintzberg on Management* (1989).

THE ENTREPRENEURIAL ORGANIZATION. . . . typically it has little or no staff, a loose division of labour, and a small managerial hierarchy. Little of its activity is formalized, and it makes minimal use of planning procedures or training routines. In a sense, it is non-structure ... [In his 1979 book *The Structuring of Organizations*, Mintzberg called this a 'simple structure' organization.] Power focuses on the chief executive, who exercises it personally. Formal controls are discouraged as a threat to that person's authority, as are strong pockets of expertise and even aspects of ideology that are not in accord with his or her vision.

THE MACHINE ORGANIZATION. ... highly specialized, routine operating tasks; very formalized communication throughout the organization; large-size operating units; reliance on the functional basis for grouping tasks; relatively centralized power for decision-making; and an elaborate administrative structure with a sharp distinction between line and staff.

THE DIVERSIFIED ORGANIZATION. ... a set of semi-autonomous units coupled together by a central administrative structure. The units are generally called divisions, and the central administration, the headquarters. ... Divisions are created to serve distinct markets and are given control over the operating functions necessary to do so. ...

Certain important tasks do, however, remain for the headquarters. One is to develop the overall corporate strategy, meaning to establish the portfolio of businesses in which the organization will operate. ... Second, the headquarters manages the movement of funds between the divisions, taking the excess profits of some to support the greater growth potential of others. Third, of course, the headquarters, through its own technostructure, designs and operates the performance control system. Fourth, it appoints and therefore retains the right to replace the division managers. ...

Finally, the headquarters provides certain support services that are common to all the divisions – a corporate public relations office or legal counsel, for example.

THE PROFESSIONAL ORGANIZATION. . . . The structure takes on the form of professional bureaucracy, which is common in universities, general hospitals, public accounting firms, social work agencies and firms doing fairly routine engineering or craft work. All rely on the skills and knowledge of their operating professionals to function; all produce standardized products or services. . . .

THE INNOVATIVE ORGANIZATION. . . . almost every major industry established since World War II relies on the innovative configuration. (One of the important exceptions is the airline industry, which seems to be a classic machine type.) Adhocracy is the structure of our age. . . .

The innovative organization cannot rely on any form of standardization for coordination. In other words, it must avoid all the trappings of bureaucratic structure, notably sharp divisions of labour, extensive unit differentiation, highly formalized behaviours and an emphasis on planning and control systems. Above all, it must remain flexible. . . .

The entrepreneurial configuration also retains a flexible, organic structure, and so is likewise able to innovate. But that innovation is restricted to simple situations, ones easily comprehended by a single leader. Innovation of the sophisticated variety requires another form of flexible structure, one that can draw together different forms of expertise. Thus the adhocracy must hire and give power to experts, people whose knowledge and skills have been highly developed in training programmes. But unlike the professional organization. . . . the adhocracy must break through the boundaries of conventional specialization and differentiation, which it does by assigning problems not to individual experts in pre-established pigeonholes but to multidisciplinary teams that merge their efforts. Each team forms around a specific project.

THE MISSIONARY ORGANIZATION. . . . What counts above all in such organizations is the mission, some endeavour that is typically (1) clear and focused, so that its members are easily able to identify with it, (2) inspiring, so that the members do, in fact, develop such identifications, and (3) distinctive, so that the organization and its members are deposited into a unique niche where the ideology can flourish. . . . At the limit, the missionary organization can achieve the purest form of decentralization: All who are accepted into the system share its power.

But that does not mean an absence of control. Quite the contrary. No matter how subtle, control tends to be very powerful in this configuration. For here, the organization controls not just people's behaviour but their very souls. The machine organization buys the 'workers'' attention through imposed rules; the missionary organization captures the 'members'' hearts through shared values.

PETER M. SENGE
The Learning Organization. From *The Fifth Discipline* (1990).

As the world becomes more interconnected and business becomes more complex and dynamic, work must become more 'learningful'. It is no longer sufficient to have one person learning for the organization, a Ford or a Sloan or a Watson. It's just not possible any longer to 'figure it out' from the top, and have everyone else following the orders of the 'grand strategist'. The organizations that will truly excel in the future will be the organizations that discover how to tap people's commitment and capacity to learn at *all* levels in an organization.

The shift to locally controlled organizations will not be complete until the new roles of corporate or central managers become clear. As local managers increasingly take on responsibility for growing and running local business units, what is left for the senior managers who formerly shared or owned outright those responsibilities? . . . One element of the role involves stewardship for the organization, 'guiding ideas', its core values and mission, and its continually evolving visions. But there are additional elements that are not yet recognized. . . .

The essence of the new role, I believe, will be what we might call *manager as researcher and designer*. What does she or he research? Understanding the organization as a system and understanding the internal and external forces driving change. What does she or he design? The learning processes whereby managers throughout the organization come to understand these trends and forces. . . .

In many ways the role of 'manager as researcher' is already starting to be practised. For example, in firms that are seriously practising total quality, local managers join with workers in the continual analysis and improvement of work processes.

This does not mean that central or corporate managers no longer participate in decision-making. On the contrary, they will be involved in many important decisions, often in conjunction with other corporate and local managers. But, designing the organization's learning processes is a unique role which cannot be delegated. It cannot be done by local managers because local managers are too involved in running their businesses and because local managers generally have less breadth of perspective to see the major, long-term issues and forces that will shape how the business evolves.

TOM PETERS
From *Liberation Management* (1992).

I try to remind myself not to use the word organization without quotes around it . . . for the brainware/software/ professional service firm is not an organization as you and I and our grandfathers have known it. Tomorrow's effective 'organization' will be conjured up anew each day. At Oticon, for example, after a quick scan of the on-line project listings, employees decide what to work on, whom to work with, and what desk to take their personal cart to for the day! At CNN, a thirty-minute, 8 a.m., nine-bureau, on-line 'meeting' invents the network for the coming day – until everything changes, which it usually does in short order. Such odd procedures will become/are becoming as commonplace in 'hardware' companies as in 'software' firms; Oticon, after all, makes hearing aids. . . .

JOHN HARVEY-JONES
From *Managing to Survive* (1993).

Organization should always be a function of the task which you wish to achieve, and should change constantly. . . .

Every individual in a business should have one person who is responsible for advising, coaching, rewarding and developing them. Indeed, the biggest change in organizational thinking is the welcome concept that the boss is no longer the supervisor responsible for overseeing the detail of your work, but is the coach, back-up, mentor and friend. . . .

As in everything else in business, there is no unique and single solution which can be applied uniformly to every company.

However, there are some principles which can be applied in drawing up organizations, and some concepts which may be of help. I feel quite strongly about one principle, which is that there should never be an organizational layer unless it is achieving some identifiable added value. This is best approached from the top down, rather than the bottom up. If you start by asking yourself what the role of the chairman is and what he can do, and then relentlessly push everything down – following that by what only the board can do, restricting board members to the unique job that only the board itself can do, and resolutely refusing to allow them the luxury of interfering and intervening in jobs which can be done below that level – you will speedily find that you are reducing the number of layers and, equally importantly, reducing the lateral numbers of people involved in each layer. . . .

In a business sense the primary goal for the nineties has to be to make an organization more than the sum of its individual parts. In itself, organizational design has to add value to the uncoordinated efforts of the mass of individuals who comprise a business. All too often organizational structures actually detract from the commitment and energy of the whole. Almost every business which carries out this 'value-added' approach will end up with a satisfyingly small number of levels, and a manageable number of people at the top. It is of the greatest possible importance that the 'value-added' exercise be done from the top down, rather than the bottom up. If you approach the exercise from the bottom up it is all too easy to persuade yourself that the person at the bottom cannot possibly take on all the responsibilities that could rightfully be theirs, and this is really a recipe for adding layers, rather than reducing them. . . .

Everybody who has worked in any company knows that the way things work in practice and the organizational chart are seldom the same thing. A sort of unofficial organization has almost always been developed over time, which finds the short cuts and tests the balance of power, and this will be constantly changed by the people who actually have to get the work done. The wise board will constantly look for the unofficial organization and for those people who feature largely in it. It is on these movers and shakers that the company's future competitiveness will depend. One of the aims of organizational change is to remove the impediments which the unofficial organization has sought to get around. This should release energy within the company to deal with the real problems outside – rather than trying to overcome the self-imposed constraints and limitations which the company has developed within itself.

NOW READ ON . . .

Drucker, Peter F., *The Practice of Management*, New York: Harper & Row (1954); London: Heinemann (1955)

Handy, Charles, *The Age of Unreason*, London: Business Books (1989), Arrow (1990)

Harvey-Jones, John, *Managing to Survive*, London: Heinemann (1993)

Jaques, Elliott, *A General Theory of Bureaucracy*, London: Heinemann (1976)

Kanter, R.M., *When Giants Learn to Dance*, New York and London: Simon & Schuster (1989)

Mintzberg, Henry, *Mintzberg on Management*, New York: The Free Press; London: Collier Macmillan (1989)

Peters, Tom, *Thriving on Chaos*, New York: Alfred A. Knopf (1987); London: Macmillan (1988)

Peters, Tom, *Liberation Management*, New York: Alfred A. Knopf; London: Macmillan (1992)

Pugh, D.S. (ed.), *Organization Theory, Selected Readings*, London: Penguin (1990)

Pugh, D.S. and Hickson, D.J. (eds.), *Writers on Organizations*, London: Penguin (1990)

Senge, Peter M., *The Fifth Discipline*, New York: Doubleday (1990); London: Century Business (1992)

Weber, Max, *The Theory of Social and Economic Organization*, translated 1947 by A.M. Henderson and I. Parsons, New York: Free Press (1924). Quoted in *Organization Theory*, ed. D.S. Pugh (above)

Chapter 2

The Craft of Management

As organizations loosen up and become lighter and more flexible in their structures, so the practice of management is evolving and adapting itself, becoming less rooted in sets of principles and more in personal qualities and skills.

We have moved from the simple elements of industrial management invented by the French mining manager Henri Fayol in the late nineteenth century (and broadly accepted by management thinkers for the next seventy-five years) to the alarmingly anarchic exhortations of Tom Peters to stop thinking like a manager and reinvent yourself.

'Am I a middle-management basher? Yes,' Peters declaims in *Liberation Management* (1992). 'Are most of the people who attend my seminars middle managers? Yes. Why do they come? Beats me. Middle Management, as we have known it since the railroads invented it right after the Civil War, is dead. Therefore, middle managers, as we have known them, are cooked geese. . . . Not every big firm is a Wal-Mart or CNN or ABB. Not every firm will be by the year 2000. But the trend is unmistakable. Frankly, I don't know how to do much more than exhort, "Build your own firm," "create your own network," "raise hell – it's that or bust".'

Holding the ring, reassuringly as ever, is Peter Drucker, the godfather of management gurus. Born in 1909, he has seen – and written – it all. His own five basic tasks of management, set out in several books in the 1950s and 1960s, refined Fayol and foreshadowed the move to a less hierarchical style of business administration. In the late 1980s he began writing and lecturing on 'flatter management structures' and using the analogy of the chief executive as orchestra conductor, drawing out the talents of his team under a guiding as well as controlling hand.

There have been perhaps ten 'big ideas' in management theory this century, culminating in the current concepts of the manager as entrepreneur (or intrapreneur), reinventing his or her tasks each day (Tom Peters), and as mentor, coach and team-builder (Peter Senge). After Fayol's five basic definitions – to forecast and plan; to organize; to command; to coordinate; and to control – and his fourteen 'General Principles of Management', one can pick out these landmarks.

- Frederick W. Taylor's 'scientific management' (1911), based on the measurement of work study and the fulfilment of optimum goals.
- Elton Mayo's theories of industrial sociology and behavioural science based on his researches at Western Electric's Hawthorne plant in Chicago in 1927-32. These experiments revealed that, regardless of working conditions, people performed better when they felt that they were part of a team and that management was paying attention to them.
- Douglas McGregor's 'Theory X and Theory Y', expounded in *The Human Side of Enterprise* (1960), positing respectively that people either naturally hate work and have to be coerced and controlled, or that they relish responsibility and respond best to the management that taps this potential. Before his early death in 1964, McGregor had the opportunity to see a Theory Y factory, with a large measure of self-direction in its workforce, prove itself at one of Procter and Gamble's plants: within a few years of its setting up, with McGregor as consultant, it was 30 per cent more productive than any of P&G's other factories. The company, says Robert Waterman in *Frontiers of Excellence* (1994), kept it a trade secret for decades.
- The motivation theories of Frederick Herzberg and Abraham Maslow, which gained recognition in the 1960s and early 1970s. Herzberg invented the concept of 'job enrichment', identifying those factors that led to working

satisfaction – achievement, recognition and personal growth – as the truly motivational ones. Apparently obvious contributors such as working conditions, salary and status were mere 'hygiene' factors, capable of causing dissatisfaction but having little positive impact. Maslow conceived the 'hierarchy of needs', in which workers progressed in their wants from the basics of food, shelter and warmth through security and a structured work environment to love, esteem and self-fulfilment. He thought Theory Y overestimated the average individual's ability to accept responsibility without direction.

- Peter Drucker's five basics of the managerial role, published in *The Practice of Management* (1954) and *Management: Tasks, Responsibilities, Practices* (1973): to set objectives, to organize, to motivate and communicate, to measure (establish yardsticks and appraise performance) and to develop people. In *People and Performance* (1973), he wrote that management's aim was to 'fulfil the specific mission and purpose of the organization; to make work productive and the worker achieving; and to manage social impacts and social responsibility.'

- Management by objectives and measurement, popular in the 1970s with Boston Consulting Group's 'learning curve' and 'growth-share matrix' that identified businesses as cash cows, stars, dogs or question marks.

- The Japanese lessons: Richard Pascale and Anthony Athos in *The Art of Japanese Management* (1981) attributed Japanese industrial success to the 'soft S' factors (staff, skills, style, shared values) in McKinsey's 'Seven S' system, whereas US management stressed the 'hard S' factors of strategy, structure, and systems. A similar message came through the hugely influential *In Search of Excellence* by Tom Peters and Robert Waterman, published the following year.

- Empowerment and the erosion of hierarchy. Rosabeth Moss Kanter's work in the 1980s, culminating in *When Giants Learn to Dance* (1989), outlined a 'post-entrepreneurial' corporate world in which managers become team leaders and staff are no longer regarded as 'overhead' but as sources of knowledge and value. This linked up with the move to flatter management advocated by Peters,

Drucker and others in the late 1980s and in a way embodies all the progressive trends of the century in industrial sociology.

- 'If it ain't broke, break it.' Pascale in *Managing on the Edge* and Peters in *Thriving on Chaos* (both 1987) evoke a new business environment of enforced change and discontinuity and argue that these can only be managed by breaking old assumptions and paradigms of past success. Peters goes so far as to describe management as a 'symbolic activity'.
- Manager as mentor, coach, team builder, project leader and the role model learner in 'the learning organization'.

Peter Drucker in 1973 identified these seven key elements in postwar management:

1. Scientific management of work as the key to productivity.
2. Decentralization as a basic principle of organization.
3. Personnel management as the orderly way of fitting people into organization structures.
4. Manager development to provide for the needs of tomorrow.
5. Managerial accounting – use of analysis and information as the foundation for firm decision-making.
6. Marketing.
7. Long-range planning.

Sir John Harvey-Jones, in *Managing to Survive* (1993), recalls from his own long career in ICI going through a different perception of management each decade – work and method study in the 1950s, systems in the 1960s, social and behavioural science in the 1970s:

The difficulty is that there can never be any single correct solution for any management problem, or any all-embracing system. . . . Most ideas on management have been around for a very long time, and the skill of the manager consists in knowing them all and, rather as he might choose the appropriate golf club for a specific situation, choosing the particular ideas which are most appropriate for the position and time in which he finds himself.

In the late 1970s the Canadian guru Henry Mintzberg broke new ground by studying exactly what managers did with their time and discovered a wide gap between actuality and managers' own perception of their work. Essentially, he found that they spent their days reacting to events and interruptions and 'firefighting' problems, and that half of their activities lasted less than nine minutes each. Mintzberg identified ten principal managerial roles under three headings – interpersonal, informational, and decisional – but found that senior managers' ability to spend more than half an hour uninterrupted on tasks only occurred once every two days.

Harvard Business School's John Kotter, in a 1982 study of general managers, also concluded that their work consisted of specific solutions to problems rather than the general application of set principles and skills.

In the roller-coaster world depicted in Peters' *Liberation Management*, prescriptives are out and the art of flying by the seat of one's pants – or, in Harvey-Jones' analogy, of choosing the right golf club for the shot – seems as good a guide to managing as we are likely to get. It is going to be much more a matter of innate abilities than acquired techniques. Harvey-Jones again, from *Managing to Survive*:

I believe that management is an art – and possibly one of the most difficult ones. Just as the artist constantly and consciously works to perfect his technique and to gain mastery of his relevant skills, so must the manager. Mere technical command of the skills does not, however, produce a virtuoso or a superb manager. It is that extra something which each of us brings from within ourselves that makes the difference – vision, judgment, awareness of the world around us, and responsiveness to that world, which leads to success. Managing is a matter of the mind and the character. . . .

KEY TEXTS

HENRI FAYOL

From *General and Industrial Management* (1916, translated 1949). Extract from *Controversies in Management*, by Alan Berkeley-Thomas (1990).

All activities to which industrial undertakings give rise can be divided into the following six groups:

1. Technical activities (production, manufacture, adaptation).
2. Commercial activities (buying, selling, exchange).
3. Financial activities (search for and optimum use of capital).
4. Security activities (protection of property and persons).
5. Accounting activities (stocktaking, balance sheet, costs, statistics).
6. Managerial activities (planning, organizing, command, co-ordination, control).

To manage is to forecast and plan, to organize, to command, to co-ordinate and to control. To foresee and provide means examining the future and drawing up the plan of action. To organize means building up the dual structure, material and human, of the undertaking. To command means maintaining activity among the personnel. To co-ordinate means binding together, unifying and harmonizing all activity and efforts. To control means seeing that everything occurs in conformity with established rule and expressed command.

Management, thus understood, is neither an exclusive privilege nor a particular responsibility of the head or senior members of the business; it is an activity spread, like all other activities, between head and members of the body corporate. The managerial function is quite distinct from the other five essential functions.

Fayol's General Principles of Management, 1916. Reproduced in *Controversies in Management*, by Alan Berkeley-Thomas.

1. *Division of work*: tasks should be divided up and

employees should specialize in a limited set of tasks so that expertise is developed and productivity increased.

2. *Authority and responsibility*: authority is the right to give orders and entails the responsibility for enforcing them with rewards and penalties; authority should be matched with corresponding responsibility.

3. *Discipline*: is essential for the smooth running of business and is dependent on good leadership, clear and fair agreements, and the judicious application of penalties.

4. *Unity of command*: for any action whatsoever, an employee should receive orders from one superior only; otherwise authority, discipline, order and stability are threatened.

5. *Unity of direction*: a group of activities concerned with a single objective should be co-ordinated by a single plan under one head.

6. *Subordination of individual interest to general interest*: individual or group goals must not be allowed to override those of the business.

7. *Remuneration of personnel*: may be achieved by various methods and the choice is important; it should be fair, encourage effort, and not lead to overpayment.

8. *Centralization*: the extent to which orders should be issued only from the top of the organization is a problem which should take into account its characteristics, such as size and the capabilities of the personnel.

9. *Scalar chain (line of authority)*: communications should normally flow up and down the line of authority running from the top to the bottom of the organization, but sideways communication between those of equivalent rank in different departments can be desirable so long as superiors are kept informed.

10. *Order*: both materials and personnel must always be in their proper place; people must be suited to their posts so there must be careful organization of work and selection of personnel.

11. *Equity*: personnel must be treated with kindliness and justice.

12. *Stability of tenure of personnel*: rapid turnover of personnel should be avoided because of the time required for the development of expertise.

13. *Initiative*: all employees should be encouraged to exercise initiative within the limits imposed by the requirements of authority and discipline.

14. *Esprit de corps*: efforts must be made to promote harmony within the organization and prevent dissension and divisiveness.

F.W. TAYLOR
From *Scientific Management* (1947).

By far the greater gain under scientific management comes from the new, the very great and the extraordinary burdens and duties which are voluntarily assumed by those on the management's side. . . .

The first of these principles, then, may be called the development of a science to replace the old rule-of-thumb knowledge of the workmen; that is, the knowledge which the workmen had, and which was, in many cases, quite as exact as that which is finally obtained by the management, but which the workmen nevertheless in 999 cases out of 1,000 kept in their heads, and of which there was no permanent or complete record. . . .

The second group of duties which are voluntarily assumed by those on the management's side, under scientific management, is the scientific selection and then the progressive development of the workmen. It becomes the duty of those on the management's side to deliberately study the character, the nature and the performance of each workman with a view to finding out his limitations on the one hand, but even more important, his possibilities for development on the other hand; and then, as deliberately and as systematically to train and help and teach this workman, giving him, wherever it is possible, those opportunities for advancement which will finally enable him to do the highest and most interesting and most profitable class of work for which his natural abilities fit him, and which are open to him in the particular company in which he is employed. . . .

The third of the principles of scientific management is the bringing of the science and the scientifically selected and trained workmen together. . . . The fourth of the principles of scientific management is perhaps the most difficult. . . . It consists of an almost equal division of the actual work of the establishment between the workmen, on the one hand, and the management, on the other hand.

Taylor proceeds to define what he means by 'science' in this context as breaking down and studying every element of a piece of work, much as every element of baseball is broken down and studied by coaches before the most effective method of performing each movement is drilled into a team. This became the basis of work-study and time-and-motion study in the 1920s and 1930s.

DOUGLAS McGREGOR
From *The Human Side of Enterprise* (1960).

The philosophy of management by direction and control – regardless of whether it is hard or soft – is inadequate to motivate because the human needs on which this approach relies are relatively unimportant motivators of behaviour in our society today. Direction and control are of limited value in motivating people whose important needs are social and egoistic. . . . So long as the assumptions of Theory X continue to influence managerial strategy, we will fail to discover, let alone utilise, the potentialities of the average human being.

PETER F. DRUCKER
From *The Practice of Management* (1954).

The function which distinguishes the manager above all others is his educational one. The one contribution he is uniquely expected to make is to give others vision and ability to perform. It is vision and moral responsibility that, in the last analysis, define the manager. . . .

Finally the manager will have to acquire a whole new set of tools – many of which he will have to develop himself. He needs to acquire economic tools to make meaningful decisions today for a long-range tomorrow. He will have to acquire the new tools of the decision-making process.

We can summarise by saying that the new demands require that the manager of tomorrow acquit himself of *seven new tasks*:

1. He must manage by objectives.
2. He must take more risks and for a longer period ahead. And risk-taking decisions will have to be made at lower levels in the organization. The manager must therefore be able to calculate each risk, to choose the most advantageous risk-alternative, to establish in advance what he expects to happen and to 'control' his subsequent course of action as events bear out or deny his expectations.
3. He must be able to make strategic decisions.
4. He must be able to build an integrated team, each member of which is capable of managing and of measuring his own performance and results in relation to the common objectives. And there is a big task ahead in developing managers equal to the demands of tomorrow.
5. He will have to be able to communicate information fast and clearly. He will have to be able to motivate people. He must, in other words, be able to obtain the responsible participation of other managers, of the professional specialists and of all other workers.
6. Traditionally a manager has been expected to know one or more functions. This will no longer be enough. The manager of tomorrow must be able to see the business as a whole and to integrate his function with it.
7. Traditionally a manager has been expected to know a few products or one industry. This, too, will no longer be enough. The manager of tomorrow will have to be able to relate his product and industry to the total environment, to find what is significant in it and to take it into account in his decisions and actions. And increasingly the field of vision of tomorrow's manager will have to take in

developments outside his own market and his own country. Increasingly he will have to learn to see economic, political and social developments on a world-wide scale and to integrate world-wide trends into his own decisions. . . .

The manager of tomorrow will not be able to remain an intuitive manager. He will have to master system and method, will have to conceive patterns and synthesize elements into wholes, will have to formulate general concepts and to apply general principles. Otherwise he will fail. In small business and in large, in general management and in functional management, a manager will have to be equipped for the Practice of Management.

From *Management: Tasks, Responsibilities, Practices* (1973).

There are five basic operations in the work of the manager. Together they result in the integration of resources into a viable growing organism.

A manager, in the first place, sets objectives. He determines what the objectives should be. He determines what the goals in each area of objectives should be. He decides what has to be done to reach these objectives. He makes the objectives effective by communicating them to the people whose performance is needed to attain them.

Second, a manager organizes. He analyses the activities, decisions, and relations needed. He classifies the work. He divides it into manageable activities and further divides the activities into manageable jobs. He groups these units and jobs into an organization structure. He selects people for the management of these units and for the jobs to be done.

Next, a manager motivates and communicates. He makes a team out of the people that are responsible for various jobs. He does that through the practices with which he works. He does it in his own relations to the men with whom he works. He does it through his 'people decisions' on pay, placement, and promotion. And he does it through constant communication, to and from his subordinates, and to and from his superior, and to and from his colleagues.

The fourth basic element in the work of the manager is measurement. The manager establishes yardsticks – and few factors are as important to the performance of the organization and of every man in it. He sees to it that each man has measurements available to him which are focused on the performance of the whole organization and which, at the same time, focus on the work of the individual and help him do it. He analyses, appraises, and interprets performance. As in all other areas of his work, he communicates the meaning of the measurements and their findings to his subordinates, to his superiors, and to colleagues.

Finally, a manager develops people, including himself.

HENRY MINTZBERG

From *The Nature of Managerial Work* (1973). Reproduced in *Controversies in Management*, by Alan Berkeley-Thomas (1990).

Characteristics: the manager at work
- Performs a great quantity of work at an unrelenting pace.
- Undertakes activities marked by variety, brevity and fragmentation.
- Has a preference for issues which are current, specific and non-routine.
- Prefers verbal rather than written means of communication.
- Acts within a web of internal and external contacts.
- Is subject to heavy constraints but can exert some control over the work.

Content: the manager's work roles
    Interpersonal roles
        Figurehead: representing the organization/unit to outsiders
        Leader: motivating subordinates, unifying effort
        Liaiser: maintaining lateral contacts
    Informational roles
        Monitor: of information flows
        Disseminator: of information to subordinates
        Spokesman: transmission of information to outsiders

Decisional roles
> *Entrepreneur*: initiator and designer of change
> *Disturbance handler*: handling non-routine events
> *Resource allocator*: deciding who gets what and who will do what
> *Negotiator*: negotiating

All managerial work encompasses these roles, but the prominence of each role varies in different managerial jobs.

From *The Nature of Managerial Work* (1973). Reproduced in *Milestones in Management* ed. H. Strage (1992).

To stimulate managers to analyse their own work, and to aid in this self-study process, the following 15 groups of guideline questions are presented:

1. Where do I get my information and how? Can I make greater use of my contacts to get information? Can other people do some of my scanning for me? In what areas is my knowledge weakest and how can I get others to provide me with the information I need? Do I have powerful enough mental models of those things within the organization and in its environment that I must understand? How can I develop more effective models?
2. What information do I disseminate into my organization? How important is it that my subordinates get my information? Do I keep too much information to myself because dissemination of it is time-consuming or inconvenient? How can I get more information to others so they can make better decisions?
3. Do I balance information-collecting with action-taking? Do I tend to act prematurely before enough information is in? Or do I wait so long for 'all' the information that opportunities pass me by and I become a bottleneck in my organization?
4. What rate of change am I asking my organization to tolerate? Is this change balanced so that our operations are neither excessively static nor overly disrupted? Have we sufficiently analysed the impact of this change on the future of our organization?

5. Am I sufficiently well informed to pass judgment on the proposals made by my subordinates? Is it possible to leave final authorization for some of them with subordinates? Do we have problems of coordination because subordinates in fact now make too many of these decisions independently?

6. What is my vision of direction for this organization? Are these 'plans' primarily in my own mind in loose form? Should they be made explicit in order to better guide the decisions of others in the organization? Or do I need flexibility to change them at will?

7. Are we experiencing too many disturbances in this organization? Would they be fewer if we slowed down the rate of change? Do disturbances reflect a delayed reaction to problems? Do we experience infrequent disturbance because we are stagnant? How do I deal with disturbances? Can we anticipate some and develop contingency plans for them?

8. What kind of leader am I? How do subordinates react to my managerial style? How well do I understand their work? Am I sufficiently sensitive to their reactions to my actions? Do I find an appropriate balance between encouragement and pressure? Do I stifle their initiative?

9. What kind of external relationships do I maintain and how? Are there certain types of people that I should get to know better? Do I spend too much of my time maintaining these relationships?

10. Is there any system to my time scheduling or am I just reacting to the pressures of the moment? Do I find the appropriate mix of activities, or do I tend to concentrate on one particular function or one type of problem just because I find it interesting? Am I more efficient with particular kinds of work at special times of the day or week and does my schedule reflect this? Can someone else (in addition to my secretary) take responsibility for much of my scheduling, and do it more systematically?

11. Do I overwork? What effect does my workload have on my efficiency? Should I force myself to take breaks or to reduce the pace of my activity?

12. Am I too superficial in what I do? Can I really shift

moods as quickly and frequently as my work patterns require? Should I attempt to decrease the amount of fragmentation and interruption in my work?

13. Do I orient myself too much toward current, tangible activities? Am I a slave to the action and excitement of my work, so that I am no longer able to concentrate on issues? Do key problems receive the attention they deserve? Should I spend more time reading and probing deeply into certain issues? Could I be more reflective?

14. Do I use the different media appropriately? Do I know how to make the most of written communication? Do I rely excessively on face-to-face communication, thereby putting all but a few of my subordinates at an informational disadvantage? Do I schedule enough of my meetings on a regular basis? Do I spend enough time touring my organization to observe activity at first hand? Am I too detached from the heart of our activities, seeing things only in an abstract way?

15. How do I blend my rights and duties? Do my obligations consume all my time? How can I free myself sufficiently from obligations to ensure that I am taking this organization where I want it to go? How can I turn my obligations to my advantage?

RICHARD PASCALE AND ANTHONY ATHOS
From *The Art of Japanese Management* (1981).

The striking differences between Matsushita and ITT lay not so much in the strategy of these two organizations as a whole, for in large part they were quite similar. The distinctions are certainly not a result of the matrix-type organizational structure that was nearly identical in both companies. Nor did the real differences reside in the systems – at least, in the formal hard copy systems, which in each case involved detailed planning and financial reports with a highly operational focus. These first three factors are insufficient to explain the differences we have seen. The real differences lay in the other elements – the management style, the staffing policies, and above all the spiritual or significant values – and, of course, the human skills to manage all of these.

THE SEVEN S's

Strategy	Plan or course of action leading to the allocation of a firm's scarce resources, over time, to reach identified goals.
Structure	Characterization of the organization chart (i.e., functional, decentralized, etc.).
Systems	Proceduralized reports and routinized processes such as meeting formats.
Staff	'Demographic' description of important personnel categories within the firm (i.e., engineers, entrepreneurs, MBAs, etc.). 'Staff' is *not* meant in line-staff terms.
Style	Characterization of how key managers behave in achieving the organization's goals; also the cultural style of the organization.
Skills	Distinctive capabilities of key personnel or the firm as a whole.
Superordinate Goals	The significant meanings or guiding concepts that an organization imbues in its members.

TOM PETERS
From *Thriving on Chaos* (1987).

Managing at any time, but more than ever today, is a symbolic activity. It involves energizing people, often large numbers of people, to do new things they previously had not thought important. Building a compelling case – to really deliver a quality product, to double investment in research and development, to step out and take risks each day (e.g., make suggestions about cost-cutting when you are already afraid of losing your job) – is an emotional process at least as much as it is a rational one.

It requires us, as managers, to persuade people quickly to share our sense of urgency about new priorities; to develop a personal, soul-deep animus toward things as they are; to get up the nerve and energy to take on the forces of inertia that work against any significant program for change. The best leaders, especially in chaotic conditions (effective generals, leaders of revolution), almost without exception and at every level, are master users of stories and symbols.

ROSABETH MOSS KANTER
From *When Giants Learn to Dance* (1989).

There are seven skills and sensibilities that must be cultivated if managers and professionals are to become true business athletes.

First they must *learn to operate without the might of the hierarchy behind them*. The crutch of authority must be thrown away and replaced by their own personal ability to make relationships, use influence, and work with others to achieve results. . . .

Second, business athletes must *know how to 'compete' in a way that enhances rather than undercuts cooperation*. They must be oriented to achieving the highest standard of excellence rather than to wiping out the competition. . . .

Third, and related, business athletes must *operate with the highest ethical standards*. While business ethics have always been important from a social and moral point of view, they also become a pragmatic requirement in the corporate Olympics. The doing-more-with-less strategies place an even greater premium on trust than did the adversarial-protective business practices of the traditional corporation. Business collaborations, joint ventures, labor-management partnerships, and other stakeholder alliances all involve the element of trust – a commitment of strategic information or key resources to the partners. . . .

A fourth asset for business athletes is to *have a dose of humility* sprinkled on their basic self-confidence, a humility that says that there are always new things to learn. . . .

Fifth, business athletes must *develop a process focus* – a respect for the process of implementation as well as the substance of what is implemented. They need to be aware that *how* things are done is every bit as important as *what* is done. . . .

Sixth, business athletes must *be multifaceted and ambidextrous*, able to work across functions and business units to find synergies that multiply value, able to form alliances when opportune but to cut ties when necessary. . . .

Seventh, business athletes must *gain satisfaction from results* and be willing to stake their own rewards on them. The accomplishment itself is really the only standard for the business athlete.

PETER M. SENGE
From *The Fifth Discipline* (1990).

The shift to locally controlled organizations will not be complete until the new roles of corporate or central managers become clear. As local managers increasingly take on responsibility for growing and running local business units, what is left for the senior managers who formerly shared or owned outright those responsibilities? One element of the role involves stewardship for the organization, 'guiding ideas', its core values and mission, and its continually evolving visions. But there are additional elements that are not yet recognized. . . .

The essence of the new role, I believe, will be what we might call *manager as researcher and designer*. What does she or he research? Understanding the organization as a system and understanding the internal and external forces driving change. What does she or he design? The learning processes whereby managers throughout the organization come to understand these trends and forces. . . .

In many ways the role of 'manager as researcher' is already starting to be practised. For example, in firms that are seriously practising total quality, local managers join with workers in the continual analysis and improvement of work processes.

This does not mean that central or corporate managers no longer participate in decision making. On the contrary, they will be involved in many important decisions, often in conjunction with other corporate and local managers. But, designing the organization's learning processes is a unique role which cannot be delegated. It cannot be done by local managers because local managers are too involved in running their businesses and because local managers generally have less breadth of perspective to see the major, long-term issues and forces that will shape how the business evolves.

NOW READ ON. . .

Drucker, Peter F., *The Practice of Management*, New York: Harper & Row (1954); London: Heinemann (1955)

Drucker, Peter F., *Management: Tasks, Responsibilities, Practices*, London: Heinemann; New York: Harper & Row (1973)

Fayol, Henri *General and Industrial Management*, translated by Constance Storrs, London: Pitman (1949). Quoted in *Controversies in Management* by Alan Berkeley-Thomas, London: Routledge (1993)

Kanter, R.M., *When Giants Learn to Dance*, New York and London: Simon & Schuster (1989)

McGregor, Douglas, *The Human Side of Enterprise*, New York: McGraw-Hill (1960)

Mintzberg, Henry, *The Nature of Managerial Work*, New York: Harper and Row (1973, 1980). First extract quoted in *Controversies in Management* by Alan Berkeley-Thomas, London: Routledge (1993)

Pascale, R.T. and Athos, A.G., *The Art of Japanese Management*, New York: Simon & Schuster (1981); London: Allen Lane (1982), Penguin Books (1986)

Peters, Tom, *Thriving on Chaos*, New York: Alfred A. Knopf (1987); London: Macmillan (1988)

Senge, Peter M., *The Fifth Discipline*, New York: Doubleday (1990); London: Century (1991)

Taylor, F.W., *Scientific Management*, New York: Harper and Row (1947). Quoted in *Organization Theory*, ed. D.S. Pugh, London: Penguin Books (1990)

Chapter 3

Managing Change

Managing change is nothing new in itself; what management is now having to live with is discontinuous change rather than steady or incremental change. Twenty years ago discontinuity in business life was an intermittent phenomenon – a war in a key strategic area, a huge interest-rate hike, the oil-price shocks of the early 1970s. It is now an inbuilt factor, the result not only of unforeseen geopolitical developments such as the collapse of European Communism with all its social and economic implications, but of ever-cheaper and smarter technology changing markets and competitive strategy underneath our feet, and of fundamental shifts in public aspirations, exemplified by the environmental revolution.

Consumer products need to respond far faster than they used to: think how quickly ozone-friendly hairsprays and deodorants have moved from being a fringe interest to a global market. It is a bit like chaos theory, where the fluttering of a butterfly's wings in the Amazonian rain forest is said eventually to cause a storm in Chicago. Consumer shifts are reflected on a much wider world stage than they used to be: as Kenichi Ohmae, Japan's guru of globalization, says: 'Sovereignty has passed from nations to consumers.'

There is no escape from the external onslaught of events and market pressures; no business is an island, and organizations are having to break the old moulds and fashion strange new ones. As Sir John Harvey-Jones writes in *Managing to Survive* (1993): 'There is unlikely to be any business or institution which will escape radical change in the nineties, and the choices before us are to manage it ourselves or have such change forced upon us.'

The most influential management books since 1985 have taken managing radical change as their theme. The titles say it all: *Thriving on Chaos, Managing on the Edge, The Age of Unreason*. We have moved a long way from the ordered certainties of Douglas McGregor's *The Human Side of Enterprise*, Alfred D. Chandler's *Strategy and Structure*, and even Peters' and Waterman's *In Search of Excellence*. Common to all the management-of-change books is the shift from hierarchical management to team-building, adhocracy, a willingness to break hallowed moulds of behaviour and 'the way it's always been done' – to 'think upside-down', in Charles Handy's phrase – and an understanding that the nature of business leadership has changed as well, to the manager as team-builder, project leader and mentor.

Other components of change in the last decade, such as the quality revolution and its indispensable ally, close attention to the customer, are by now a conventional part of business wisdom, though in practice many managers are still grappling with the day-to-day problems that a quality drive, for example, throws up.

Change management in the early, recessionary 1990s also embraced something else, which is examined later in this book; the radical overhaul of organizations known as 'business re-engineering' or 'business process redesign'. Again, this involves wholesale and discontinuous rather than piecemeal change, though this is no new phenomenon. Companies have been taken apart and restructured since Alfred D. Sloan took on the ailing, fragmented car companies of early 1920s America and forged them into General Motors, the world's biggest and most powerful industrial corporation.

Harvey-Jones implemented many radical changes at ICI in the early 1980s, effectively 're-engineering' a new divisional and board structure and ethos. In *Managing to Survive*, he speaks from experience when he writes: 'It is impossible to change organizations which do not accept the danger of their present way of doing things. . . . Organizations only change when the people in them change, and people will only change when they accept in their hearts that change must occur.'

Leadership is therefore at the heart of managing change.

This is a subject dealt with separately in this book, because leadership studies have gained in importance since the 1970s, and the concept has evolved along with the destructuring, 'de-bossing' and informalization of the business organization. But its importance in gaining the acceptance of change, and in managing the hugely more challenging business problems of the 1990s, cannot be overestimated.

KEY TEXTS

ROSABETH MOSS KANTER
From *The Change Masters* (1983).

The first step in change mastery is understanding how individuals can exert leverage in an organization – the skills, strategies, power tools, and power tactics successful corporate entrepreneurs use to turn ideas into innovations. Getting a promising new idea through the system – or pushing others to do it – is the way in which corporate citizens with an entrepreneurial spirit make a difference for their organizations.

'Corporate entrepreneurs' are the people who test limits and create new possibilities for organizational action by pushing and directing the innovation process. They may exercise their power skills in a number of realms – not only those which are defined as 'responsible for innovation', like product development or design engineering.

I have found corporate entrepreneurs in every function, bringing about a variety of changes appropriate for their own territories. Some were *system builders* (e.g., designers of new market-research departments in insurance companies, of long-range financial-planning and budgeting systems in rapidly growing computer firms). Others were *loss cutters* (e.g., prime movers behind getting foundering products into production faster, behind replacing obsolete quality-control systems in record time). Still others were *socially conscious pioneers* (e.g., developers of task forces to reduce the turnover of women in sales, of new structures to engage employees in solving productivity problems).

And there were *sensitive readers of cues about the need for strategy shifts* (e.g., fighters for reduced manufacturing of favored products because of anticipated market decline, for culling out the losers among 1,200 product options offered to customers).

These 'new entrepreneurs' do not start businesses; they improve them. They push the creation of new products, lead the development of new production technology, or experiment with new, more humanly responsive work practices. . . .

Change masters are – literally – the right people in the right place at the right time. The *right people* are the ones with the ideas that move beyond the organization's established practice, ideas they can form into visions. The *right places* are the integrative environments that support innovation, encourage the building of coalitions and teams to support and implement visions. The *right times* are those moments in the flow of organizational history when it is possible to reconstruct reality on the basis of accumulated innovations to shape a more productive and successful future.

TOM PETERS
From *Thriving on Chaos* (1987).

'What have you changed lately?' 'How fast are you changing?' and 'Are you pursuing bold enough change goals?' must become pressing questions asked of any manager, at any level, in any function, as a matter of course. For instance, during each staff meeting, go around the table posing the question to each colleague. Don't spend much time, perhaps no more than ten minutes for ten people. But do it, ritualistically. Make the simple question a prime element in your formal performance appraisal system, as well as in your informal monthly sit-down appraisal: 'What have you changed? How much have you changed? What are you planning to change next? What are your direct reports changing? What have they changed in the last two days, two weeks, two months? How bold are the goals of your change program?'

My assessment of the surprising continued vitality of 3M, PepsiCo, and Citicorp, arguably three of the fastest-moving giant firms in the United States, is that they are, above all, impatient. They'll reorganize on a dime, while others barely have the energy to do so every half-dozen years. In fact, my own measure is that *if you aren't reorganizing, pretty substantially, once every six to twelve months, you're probably out of step with the times. . . .*

Lately I've been ending my speeches with a snide observation which directly concerns this prescription: 'If you are interested in keeping your jobs, ask yourself at the end of the day, every day, 'What exactly and precisely and explicitly is being done in my work area differently from the way it was done when I came to work in the morning?' The average manager starts each and every day as an expense item ('wealth dissipator', in the words of Brunswick's Jack Reichert), not a revenue enhancer. You must earn the right to draw your substantial managerial salaries. The only way to do so is by making things different and better. Different and better today can only mean – changed, acted upon. If you can't put your hands on something – a coaching session that's leading to demonstrably new behavior, a changed form or eliminated rule – that's being done differently in the afternoon from the way it was done in the morning, then you haven't been alive.' Furthermore, that specific something changed today had better have been changed in pursuit of a very bold goal (i.e., a 90 per cent decrease in defects in the next thirty-six months). That is, the moment's tangible change must be in pursuit of dramatic change.

It's tough medicine. The manager, in today's world, doesn't get paid to be a 'steward of resources', a favored term not so many years ago. He or she gets paid for one and only one thing – to make things better (incrementally and dramatically), to change things, to act – today.

JOHN HARVEY-JONES
From *Making It Happen* (1988).

> Management . . . is not about the preservation of the status quo, it is about maintaining the highest rate of change that the organization and the people within it can stand.

From *Managing to Survive* (1993).

In my belief, the greatest personal skill needed for this decade will be to manage radical change. There is unlikely to be any business or institution which will escape radical change in the nineties and the choices before us are to manage it ourselves or to have such change forced upon us. . . . It is impossible to change organizations which do not accept the dangers of their present way of doing things. It is certainly true that the greatest risk of all is making no change, because it is inevitable that others will overtake you – but this is a truism that is not always easy to accept. Organizations only change when the people in them change, and people will only change when they accept in their hearts that change must occur. Change is a 'hearts and minds' job and the engines of change are dissatisfaction with, and fear of, maintaining the status quo. It is very difficult indeed to change against the grain of the belief of your people. . . .

It is important to recognize two major limitations on managing change. The first, and perhaps most fundamental of all, is that no one 'manages' change – but rather releases and guides it. Management, in most people's eyes, has a pleasing ring of precision, prescience and control. If change is to occur there must be a relaxation on all three of those characteristics. . . . Organizations do not change until the people in those organizations have – and people do not change their ideas and values quickly. Even the best manager's programme for change is very lucky to have achieved its aims in three years – and five years is a more realistic time-scale. . . .

All natural organizational forces lead to more complexity, more centralization, less delegation and longer and more diffuse chains of command. Endless hierarchical levels are used as a part of the reward system, and promotions, even if almost entirely titular, are seen as the major motivator. Such promotions are used in lieu of praise, reward and recognition of jobs well done, and the withholding of promotion is used instead of reprimands and counselling. Change is almost impossible without tackling many of these issues head on. To a large extent the questions of numbers, organization, hierarchy and control are intermingled and must be worked on as parts of an interdependent whole. The best place to start is probably with the control systems. The removal of controls leads to dancing in the streets and places responsibility unambiguously where it should actually lie. Secondly it gives a lot of very desirable messages about change and trust, and thirdly the control system, or at least parts of it, is within your own command. . . .

Money is saved, speed enhanced, and efficiency increased by passing full financial responsibility as far down the line as possible. Full financial responsibility can only be exercised if information is available in order to exercise it, and it can only work if it is accompanied by freedoms to buy elsewhere, to hire in outside services or staff, to affect the numbers and rewards of the people employed, and so forth. . . .

Little is gained by attempting to 'make people work harder'. Most people have a natural rate of working, which they will maintain in any event. The first key to reducing numbers is to cut out whole areas of activity completely. The second key is to start at the top. People create work for other people, and excess people create extra work. Undermanned organizations are forced to concentrate on the important issues. . . .

In principle, there should not be a task, role or hierarchical position which does not 'add value' by doing something different to the ones beneath it. The chief executive has unique roles and responsibilities that only he can do. Better by far that he concentrate on these, instead of 'helping' everyone else by doing their jobs as well. If you approach your organizational model by applying these concepts, you will find that layers and levels disappear, almost as if by magic. The numbers needed at the top, for that is where the examination should start, will be rapidly reduced, and the spin-off from that alone is enormous. In the process more responsibility is unequivocally passed down the line – and with it the power and clarity of intent to actively meet the demands which will be put upon the individuals. Reduced layers, reduced numbers, fewer controls and more clarity all produce a virtuous circle which releases energy and increases both the ability to change and the speed with which change can be accomplished.

NOW READ ON . . .

Harvey-Jones, John, *Making it Happen*, Glasgow: William Collins (1988)
Harvey-Jones, John, *Managing to Survive*, London: Heinemann (1993)
Kanter, R.M., *The Change Masters*, New York: Simon & Schuster (1983); London: Allen & Unwin (1984)
Peters, Tom, *Thriving on Chaos*, New York: Alfred A. Knopf (1987); London: Macmillan (1988)

Chapter 4

Managing People

Managing is about people or it is nothing; even F.W. Taylor, now associated with mechanistic systems of work study, recognized the importance of developing each worker's abilities to be 'first class' at some task. Peter Drucker's constant theme throughout his long career as a management writer has been the effective use of human resources as the key to creating and sustaining a successful organization. Yet there is a strange gap on the subject in the literature of management; it is as if the theory and practice of managing people is too complex and volatile to be contained within a book. Plenty has been written since the 1960s on motivation and behaviour in the workplace, but for the wider issue of developing people to their full potential, one has to search for the sideways view, under the labels of empowerment, participation, team-building or leadership, which by definition depends on drawing out the allegiance of other people.

In the beginning of nineteenth-century management (leadership, of course, is timeless), people were of small account, other than as units of productive labour. Systems were all, in the US initially to make the railroads run on time and in connection with each other, and everywhere in the industrialized world to bend the workforce to the ends of the company that employed it.

Henri Fayol, the French mining manager who first attempted to codify the tasks of management, recognized the need to instil a sense of equity and *esprit de corps* among employees, and possibly the sacrifice of some personal vanity by managers in order to give subordinates the satisfaction of feeling they had partly created a plan of action. 'Real talent is needed,' he observed, 'to coordinate effort, encourage keenness, use each person's abilities and reward each one's merit without arousing possible jealousies and disturbing harmonious relations.' But at the same time he advocated 'subordination of individual to general interest', involving 'constant supervision'.

Early managerial theory, as Richard Pascale has pointed out, was significant for what it left out. 'There was almost a total absence of emphasis on building a corporate team. There was little attention given to the importance of selection, training and socialization. There was little or no recognition that the "field infantry" composed of lower-level managers and workers could add value through initiatives and ideas if empowered to do so.' (*Managing on the Edge*, Ch. 4.)

Where any of these subjects were touched on, as in Taylor's comments on selection and training in *Principles of Scientific Management*, the relations between management and workforce were of the master-servant or parent-child variety. Such top-down assumptions of management would endure for more than fifty years after Taylor's work first saw print.

New concepts of managing people, human relations or industrial sociology, broke ground in the 1930s with the work of Australian-born Elton Mayo of Harvard, specifically in his studies of behavioural patterns at the Hawthorne Works of Western Electric in Chicago during the years 1927-32. Mayo's findings – that groups of workers improved productivity after discussions with management on their working conditions, whether those conditions were improved or not – opened up a whole new field of research into employees' relationships with each other as well as with management, and led to much influential writing on the springs of people's motivation at work from thinkers such as Abraham Maslow, Frederick Herzberg and Douglas McGregor.

In McGregor's famous 'Theory X and Theory Y', first published in 1960 in *The Human Side of Enterprise*, we see the first glimmerings of the modern idea of empowering individuals in the workplace to take more responsibility. It was not until the late 1980s, however, that Rosabeth Moss Kanter, then editor of the *Harvard Business Review* as well as a noted Harvard professor and management consultant, identified 'empowerment' as one of the key factors that would mark the successful 'post-entrepreneurial corporation' in its fight to be faster on its feet than its global competitors. The old hierarchies and the elaborate structures they supported could not be carried in these new lightweight companies, any more than the monumental marble fireplaces of the *Titanic* could be installed into the *Queen Elizabeth 2*.

The catalyst of change was more than external trading threats and an explosion of new markets. At bottom it was the arrival of the information age and the knowledge worker. Great companies could now be built on a brilliant idea and a handful of talented people, rather than on a manufacturing process and a pyramid of management to oversee it. CNN, Ted Turner's round-the-clock TV news service, was one of the new corporate stars: Ross Perot's Electronic Data Systems was another. At last that threadbare piece of chairman's cant in the annual report about 'our people are our greatest asset' was being challenged by companies that actually practised it.

Within a few years, the fossilized structures of personnel administration or personnel management, virtually unchanged in their functions since they were invented in the wake of World War I, have given way to the concept of human resources. In the knowledge industries, these are the only resources, apart from capital investment, that a business enterprise has.

Even in traditional manufacturing areas, however, human resources are being used more creatively. Multidisciplinary teams, with their strong self-motivation and contributions to continuous improvement, have long been a feature of the Japanese shop floor and are now being adopted as Western industrial companies 're-engineer' themselves to meet tougher competition and economic conditions. Team-building will be one of the key management skills of the 1990s, but one no longer exclusive to management: its success ultimately depends on each member of the team, a true measure of empowerment.

KEY TEXTS

PETER F. DRUCKER
From *The Practice of Management* (1954).

'Working' the human being always means developing him. And the direction this development takes decides whether the human being – both as a man and as a resource – will become more productive or cease, ultimately, to be productive at all. This applies, as cannot be emphasized too strongly, not alone to the man who is being managed, but also to the manager. Whether he develops his subordinates in the right direction, helps them to grow and become bigger and richer persons, will directly determine whether he himself will develop, will grow or wither, become richer or become impoverished, improve or deteriorate.

One can learn certain skills in managing people, for instance, the skill to lead a conference or to conduct an interview. One can set down practices that are conducive to development – in the structure of the relationship between manager and subordinate, in a promotion system, in the rewards and incentives of an organization. But when all is said and done, developing men still requires a basic quality in the manager which cannot be created by supplying skills or by emphasizing the importance of the task. It requires integrity of character.

W. EDWARDS DEMING
From *Out of the Crisis* (1982).

In my experience, people can face almost any problem except the problems of people. They can work long hours, face declining business, face loss of jobs, but not the problems of people. Faced with problems of people (management included), management, in my experience, go into a state of paralysis, taking refuge in formation of QC-Circles and groups for EI, EP, and QWL (Employee

Involvement, Employee Participation, and Quality of Work Life). These groups predictably disintegrate within a few months from frustration, finding themselves unwilling parties to a cruel hoax, unable to accomplish anything, for the simple reason that no one in management will take action on suggestions for improvement. These are devastatingly cruel devices to get rid of the problems of people. There are of course pleasing exceptions, where the management understands their responsibilities, where the management participates with advice and action on suggestions for removal of barriers to pride of workmanship.

The possibility of pride of workmanship means more to the production worker than gymnasiums, tennis courts, and recreation areas.

Give the work force a chance to work with pride, and the 3 per cent that apparently don't care will erode itself by peer pressure.

ROSABETH MOSS KANTER
From *The Change Masters* (1983).

Teamwork is not just a high-tech touch. In older industries as well, practice in the use of integrative team mechanisms may account for successful problem solving and innovation. In 1981, for example, a terrible year for retailing, J.C. Penney stood out for its superior financial performance (an earnings rise of 44 per cent on a mere 4.5-per cent increase in sales). Success was attributed by top executives to a 'new management style involving teamwork' and 'creating developmental opportunities by helping people understand what happens at different levels of the organization', as the chairman put it. The mechanisms for teamwork involved a set of overlapping permanent and ad hoc committees, the groundwork for which dates at least back to the early 1970s, but which flowered fully a decade later: a management committee of the fourteen top officers; seven permanent subcommittees on key issues such as strategic planning, transitional planning, personnel, and economic affairs; and task forces on operating problems composed so that diverse points of view would be available. The leaders appeared aware that such team vehicles not only paid off in immediate problem solving but laid the foundation for a more informed, versatile, and integrated management.

TOM PETERS
From *Thriving on Chaos* (1987)

- Involve all personnel at all levels in all functions in virtually everything: for example, quality improvement programs and 100 per cent self-inspection; productivity improvement programs; measuring and monitoring results; budget development, monitoring, and adjustment; layout of work areas; assessment of new technology; recruiting and hiring; making customer calls and participating in customer visit programs.
- Be guided by the axiom: There are no limits to the ability to contribute on the part of a properly selected, well-trained, appropriately supported, and, above all, committed person.

Involving everyone in virtually everything means just that. If the supporting elements are in place, then this prescription can be translated into reality, surprisingly quickly. Productivity gains of several hundred per cent can ensue. . . .

Set an objective of an increase of 100 per cent in productivity over the next three years – led by people-participation programs.

To achieve the level of involvement . . . which is necessary to become appropriately flexible, quality-conscious, and thence competitive, we must:

- Organize as much as possible around teams, to achieve enhanced focus, task orientation, innovativeness, and individual commitment.

The modest-sized, task-oriented, semi-autonomous,

mainly self-managing team should be the basic organization building block. Be aware that the wholesale use of a self-managing team structure probably calls for elimination of the traditional first-line supervisor's job.

Regardless of whether or not the fit is perfect, organize *every function* into ten- to thirty-person, largely self-managing teams. Eliminate all first-line supervision as we know it. . . .

Train and retrain. We must:

- Invest in human capital as much as in hardware.
- Train entry-level people; retrain them as necessary.
- Train everyone in problem-solving techniques to contribute to quality improvement.
- Train extensively following promotion to the first managerial job; then train managers every time they advance.
- Use training as a vehicle for instilling a strategic thrust.
- Insist that all training be line-driven – radically so; all programs should consist primarily of input from the line, be piloted in several line locations, and be taught substantially by line people.

Work-force training and constant retraining – and the larger idea of the work force as an appreciating (or depreciating) package of appropriate (or inappropriate) skills – must climb to the top of the agenda of the individual firm and the nation. Value added will increasingly come through people, for the winners. Only highly skilled – that is, trained and continuously retrained – people will be able to add value.

JOHN HARVEY-JONES
From *Making It Happen* (1988).

One of our major industrial problems is that we usually do not ask enough of our people. People at all levels of the organization can accomplish very much more than they are asked to under contemporary conventions. You have only got to see what your people can achieve when you are in an enormous period of expansion. Some of us have only got to look back to what was achieved by people during the last war. . . .

The reality is that we are conservative in our appreciation of others' abilities and we are reticent and uncertain about our own. Not only is it necessary organizationally to stretch others, but it is also necessary that we should stretch ourselves. How many times have you told yourself you could not do something but when you ultimately faced up and had a go, to your amazement you succeeded. The art of 'growing people' lies to a great degree in this stretching process. First, everybody in a well-run organization should feel himself under some pressure. Nothing is worse for young people when they start work, particularly if they join large companies, than to spend a year or so sitting with Nelly before they are trusted to do anything. A characteristic I look for is that young people coming just out of university should be frightened by the responsibility they are given, rather than bored by the lack of demand that is made on them. People's self-confidence grows when they achieve more. Each time they achieve more, an even more ambitious or difficult target needs to be set. I am firmly of the belief that most people in this world achieve only a fraction of what they are capable of. . . .

If we do not stretch people enough at work it is inevitable that they will do more outside. It is the responsibility of the leadership and the management to give opportunities and put demands on people which enable them to grow as human beings in their work environment.

ROBERT H. WATERMAN Jr.
From *The Renewal Factor* (1987).

Teamwork is a tricky business; it requires people to pull together toward a set of shared goals or values. To strengthen the sense of teamwork at your company, take the following steps:

1. *Hire people who both qualify for the job and fit into the culture.*
2. *Destroy at least one we-they barrier a year.*
3. *Encourage direct talk across the we-they boundaries.*
4. *Look outside the company for needless we-they barriers.*
5. *Use training programmes to build relationships.*
6. *Build networks.*
7. *Think of the political process as one of conflict resolution.*
8. *Share the facts.*
9. *Win support from the boss.*
10. *Discourage political behaviour that is purely self-serving.*
11. *Come down hard on political infighting.*
12. *Promote transforming leaders at all levels of the organization.*
13. *Do not tolerate lack of integrity or of trustworthy behaviour.*
14. *If your company runs on mistrust, leave.*

PETER M. SENGE
From *The Fifth Discipline* (1990).

There has never been a greater need for mastering team learning in organizations than there is today. Whether they are management teams or product development teams or cross-functional task forces, teams, 'people who need one another to act', in the words of Arie de Geus, former coordinator of Group Planning at Royal Dutch/Shell, are becoming the key learning unit in organizations. This is so because almost all important decisions are now made in teams, either directly or through the need for teams to translate individual decisions into action. Individual learning, at some level, is irrelevant for organizational learning. Individuals learn all the time and yet there is no organizational learning. But if teams learn, they become a microcosm for learning throughout the organization. Insights gained are put into action. Skills developed can propagate to other individuals and to other teams (although there is no guarantee that they will propagate). The team's accomplishments can set the tone and establish a standard for learning together for the larger organization. . . .

Dialogue can occur only when a group of people see each other as colleagues in mutual quest for deeper insight and clarity. Thinking of each other as colleagues is important because thought is participative. The conscious act of thinking of each other as colleagues contributes toward interacting as colleagues. This may sound simple, but it can make a profound difference.

Seeing each other as colleagues is critical to establish a positive tone and to offset the vulnerability that dialogue brings. In dialogue people actually feel as if they are building something, a new deeper understanding. Seeing each other as colleagues and friends, while it may sound simple, proves to be extremely important. We talk differently with friends from the way we do with people who are not friends. Interestingly, as dialogue develops, team members will find this feeling of friendship developing even towards others with whom they do not have much in common. What is necessary going in is the *willingness* to consider each other as colleagues. In addition, there is a certain vulnerability to holding assumptions in suspension. Treating each other as colleagues acknowledges the mutual risk and establishes the sense of safety in facing the risk.

Colleagueship does not mean that you need to agree or share the same views. On the contrary, the real power of seeing each other as colleagues comes into play when there are differences of view. It is easy to feel collegial when everyone agrees. When there are significant disagreements, it is more difficult. But the payoff is also much greater. Choosing to view 'adversaries' as 'colleagues with different views' has the greatest benefits.

NOW READ ON . . .

Deming, W.E., *Out of the Crisis*, Cambridge, Mass.: MIT Center for Advanced Engineering Study (1982); Cambridge, England: Cambridge University Press (1986)
Drucker, Peter F., *The Practice of Management*, New York: Harper & Row (1954); London: Heinemann (1955)

Harvey-Jones, John, *Making it Happen*, Glasgow: William Collins (1988)

Kanter, R.M., *The Change Masters*, New York: Simon & Schuster (1983); London: Allen & Unwin (1984)

Peters, Tom, *Thriving on Chaos*, New York: Alfred A. Knopf (1987); London: Macmillan (1988)

Senge, Peter M., *The Fifth Discipline*, New York: Doubleday (1990); London: Century (1992)

Waterman, Robert H. Jr., *The Renewal Factor*, New York: Bantam (1987)

Chapter 5

Managing Knowledge

The term 'knowledge industries', meaning those which produce and distribute ideas and information rather than goods and services, appears to have been invented in 1962 by Fritz Machlup, an economist working at Princeton University, in a book called *The Production and Distribution of Knowledge in the US*. As usual, however, it was the prescient Peter Drucker who picked the new coinage up and examined its implications in his remarkable book *The Age of Discontinuity* (1969), which anticipated many developments of the 1980s.

Drucker observed, even then, that in the years since World War II, the US had changed from 'an economy of goods' into 'a knowledge economy'. Where in 1939 the assembly-line worker had been at the heart of the American workforce, thirty years on the individual at the centre was 'the knowledge worker, the man or woman who applies to productive work ideas, concepts and information rather than manual skill or brawn.'

In 1900, he pointed out, the largest single group of working people in America made their living in agriculture; by 1960, this had given way to 'professional, managerial and technical people, that is, knowledge workers. By 1975, or at the latest, by 1980, this group will embrace the majority of Americans at work in the civilian labour force.'

At the core of *The Age of Discontinuity* lay Drucker's conviction that knowledge was increasingly becoming 'the key factor in a country's international economic strength'; the primary industry that supplied the economy with its 'essential and central resource of production'. The computer age had barely begun when *Discontinuity* was written, but Drucker foresaw the explosive demand for workers to feed the information industry – programmers, systems engineers, systems designers and specialists of all kinds – along with a burgeoning healthcare sector that required skills founded on knowledge.

For years it seemed that no one except Peter Drucker was thinking and writing about this fundamental shift in the economy, and specifically about managing this key resource. He returned to the theme in several more books, notably *Managing for the Future* in 1992. In the meantime, Britain's Charles Handy, in *The Future of Work*, had outlined a world where virtually the only employment would be in the knowledge industries. Those who depended upon the labour of hand and muscle would become one with the dinosaurs.

The advent of a world in which more and more companies had to concede that their primary assets went down in the lift and out of the building each night forced new thinking across the spectrum of human resource management; not only how to attract, motivate and retain key knowledge workers, but how to reinvent careers when the loyalty of an employee was to his or her 'brainware' rather than to a corporation and a ladder of promotion. Rosabeth Moss Kanter of Harvard broke new ground in this area in *When Giants Learn to Dance* (1989), a book which explored the then novel concept of 'empowerment' both as a motivating tool and as a catalyst for change and renewal in the corporation, and which spoke for the first time of managers needing to switch the role of boss for that of partner.

In *Managing for the Future*, Drucker states categorically that 'in knowledge and service work, partnership with the responsible workers is the only way; nothing else will work at all.'

There still remained a gap in management bookshelves when it came to the practical business of how this was to be done. A well-known London advertising man, Winston Fletcher, published a book in 1990 called *Creative People*, which naturally focused on the worlds he knew best, those of advertising and design. Then in 1993 Philip Sadler, vice-president and former chief executive of Ashridge Management College, brought out *Managing Talent*, in which he analysed the experience of more than fifty 'talent-intensive' organizations from Sotheby's to Intel, British Airways to Colgate-Palmolive, and attempted to distil a management success strategy from the case studies.

Sadler, whose thinking was deeply influenced by Drucker's *Age of Discontinuity*, differentiates talent from knowledge – a resource that is freely available and accessible to all. Talent, he argues, is the only true scarce remaining resource and therefore the true source of competitive advantage.

The central paradox Sadler addresses in his book is that many talented workers are highly individualistic, while conventional management, nurtured in hierarchical corporations, would prefer to minimize rather than encourage individuality. But the traditional corporation is changing and fragmenting, partly under the pressures of the knowledge-based economy. The new skills required of management, particularly in the building and managing of teams in flexible, project-oriented organizations, are much closer to those required, as the subtitle to Sadler's book puts it, for 'making the best of the best'.

KEY TEXTS

PETER F. DRUCKER
From *The Age of Discontinuity* (1969).

Though the knowledge worker is not a 'labourer', and certainly not a 'proletarian', he is still an 'employee'. He is not a 'subordinate' in the sense that he can be told what to do; he is paid, on the contrary, for applying his knowledge, exercising his judgement, and taking responsible leadership. Yet he has a 'boss' – in fact, he needs to have a boss to be productive. And the boss is usually not a member of the same discipline but a 'manager' whose special competence is to plan, organize, integrate, and measure the work of knowledge people regardless of their discipline or area of specialization.

The knowledge worker is both the true 'capitalist' in the knowledge society and dependent on his job. Collectively the knowledge workers, the employed educated middle-class of today's society, own the means of production through pension funds, investment trusts, and so on. These funds are the true 'capitalists' of modern society with which no private individual, were he richer than Croesus, Rothschild, and Morgan combined, could compete. But individually the knowledge worker is dependent on his salary, on the pension benefits and health insurance that go with it, and altogether on having a job and getting paid. Individually he is an 'employee', even though there is no other 'employer' in our society.

But the knowledge worker sees himself as just another 'professional', no different from the lawyer, the teacher, the preacher, the doctor, or the government servant of yesterday. He has the same education. He has more income. He has probably greater opportunities as well. He may realize that he depends on the organization for access to income and opportunity, and that without the investment the organization has made – and a high investment at that – there would be no job for him. But he also realizes, and rightly so, that the organization equally depends on him.

From *Managing for the Future* (1992).

From now on the key is knowledge. The world is becoming not labour intensive, not materials intensive, not energy intensive, but knowledge intensive.

Japan today produces two and a half times the quantity of manufactured goods it did 25 years ago with the same amount of energy and less raw material. In large part this is due to the shift to knowledge-intensive work. The representative product of the 1920s, the automobile, at the time had a raw material and energy content of 60 per cent. The representative product of the 1980s is the semiconductor chip, which has a raw material and energy content of less than 2 per cent. The 1990s equivalent will be biotechnology, also with a content of about 2 per cent in materials and energy, but with a much higher knowledge content.

The first question in increasing productivity in knowledge

and service work has to be: *What* is the task? *What* do we try to accomplish? *Why* do it at all? The easiest – but perhaps also the greatest – increases in productivity in such work come from redefining the task, and especially from eliminating what needs not to be done.

Nowadays, while still far from being widely practised, it is at least generally accepted in theory that the workers' knowledge of their job is the starting point for improving productivity, quality, and performance altogether.

In making and moving things, partnership with the responsible worker is, however, only the *best* way – after all, Taylor's telling them worked, too, and quite well. In knowledge and service work, partnership with the responsible worker is the *only* way; nothing else will work at all. . . .

And equally important, an insight of the last few years: knowledge people and service people learn the most when they teach. The best way to improve the productivity of the star salesperson is for him or her to present 'the secrets of my success' at a sales convention. . . .

It is often being said that in the information age every enterprise has to become a learning institution. It also has to become a teaching institution.

PHILIP SADLER
From *Managing Talent* (1993).

The higher the level of talent, the greater the challenge to companies to find more effective ways of managing it for productivity and performance. . . .

Making gifted people productive for their organizations is not, in most instances, a matter of getting them to work harder or smarter. They are usually so involved in their work and so bright that such interventions are irrelevant. The managerial task is much more to do with dismantling barriers to performance and productivity and channelling efforts into avenues which will directly contribute to the achievement of the organization's goals.

Thus performance management in the case of highly talented people is best looked upon as a process of influence. The outcome should be for them to understand and identify with the organization's objectives and see how their own contribution can be enhanced.

In exercising this process managers must take full account of the preferred ways of working of talented people. . . .

The organization must, initially, establish an overall framework in terms of structure, culture and style of management which offers an ambience in which talent can flourish. . . .

Within such a framework the specific actions called for are as follows.

- The identification and recognition of outstanding talent wherever it is to be found. It is increasingly recognized that both for reasons of equity and to deal with severe shortages of certain kinds of talent, companies must widen the search for talent beyond the traditional institutional sources – Oxbridge, the *grandes écoles*, the Ivy League – and beyond the traditional white, male-dominant group. They must discover the talent emerging from regional or specialist colleges, talented women, talented Asians and blacks and talent already in the business but trapped at shop-floor level. . . .

- Setting, in partnership with the individuals concerned, clear task objectives and performance standards.

- The provision of a range of supportive and developmental processes designed both to monitor performance and to provide paths to its improvement. These include appraisal, counselling, coaching, mentoring and feedback in various forms.

- The provision of a range of incentives, rewards and reinforcement processes designed to meet the motivational patterns of the types of talented people concerned.

- Investing in the maintenance and further development of talent. Such investment involves not only the financial outlay involved in providing for places on formal training courses. Of greater significance still is the investment in the form of top management time and commitment. . . .

The process of influencing the performance of highly talented people performing unprogrammable tasks is best described as developmental. It will involve a whole range of tools.

- **Appraisal.** By the individual of his or her own performance and by peers, as well as by others who have more experience or carry overall responsibility for the individual's performance and development.
- **Coaching.** By the line manager or other appropriate persons.
- **Mentoring.** In the case of the really top talent, mentoring should involve the most senior line managers.
- **Providing feedback.** This can be done in a range of ways including subordinate and peer-group attitude surveys or ratings, psychometric test scores or opportunities to 'calibrate' an individual's performance and achievements alongside people doing similar jobs in other organizations. . . .

If companies really do see talented people as the most important form of investment for the future they will tend to do all or most of the following things.

- Senior line management, often including the chief executive officer, will be directly and regularly involved in such activities as recruiting, acting as assessors at assessment centres, as mentors for young persons with high potential and as tutors on formal management development programmes. . . .
- There will be a 'no layoffs' policy or at least a policy of resorting to layoffs only as a desperate last resort. . . .
- The company will invest substantially in continuing education, training and development. . . .
- There will exist processes for the maintenance and nurturing of talented people suffering from stress, mid-life crisis or burn-out. These include employee assistance

programmes, internal counselling services and sabbatical leave. . . .

- The company will have positive policies to ensure that rich sources of talent are not overlooked because of discrimination on the grounds of sex, race or religion. No company which consistently ignores the potential talent existing in the female population, for example, can be validly described as one which truly places a high value on talent. . . .

For talent-intensive companies there is no future in trying to be the lowest-cost producer. The whole purpose of attracting talented people is to add value by differentiation, not reduce cost. . . . The ability of any enterprise to build a sustainable competitive advantage and defend its chosen positioning will be a function of its ability to stay ahead of the competition in terms of such things as product development, product innovation, quality of product or service and level of customer service. The ability of a company to do these things will rest in turn upon its ability to attract, retain, develop and motivate the best available talent.

NOW READ ON . . .

Drucker, Peter F., *The Age of Discontinuity*, London: Heinemann (1969)
Drucker, Peter F., *Managing for the Future*, Oxford: Butterworth-Heinemann (1992)
Sadler, Philip, *Managing Talent*, London: The Economist Books (1993)

Chapter 6

Motivation

Motivation, a word that lies at the very heart of management today, was virtually unknown in management circles outside the United States before the 1940s. It did not figure in the early prescriptions of management functions, and when incentives were considered at all, it was only in terms of monetary reward. A wider understanding of what makes people give of their best at work had to wait until the Hawthorne Experiments of Elton Mayo in the late 1920s and early 1930s, which rank among the great watersheds of management theory.

Mayo, an Australian philosophy teacher who joined Harvard University in 1926 as Associate Professor of Industrial Research, led a series of experiments at Western Electric's Hawthorne Works in Chicago between 1927 and 1932 (the programme continued until 1937) which demonstrated, unexpectedly, that production among test groups of workers rose when their working conditions were discussed with the research scientists – whether or not the subsequent changes were an improvement.

Mayo deduced that what made the difference was the satisfaction of feeling part of a team, working together with the researchers – as surrogate managers – rather than receiving imposed conditions from above. Every worker in the experiments felt more valued and more responsible for her performance and for that of her group. From this, Mayo later concluded, 'the desire to stand well with one's fellows, the so-called human instinct of association, easily outweighs the merely individual interest and the logic of reasoning upon which so many spurious principles of management are based.' (Elton Mayo, *The Social Problems of an Industrial Civilization*, 1949.)

Mayo's findings were to revolutionize management thinking and become the foundation stone of human relations in industry. Workers were henceforth understood to be part of a social organism rather than individual cogs performing tasks, and to value the social benefits of belonging to a productive group as much as (sometimes more than) financial rewards for high individual performance.

By the late 1950s, investigations into motivation at work were occupying a number of distinguished minds in US universities. Abraham Maslow and Frederick Herzberg separately studied the needs of the human personality as they progressed from food, shelter, and other physiological imperatives through security to a sense of belonging, recognition, self-esteem and personal development.

Maslow called his structure the 'hierarchy of needs'. The key to it was the understanding that as each need was satisfied, the satisfaction itself ceased to be important. Peter Drucker, however, pointed out a significant omission in the theory; that, although economic rewards became less important as they were attained, failure to attain them created a proportionately greater sense of dissatisfaction. The implication for management was that an ever-increasing spiral of incentives would be required to maintain satisfaction.

Herzberg based his 1959 book *The Motivation to Work* on a study of 203 engineers and accountants in Pittsburgh, questioning them about the factors in their work that made them feel good or bad. He singled out those motivators with diminishing returns – company policy, supervision, salary status, working conditions – as 'hygiene factors', as distinct from the true 'motivation' factors – achievement, recognition, satisfaction in the work being done, progress and personal development. 'Man has two sets of needs,' he explained in *Work and the Nature of Man* (1966), 'his need as an animal to avoid pain and his need as a human to grow psychologically.'

In a famous article for *Harvard Business Review* two years later, Herzberg cited a survey of 1,685 employees which confirmed that motivators were the primary cause of satisfaction and hygiene factors the primary cause of unhappiness on the job. ('One More Time: How Do You Motivate Employees?' *HBR*, 1968.)

Herzberg associated his ideas with Biblical examples; Abraham representing motivation through achievement and personal development, and Adam representing the 'hygiene' factors, forced to work for bodily needs after expulsion from Eden. To encourage the Abraham factor in industry, Herzberg devised the theory of 'job enrichment', which is now built into management theory and practice at levels ranging from flexible working hours and 'cafeteria' benefits (where the employee chooses from a 'menu' of benefit options) all the way up to 'empowerment'.

Maslow had been deeply influenced by the work of Douglas McGregor, the inventor of Theory X and Theory Y. 'Man is a wanting animal – as soon as one of his needs is satisfied, another appears in its place,' McGregor wrote in *The Human Side of Enterprise* (1960), the seminal work on industrial motivation. 'Human needs are organized in a series of levels – a hierarchy of importance. . . . A satisfied need is not a motivator of behaviour. This is a fact of profound significance. It is a fact which is unrecognized in Theory X and is, therefore, ignored in the conventional approach to the management of people.'

Theory X was McGregor's encapsulation of the traditional view of direction and control in organizations. It assumed that the average human being disliked work, shunned responsibility and needed to be coerced and directed with carrot and stick to make him perform adequately. Theory Y, by contrast, viewed the individual as naturally welcoming work and responsibility, believed that 'commitment to objectives is a function of the rewards associated with their achievement', and stated that under the Theory X conditions of modern industrial life, 'the intellectual potentialities of the average human being are only partially utilized'.

Theory Y was first put into action at a California electronics factory and Maslow studied it there, eventually disagreeing with McGregor on its workability. He concluded that not every individual was able or willing to assume full participative responsibility; some would always need an element of the structured security and direction provided by Theory X.

McGregor's belief in Theory Y was, however, vindicated at a purpose-built detergent factory owned by Procter and Gamble in Augusta, Georgia. David Swanson, a P&G executive newly returned from the Korean War and determined not to carry military-style control into industry, called in McGregor as a consultant and the plant ran successfully on self-directed teams – Procter and Gamble being probably the first company to introduce this now-fashionable concept, forty years ago. The factory proved a third more productive than any other in the company, and P&G kept it a trade secret until the 1990s, believing that McGregor's concept gave it a competitive advantage. The story was finally revealed in Robert Waterman's *Frontiers of Excellence* (1994).

Motivation theory largely revolved around Herzberg, Maslow and McGregor throughout the 1960s and 1970s. In Europe, influential earlier research had come from London's Tavistock Institute of Human Relations and its founder member Elliott Jaques, the Canadian industrial psychologist who initiated the famous Glacier Metals study of group behaviour in the workplace. Jaques' book based on this research, *The Changing Culture of a Factory* (1951), found that a key factor in avoiding stress and demotivation at both shop-floor and management levels was to have clearly defined roles and responsibilities which were accepted by the individual workers and their colleagues. Confusion or lack of clear boundaries led to frustration, insecurity and a tendency to avoid accountability.

In the early 1960s the Tavistock Institute worked on projects in Norway involving early models of industrial democracy, and identified a number of guidelines for maintaining employee motivation. These included: the job being reasonably varied and demanding in terms other than physical endurance; giving the worker an opportunity to learn while working (and an area of responsibility or decision-making), and holding out some prospects for the future beyond those of promotion, in other words some hope of self-development.

Newport University

City Campus

01633 435079

Borrowed Items 24/10/2011 20:19

XXXXX1341

Item Title	Due Date
Mastering management skills	11/11/2011
Introduction to management	11/11/2011
* Managing with the gurus : t	14/11/2011

* Indicates items borrowed today

Thankyou for using this unit

Please don't forget to unlock
DVD and CD cases

The Tavistock went on to develop concepts of industrial democracy that were advanced for their time, and not taken seriously in industry until the end of the 1970s. Today, the concept of empowerment, of pushing responsibility and autonomy down and throughout the organization, is an integral part of the team-building, unhierarchical style of management advocated by Tom Peters, Bob Waterman and others. But the problem that Maslow identified in Theory Y remains as challenging as in the 1960s: some individuals capable of contributing value to their organization will be less comfortable in an unstructured system and will feel exposed by empowerment.

As more and more companies redesign their processes and career structures in search of the lean, efficient organization run by self-motivated individuals, motivation studies will have to address this problem increasingly in the future, along with all the ramifications of pay-by-performance and the motivating or demotivating effects of performance measurement systems. The field is still wide open and it does, after all, deal with the most essential assets of any business organization – the assets that go home each night.

KEY TEXTS

PETER F. DRUCKER
From *The Practice of Management* (1954).

What we need is to replace the externally imposed spur of fear with an internal self-motivation for performance. *Responsibility – not satisfaction – is the only thing that will serve*.

One can be satisfied with what somebody else is doing; but to perform one has to take responsibility for one's own actions and their impact. To perform, one has, in fact, to be dissatisfied, to want to do better.

Responsibility cannot be bought for money. Financial rewards and incentives are, of course, important, but they work largely negatively. Discontent with financial rewards is a powerful disincentive, undermining and corroding responsibility for performance. But satisfaction with monetary rewards is not, the evidence indicates, a sufficient positive motivation. It motivates only where other things have made the worker ready to assume responsibility. One can see this quite clearly when studying incentive pay for increased work. The incentive pay produces better output where there is already a willingness to perform better; otherwise it is ineffectual, is indeed sabotaged. . . .

There are four ways by which we can attempt to reach the goal of the responsible worker. They are careful placement, high standards of performance, providing the worker with the information needed to control himself, and with opportunities for participation that will give him a managerial vision. All four are necessary. . . .

Nothing challenges men so effectively to improved performance as a job that makes high demands on them. Nothing gives them more pride of workmanship and accomplishment. To focus on the minimum required is always to destroy people's motivation. To focus on the best that can just be reached by constant effort and ability always builds motivation. . . .

To motivate the worker to peak performance, it is equally important that management set and enforce on itself high standards for its own performance of those functions that determine the worker's ability to perform.

DOUGLAS McGREGOR
From *The Human Side of Enterprise* (1960).

Theory X: The Traditional View of Direction and Control

1. *The average human being has an inherent dislike of work and will avoid it if he can.*
2. *Because of this human characteristic of dislike of work, most people must be coerced, controlled, directed, threatened with punishment to get them to put forth adequate effort toward the achievement of organizational objectives.*

3. *The average human being prefers to be directed, wishes to avoid responsibility, has relatively little ambition, wants security above all.*

Man is a wanting animal – as soon as one of his needs is satisfied, another appears in its place. This process is un-ending. It continues from birth to death. Man continuously puts forth effort – works, if you please – to satisfy his needs. . . .

A satisfied need is not a motivator of behavior! This is a fact of profound significance. It is a fact which is unrecog-nized in Theory X and is, therefore, ignored in the conventional approach to the management of people. . . .

When the physiological needs are reasonably satisfied, needs at the next higher level begin to dominate man's be-havior – to motivate him. These are the safety needs, for protection against danger, threat, deprivation. Some people mistakenly refer to these as needs for security. However, unless man is in a dependent relationship where he fears arbitrary deprivation, he does not demand security. The need is for the 'fairest possible breaks'. When he is confident of this, he is more than willing to take risks. But when he feels threatened or dependent, his greatest need is for protection, for security. . . .

When man's physiological needs are satisfied and he is no longer fearful about his physical welfare, his social needs become important motivators of his behavior. These are such needs as those for belonging, for associa-tion, for acceptance by one's fellows, for giving and receiving friendship and love. . . .

Above the social needs – in the sense that they do not usually become motivators until lower needs are reason-ably satisfied – are the needs of greatest significance to management and to man himself. They are the egoistic needs, and they are of two kinds:

1. Those that relate to one's self-esteem: needs for self-respect and self-confidence, for autonomy, for achieve-ment, for competence, for knowledge
2. Those that relate to one's reputation: needs for status,

for recognition, for appreciation, for the deserved respect of one's fellows.

Unlike the lower needs, these are rarely satisfied; man seeks indefinitely for more satisfaction of these needs once they have become important to him. . . .

Consideration of the rewards typically provided the worker for satisfying his needs through his employment leads to the interesting conclusion that most of these rewards can be used for satisfying his needs *only when he leaves the job*. Wages, for example, cannot be spent at work. The only contribution they can make to his satisfaction on the job is in terms of status differences resulting from wage differentials. . . .

Most fringe benefits – overtime pay, shift differentials, vacations, health and medical benefits, annuities, and the proceeds from stock purchase plans or profit-sharing plans – yield needed satisfaction only when the individual leaves the job. Yet these, along with wages, are among the major rewards provided by management for effort. It is not surprising, therefore, that for many wage earners *work is perceived as a form of punishment* which is the price to be paid for various kinds of satisfaction away from the job. To the extent that this is their perception, we would hardly expect them to undergo more of this punishment than is necessary. . . .

The 'carrot and stick' theory of motivation which goes along with Theory X works reasonably well under certain circumstances. The *means* for satisfying man's physiological and (within limits) safety needs can be provided or withheld by management. Employment itself is such a means, and so are wages, working conditions, and benefits. By these means the individual can be controlled so long as he is struggling for subsistence. Man tends to live for bread alone when there is little bread.

But the 'carrot and stick' theory does not work at all once man has reached an adequate subsistence level and is motivated primarily by higher needs. Management cannot provide a man with self-respect, or with the respect of his fellows, or with the satisfaction of needs for self-fulfillment. We can create conditions such that he is encouraged and enabled to seek such satisfactions for himself, or we can thwart him by failing to create those conditions. . . .

The philosophy of management by direction and control – *regardless of whether it is hard or soft* – is inadequate to motivate because the human needs on which this approach relies are relatively unimportant motivators of behavior in our society today. Direction and control are of limited value in motivating people whose important needs are social and egoistic.

The Assumptions of Theory Y

1. *The expenditure of physical and mental effort in work is as natural as play or rest.*
2. *External control and the threat of punishment are not the only means for bringing about effort toward organizational objectives. Man will exercise self-direction and self-control in the service of objectives to which he is committed.*
3. *Commitment to objectives is a function of the rewards associated with their achievement.*
4. *The average human being learns, under proper conditions, not only to accept but to seek responsibility.*
5. *The capacity to exercise a relatively high degree of imagination, ingenuity, and creativity in the solution of organizational problems is widely, not narrowly, distributed in the population.*
6. *Under the conditions of modern industrial life, the intellectual potentialities of the average human being are only partially utilized.*

Above all, the assumptions of Theory Y point up the fact that the limits on human collaboration in the organizational setting are not limits of human nature but of management's ingenuity in discovering how to realize the potential represented by its human resources. Theory X offers management an easy rationalization for ineffective organizational performance: It is due to the nature of the human resources with which we must work. Theory Y, on the other hand, places the problem squarely in the lap of management. If employees are lazy, indifferent, unwilling to take responsibility, intransigent, uncreative, uncooperative, Theory Y implies that the cause lies in the management's methods of organization and control. . . .

There is substantial evidence for the statement that the potentialities of the average human being are far above those which we typically realize in industry today. If our assumptions are like those of Theory X, we will not even recognize the existence of these potentialities and there will be no reason to devote time, effort, or money to discovering how to realize them. If, however, we accept assumptions like those of Theory Y, we will be challenged to innovate, to discover new ways of organizing and directing human effort, even though we recognize that the perfect organization, like the perfect vacuum, is practically out of reach. . . .

Acceptance of Theory Y does not imply abdication, or 'soft' management or 'permissiveness'. . . . Theory Y assumes that people will exercise self-direction and self-control in the achievement of organizational objectives *to the degree that they are committed to those objectives*. If that commitment is small, only a slight degree of self-direction and self-control will be likely, and a substantial amount of external influence will be necessary. If it is large, many conventional external controls will be relatively superfluous, and to some extent self-defeating. Managerial policies and practices materially affect this degree of commitment.

Authority is an inappropriate means for obtaining commitment to objectives. Other forms of influence – help in achieving integration, for example – are required for this purpose. Theory Y points to the possibility of lessening the emphasis on external forms of control to the degree that commitment to organizational objectives can be achieved. Its underlying assumptions emphasize the capacity of human beings for self-control, and the consequent possibility of greater managerial reliance on other means of influence. Nevertheless, it is clear, that authority *is* an appropriate means for control under certain circumstances – particularly where genuine commitment to objectives cannot be achieved. The assumptions of Theory Y do not deny the appropriateness of authority, but they do deny that it is appropriate for all purposes and under all circumstances.

FREDERICK HERZBERG

From 'One More Time: How Do You Motivate Employees?' (*Harvard Business Review*, 1968). Reproduced in *Milestones in Management* ed. H. Strage, (1992).

In attempting to enrich an employee's job, management often succeeds in reducing the man's personal contribution, rather than giving him an opportunity for growth in his accustomed job. Such an endeavor, which I shall call horizontal job loading (as opposed to vertical loading, or providing motivator factors), has been the problem of earlier job enlargement programs. This activity merely enlarges the meaninglessness of the job. Some examples of this approach, and their effect, are:

- Challenging the employee by increasing the amount of production expected of him. If he tightens 10,000 bolts a day, see if he can tighten 20,000 bolts a day. The arithmetic involved shows that multiplying zero by zero still equals zero.
- Adding another meaningless task to the existing one, usually some routine clerical activity. The arithmetic here is adding zero to zero.
- Rotating the assignments of a number of jobs that need to be enriched. This means washing dishes for a while, then washing silverware. The arithmetic is substituting one zero for another zero.
- Removing the most difficult parts of the assignment in order to free the worker to accomplish more of the less challenging assignments. This traditional industrial engineering approach amounts to subtraction in the hope of accomplishing addition.

Steps to Job Enrichment
1. Select those jobs in which (a) the investment in industrial engineering does not make changes too costly, (b) attitudes are poor, (c) hygiene is becoming very costly, and (d) motivation will make a difference in performance.

2. Approach these jobs with the conviction that they can be changed. . . .

3. Brainstorm a list of changes that may enrich the jobs, without concern for their practicality.

4. Screen the list to eliminate suggestions that involve hygiene, rather than actual motivation.

5. Screen the list for generalities, such as 'give them more responsibility', that are rarely followed in practice. . . .

6. Screen the list to eliminate any *horizontal* loading suggestions.

7. Avoid direct participation by the employees whose jobs are to be enriched. Ideas they have expressed previously certainly constitute a valuable source for recommended changes, but their direct involvement contaminates the process with human relations *hygiene* and, more specifically, gives them only a *sense* of making a contribution. The job is to be changed, and it is the content that will produce the motivation, not attitudes about being involved or the challenge inherent in setting up a job. . . .

8. In the initial attempts at job enrichment, set up a controlled experiment. At least two equivalent groups should be chosen, one an experimental unit in which the motivators are systematically introduced over a period of time, and the other one a control group in which no changes are made. . . .

9. Be prepared for a drop in performance in the experimental group the first few weeks. . . .

10. Expect your first-line supervisors to experience some anxiety and hostility over the changes you are making. . . .

After a successful experiment, however, the supervisor usually discovers the supervisory and managerial functions he has neglected, or which were never his because all his time was given over to checking the work of his subordinates.

Job enrichment will not be a one-time proposition, but a continuous management function. The initial changes, however, should last for a very long period of time. There are a number of reasons for this:

● The changes should bring the job up to the level of challenge commensurate with the skill that was hired.

- Those who have still more ability eventually will be able to demonstrate it better and win promotion to higher-level jobs.
- The very nature of motivators, as opposed to hygiene factors, is that they have a much longer-term effect on employees' attitudes. Perhaps the job will have to be enriched again, but this will not occur as frequently as the need for hygiene.

Not all jobs can be enriched, nor do all jobs need to be enriched. If only a small percentage of the time and money that is now devoted to hygiene, however, were given to job enrichment efforts, the return in human satisfaction and economic gain would be one of the largest dividends that industry and society have ever reaped through their efforts at better personnel management.

The argument for job enrichment can be summed up quite simply: If you have someone on a job, use him. If you can't use him on the job, get rid of him, either via automation or by selecting someone with lesser ability. If you can't use him and you can't get rid of him, you will have a motivation problem.

TOM PETERS AND ROBERT H. WATERMAN Jr.
From *In Search of Excellence* (1982).

The lesson that the excellent companies have to teach is that . . . most of their people are made to feel that they are winners. Their populations are distributed around the normal curve, just like every other large population, but the difference is that their systems reinforce degrees of winning rather than degrees of losing. Their people by and large make their targets and quotas, because the targets and quotas are set (often by the people themselves) to allow that to happen.

JOHN HARVEY-JONES
From *Making It Happen* (1988).

People are self-motivated. They do their best work when they have come to believe, through their own processes, that what they are going to do is worthwhile. The free man is always better than the slave.

JOHN P. KOTTER
From *A Force For Change* (1990).

The motivational aspect of leadership can manifest itself in many different ways. But more often than not, it comes in a package that includes (1) the articulation of a vision in a manner that stresses the values of the audience being addressed (and thus makes the work important to these individuals), (2) the involvement of those people in deciding how to achieve that vision or the part of the vision that is most relevant to them (giving people a sense of control), (3) the enthusiastic support of their efforts at achieving that vision, supplemented by coaching, feedback, and role modeling (which helps them grow professionally and enhances their self-esteem), and (4) the public recognition and rewarding of all their successes (providing them with recognition, a sense of belonging to an organization that cares about them, and a feeling of accomplishment). In a sense, when this is done, the work itself seems intrinsically motivating.

Motivating people for a short period of time is not very difficult. A crisis will often do just that, or a carefully planned special event. Motivating people over a longer period of time, however, is far more difficult. It is also far more important in today's business environment.

Motivation over time requires, first, that visions and strategies be communicated on a continuous basis, not just once or occasionally. . . . That communication must go beyond just informing; it must excite people by connecting to their values. . . . People's involvement in deciding how to implement the vision must be real, not manipulative. ... The right kind of support must be forthcoming so that individuals can succeed in making progress toward that vision.

NOW READ ON ...

Drucker, Peter F., *The Practice of Management*, New York: Harper & Row (1954); London: Heinemann (1955)

Harvey-Jones, John, *Making it Happen*, Glasgow: William Collins (1988)

Herzberg, Frederick, 'One More Time: How Do You Motivate Employees?' in *Harvard Business Review*, Cambridge, Mass. (1968)

Kotter, John P., *A Force for Change*, New York: The Free Press (1990)

McGregor, Douglas, *The Human Side of Enterprise*, New York: McGraw-Hill (1960)

Peters, Tom and Waterman, Robert H. Jr., *In Search of Excellence*, New York and London: Harper & Row (1982)

Chapter 7

Leadership

'Never have so many laboured so long to say so little,' wrote Warren Bennis and Burt Nanus in *Leaders: The Strategies for Taking Charge*, published in 1985. James McGregor Burns, the US political scientist who identified the far-reaching difference between 'transactional' and 'transformational' leadership, described the subject as 'one of the most observed and least understood phenomena on earth'.

In spite of the volume of writing on leadership – mostly in monographs or as part of a wider treatment of management – there remains surprisingly little practical analysis of what it means in a business context. Time and again the old military analogies are rolled out, from Alexander the Great to Nelson, Montgomery and in due course, no doubt, General H. Norman Schwarzkopf in the Gulf War of 1991. Business leadership is evidently harder to recognize and define than the 'follow me' qualities that identify a leader on the battlefield.

Warren Bennis, who did much to popularize leadership studies in the US, told *Director* magazine in 1991: 'Leadership is an endless subject and endlessly interesting because you can never get your conceptual arms fully around it. I always feel rather like a lepidopterist chasing a butterfly. There's nothing in the realm of human behaviour that doesn't in some way impinge on the subject of leadership and followership.'

Certainly there are business situations where a leader needs similar qualities to those of the bold commander able to inspire others to follow him on a risky mission. (With no apparent sense of irony, one of Britain's more inept business figures in the 1970s, who fancied himself as a leader of vision, was once heard to lament that his only problem was a lack of followers.)

One such situation is the hostile takeover; another is 're-structuring', 'downsizing' or any of the other sanitized labels for a process by which jobs and people are taken out of an organization. A third, which goes deeper, is the radical transformation of a company by 're-engineering' or 'business process redesign' (see Chapter 19).

Such a transformation, involving serious challenges to the 'turf' of existing managers, radical changes in work practices and often substantial redundancies, cannot work without committed leadership. Michael Hammer, the dynamic MIT mathematician who claims to have invented re-engineering and now pursues a lucrative new career teaching the process, likes to quote the battle-eve rhetoric of Bob Stark, CEO of Hallmark Cards, prior to that company's re-engineering: 'We are going on a journey. We will carry our wounded and shoot the stragglers.'

This, in Hammer's eyes, epitomizes leadership: warning that the way ahead will be hard but unavoidable, that people who fail through no fault of their own will be helped, but those unwilling to make the effort can expect short shrift. 'Without leadership,' Hammer tells his seminars, 'nothing happens.' And he defines a leader as someone who makes others want what he wants, not merely do what he wants – 'that's a dictator.'

Before the 1930s, Douglas McGregor wrote in *The Human Side of Enterprise*, 'it was widely believed that leadership was a property of the individual, that a limited number of people were uniquely endowed with abilities and traits which made it possible for them to become leaders. Moreover, these abilities and traits were believed to be inherited rather than acquired.' Research therefore concentrated on identifying the supposed universal characteristics of leadership.

World War II heightened public awareness of leadership, and one of the first events organized by the newly formed British Institute of Management in 1948 was a series of lectures in Sheffield City Hall to 1,200 British managers under the title 'Management Through Leadership'. One of the speakers was Field Marshal Sir William Slim, who argued that the principles of modern military leadership could be applied successfully to industry.

Business and military leaders certainly have one great attribute in common: they are *visible*. Think of Nelson on the deck of HMS *Victory*, Montgomery touring the units of the Eighth Army before Alamein with his brisk cricket-captain's pep-talk: 'We're going to hit the enemy for six.' Not for them the safety of the admiral's cabin or the equivalent of a First World War general's château behind the lines.

Similarly, the chief executives who make a difference – Sir John Harvey-Jones, Lee Iacocca, Percy Barnevik of Asea Brown Boveri – have been those who rarely sit in panelled offices, but 'manage by walking around', talking, listening and winning hearts and minds to difficult new directions.

There is a broad consensus among management writers on a number of other essential qualities. Energy, stamina, vision, self-confidence, imagination, daring, ability to tolerate stress and adaptability are cited by Philip Sadler ('Leaders: Born or Bred?', *Frontiers of Leadership*, 1992), in a list few would disagree with. Role-modelling, through the way a leader performs even in mundane matters – consistently arriving at his desk ahead of his staff, for example – is another trait, and one that can be developed with training.

In many ways the personal characteristics typical of a leader have changed remarkably little since Nelson, whose contemporaries praised his enthusiasm, ability to create harmony of purpose, to inspire confidence and to communicate well. The leadership guru John Adair writes of Nelson: 'He gave clear directions; he built teams, and he showed a real concern for the individual. . . . it also became clear that he possessed a great leader's gift for drawing out the best from people.' Another inspirational quality was his willingness to share the privations of his men, telling the surgeon at Aboukir Bay who broke off from attending a wounded sailor to treat Nelson's injured eye, 'No, I will take my turn with my brave fellow.' Nelson was always visible in the thick of battle; it literally caused his death.

The line between manager and leader is forever being redefined, but Warren Bennis' well-known list, quoted in this

chapter's Key Texts, is fairly definitive, ending in his celebrated dictum: 'The manager does things right; the leader
does the right thing.'

Bennis professes himself still 'very puzzled' by the myster-
ies of leadership and followership, of why some individuals
fall naturally into the former and others into the latter.
'Leaders expect the best of the people around them,' he has
written. 'Leaders know that the people around them change
and grow. If you expect great things, your associates will
give them to you. . . . At the same time, leaders are realistic
about expectations. Their motto is, stretch, don't strain.'

In a rapidly changing management world, Bennis offers
the paradox that successful leadership will involve 'more
listening than speaking; learning how to be vulnerable.'
Those who will lead in the twenty-first century, he thinks,
will be 'people who are continuous learners, who have their
eyebrows always raised in curiosity, who can embrace diversity, who are basically children of chaos and feel comfortable
with ambiguity and chaos' (*Director*, June 1991).

The concept of the leader has already significantly changed
since the postwar era, when military heroes translated effort-
lessly to politics (Presidents Eisenhower and de Gaulle) and
quasi-military concepts of strategy were transferred to business, an extension of 'scientific management'. From Thomas
Carlyle's 'great man' we have moved to a more collegiate
style of leadership, drawing on the strength of the team
(though Warren Bennis admits he still believes influence is
spread by the 'lengthened shadow of one great person').

The principal breakthrough in leadership theory remains
that of James McGregor Burns, who worked for John F.
Kennedy in his presidential campaign. Burns explained that
most leaders are 'transactional' with their followers: that is,
they offer something in exchange – jobs or some other benefit in return for allegiance. 'Transformational' leadership is of
a different magnitude.

'Transforming leadership, while more complex than transactional leadership, is more potent,' wrote Burns. 'The
transforming leader recognizes an existing need or demand of
a potential follower. But, beyond that, the transforming
leader looks for potential motives in followers, seeks to

satisfy higher needs, and engages the full person of the follower.'

Tom Peters in *Thriving on Chaos* puts it succinctly: 'The most effective leaders, political or corporate, empower others to act – and grow – in support of a course that both leaders and followers find worthy.'

Business leadership has grown in its perceived importance over the last few years. The roller-coaster of chaotic change that has forced a rethink of long-accepted business structures and practices has produced a demand for 'managing change' that is all about leadership. John Kotter, the Harvard Professor of Organizational Behaviour who is an acknowledged authority on executive leadership and cultural change in organizations, says: 'The single most visible factor that distinguishes major cultural changes that succeed from those that fail is competent leadership at the top. . . . Unlike even the very best management process, leadership has as its primary function the production of change.'

At the same time the qualities required of business leadership have undergone a subtle change, or, rather, an additional dimension. It is still necessary to be visible, to be committed, to think and talk of management and workforce as 'we' (one of the worst failures of leadership in World War II was the Whitehall propaganda poster that ran: 'Your courage, your fortitude, your resolution will bring us victory', unconsciously separating 'you' from 'us'). If anything, those qualities are even more needed as the leader becomes less the 'boss' than the 'coach' or the 'mentor'.

Leaders, says Bennis, 'manage the dream' in an organization: they have the capacity to 'create a compelling vision, one that takes people to a new place, and then to translate that vision into reality.' Peter Drucker states that the first task of the leader is to define the mission (see Chapter 11).

As organizations flatten out and hierarchies of middle managers are stripped away in favour of 'team-building' and 'project work', the 'follow me' ethos is giving way to that of 'join me'. The leader who learns as much as he imparts is the key to the 'learning organization' now held up as a model for the nineties. Peter Senge, the most influential advocate of the 'learning organization', says we have moved from the age of heroes to that of 'designers, stewards and teachers'.

John Adair, Britain's sole guru in the leadership field, and the UK's first Professor of Leadership Studies, has always maintained that 'leadership is about teamwork, creating teams'. His Action–Centred Learning model, developed first out of lectures at Sandhurst Military College and later at The Industrial Society, takes as its core three overlapping circles – task, team and individual. Each interacts with the other two, so that failure, for example, to complete a task, or the lack of one, affects both the sense of team achievement and that of the individual.

Adair believes that leadership skills can be acquired through training, though John Kotter would argue that not everyone has the potential: Warren Bennis has summarized his position as 'Leaders are born, *then* made.'

Leadership development is increasingly seen as an investment in the future. Bennis stresses the importance of offering executives leadership opportunities early in their careers 'because they build drive, trigger a can-do spirit and inspire self-confidence.'

KEY TEXTS

PETER F. DRUCKER
From *The Practice of Management* (1954).

There is no substitute for leadership. But management cannot create leaders. It can only create the conditions under which potential leadership qualities become effective; or it can stifle potential leadership. The supply of leadership is much too limited and unpredictable to be depended upon for the creation of the spirit the business enterprise needs to be productive and to hold together. Management must work on creating the spirit by other means. These means may be less effective and more pedestrian. But at least they are available and within management's control. In fact, to concentrate on leadership may only too easily lead management to do nothing at all about the spirit of its organization.

Leadership requires aptitude – and men who are good

chief engineers or general managers are rare enough even without aptitude for leadership. Leadership also requires basic attitudes. And nothing is as difficult to define, nothing as difficult to change, as basic attitudes (quite apart from the question whether the employment contract confers on management the right to attempt to manipulate what is in effect an employee's basic personality). To talk of leadership as the unique key to spirit therefore only too often means neither action nor results.

DOUGLAS McGREGOR
From *The Human Side of Enterprise* (1960).

There are at least four major variables now known to be involved in leadership: (1) the characteristics of the leader; (2) the attitudes, needs, and other personal characteristics of the followers; (3) characteristics of the organization, such as its purpose, its structure, the nature of the tasks to be performed; and (4) the social, economic, and political milieu. The personal characteristics required for effective performance as a leader vary, depending on the other factors.

This is an important research finding. *It means that leadership is not a property of the individual, but a complex relationship among these variables*. The old argument over whether the leader makes history or history makes the leader is resolved by this conception. Both assertions are true within limits. . . .

It does not follow . . . that *any* individual can become a successful leader in a given situation. It *does* follow that successful leadership is not dependent on the possession of a single universal pattern of inborn traits and abilities. It seems likely that leadership potential (considering the tremendous variety of situations for which leadership is required) is broadly rather than narrowly distributed in the population.

Research findings to date suggest, then, that it is more fruitful to consider leadership as a relationship between the leader and the situation than as a universal pattern of characteristics possessed by certain people. The differences in requirements for successful leadership in different situations are more striking than the similarities. Moreover, research studies emphasize the importance of leadership skills and attitudes which can be acquired and are, therefore, not inborn characteristics of the individual. . . .

If we accept the point of view that leadership consists of a relationship between the leader, his followers, the organization, and the social milieu, and if we recognize that these situational factors are subject to substantial changes with time, we must recognize that we cannot predict the personal characteristics of the managerial resources that an organization will require a decade or two hence. Even if we can list the positions to be filled, we cannot define very adequately the essential characteristics of the people who will be needed in those situations at that time. *One of management's major tasks, therefore, is to provide a heterogeneous supply of human resources from which individuals can be selected to fill a variety of specific but unpredictable needs.*

TOM PETERS AND ROBERT H. WATERMAN Jr.
From *In Search of Excellence* (1982)

Leadership is many things. It is patient, usually boring coalition-building. It is the purposeful seeding of cabals that one hopes will result in the appropriate ferment in the bowels of the organization. It is meticulously shifting the attention of the institution through the mundane language of management systems. It is altering agendas so that new priorities get enough attention. It is being visible when things are going awry, and invisible when they are working well. It's building a loyal team at the top that speaks more or less with one voice. It's listening carefully much of the time, frequently speaking with encouragement, and reinforcing words with believable action. It's being tough when necessary, and it's the occasional naked use of power – or the 'subtle accumulation of nuances, a hundred things done a little better,' as Henry Kissinger once put it. . . .

We are fairly sure that the culture of almost every excellent company ... can be traced to transforming leadership somewhere in its history. While the cultures of these companies seem today to be so robust that the need for transforming leadership is not a continuing one, we doubt such cultures ever would have developed as they did without that kind of leadership somewhere in the past, most often when they were relatively small.

TOM PETERS
From *Thriving on Chaos* (1987).

The most effective leaders, political or corporate, empower others to act – and grow – in support of a course that both leaders and followers find worthy. The leader's job is at once to articulate the empowering vision, and to stay in touch with followers to ensure that she or he is in tune with the needs of the real world where the vision is implemented. Studies of effective leaders demonstrate that they do not induce narrow obedience to a precise objective among followers. To the contrary, powerful leaders make followers more powerful in pursuit of a commonly held dream, jointly defined. Furthermore, the listening leader inspires other leaders (managers at all levels) to be listeners too. The listening organization is in turn the one most likely to pick up quickly on changes in its environment.

JOHN HARVEY-JONES
From *Making It Happen* (1988).

The aim of the business leader must be to be the best, for only the best command their own destiny and achieve the sort of rewards that are sought for themselves and their people. In a cycle of reinforcement, the best people wish to join the best companies. The best companies are able more readily to make alliances or purchase technology or be welcomed into countries other than their own, or obtain financial consideration from banks or shareholders, or escape some of the more scathing criticisms which can be so damaging to a company if produced in the public arena.

WARREN BENNIS
From *On Becoming a Leader* (1989).

There are three basic reasons why leaders are important. First, they are responsible for the effectiveness of organizations. The success or failure of all organizations, whether basketball teams, moviemakers, or automobile manufacturers, rests on the perceived quality at the top. Even stock prices rise and fall according to the public perception of how good the leader is.

Second, the change and upheaval of the past years has left us with no place to hide. We need anchors in our lives, something like a trim-tab factor, a guiding purpose. Leaders fill that need.

Third, there is a pervasive, national concern about the integrity of our institutions. Wall Street was, not long ago, a place where a man's word was his bond. The recent investigations, revelations, and indictments have forced the industry to change the way it conducted business for 150 years.

- The first basic ingredient of leadership is a *guiding vision*. The leader has a clear idea of what he wants to do – professionally and personally – and the strength to persist in the face of setbacks, even failures. Unless you know where you're going, and why, you cannot possibly get there. . . .
- The second basic ingredient of leadership is *passion* – the underlying passion for the promises of life, combined with a very particular passion for a vocation, a profession, a course of action. The leader loves what he does and loves doing it. . . .
- The next basic ingredient of leadership is *integrity*. I think there are three essential parts of integrity: self-knowledge, candor, and maturity. . . .
- Two more basic ingredients of leadership are *curiosity*

and *daring*. The leader wonders about everything, wants to learn as much as he can, is willing to take risks, experiment, try new things. He does not worry about failure, but embraces errors, knowing he will learn from them.

- The manager administers; the leader innovates.
- The manager is a copy; the leader is an original.
- The manager maintains; the leader develops.
- The manager focuses on systems and structure; the leader focuses on people.
- The manager relies on control; the leader inspires trust.
- The manager has a short-range view; the leader has a long-range perspective.
- The manager asks how and when; the leader asks what and why.
- The manager has his eye always on the bottom line; the leader has his eye on the horizon.
- The manager imitates; the leader originates.
- The manager accepts the status quo; the leader challenges it.
- The manager is the classic good soldier; the leader is his own person.
- The manager does things right; the leader does the right thing.

PETER F. DRUCKER
From *Managing the Non-Profit Organization* (1990). Extracted from *The Frontiers of Leadership*, ed. M. Syrett and C. Hogg (1992).

There are simply no such things as 'leadership traits' or 'leadership characteristics'. Of course, some people are better leaders than others. By and large, though, we are talking about skills that perhaps cannot be taught but they can be learned by most of us. True, some people genuinely cannot learn the skills. They may not be important to them; or they'd rather be followers. But most of us can learn them.

The leaders who work most effectively, it seems to me, never say 'I'. And that's not because they have trained themselves not to say 'I'. They don't *think* 'I'. They think 'we'; they think 'team'. They understand their job to be to make the team function. They accept the responsibility and don't sidestep it, but 'we' gets the credit. There is an identification (very often, quite unconscious) with the task and with the group. This is what creates trust, what enables you to get the task done. . . .

As the first basic competence, I would put the willingness, ability, and self-discipline to listen. Listening is not a skill; it's a discipline. Anybody can do it. All you have to do is keep your mouth shut. The second essential competence is the willingness to communicate, to make yourself understood. That requires infinite patience. We never outgrow age three in that respect. You have to tell us again and again and again. And demonstrate what you mean. The next important competence is not to alibi yourself. Say: 'This doesn't work as well as it should. Let's take it back and re-engineer it.' We either do things to perfection, or we don't do them. We don't do things to get by. Working that way creates pride in the organization.

The last basic competence is the willingness to realize how unimportant you are compared to the task. Leaders need objectivity, a certain detachment. They subordinate themselves to the task, but don't identify themselves with the task. The task remains both bigger than they are, and different. The worst thing you can say about a leader is that on the day he or she left, the organization collapsed. When that happens, it means the so-called leader has sucked the place dry. He or she hasn't built. They may have been effective operators, but they have not created vision.

JOHN P. KOTTER
From *A Force for Change* (1990).

Leadership produces change. That is its primary function.

In cases of effective leadership, the direction of that change is carefully selected in an activity that is at the core of what leadership is all about. To understand that activity, it is absolutely essential to recognize what it is not. Setting direction is never the same as planning or long-term planning, although people regularly confuse the two. Planning is a management process, fundamentally deductive in nature, and primarily designed to help produce orderly results, not change. That is quite different from the direction-setting aspect of leadership. . . .

Leadership within a complex organization achieves this function through three subprocesses which can briefly be described as:

1. Establishing direction – developing a vision of the future, often the distant future, along with strategies for producing the changes needed to achieve that vision.
2. Aligning people – communicating the direction to those whose cooperation may be needed so as to create coalitions that understand the vision and that are committed to its achievement.
3. Motivating and inspiring – keeping people moving in the right direction despite major political, bureaucratic, and resource barriers to change by appealing to the very basic, but often untapped, human needs, values, and emotions.

People who provide effective leadership always seem to have above-average energy levels, often much above average. They appear to thrive on achieving something important and being in a position of influencing others to achieve. This inner drive is often associated with high personal standards, a certain dissatisfaction with the status quo, and a tendency to push for continuing improvements (what the Japanese call 'Kaizen'). . . .

Intellectual skills and abilities are probably especially important to direction setting. Assimilating a huge quantity of diverse information and sensing relevant patterns in that information is a task of considerable cognitive complexity. . . .

The Difference Between Management and Leadership

Management	Leadership
Planning and Budgeting – establishing detailed steps and timetables for achieving needed results, and then allocating the resources necessary to make that happen	Establishing direction – developing a vision for the future, often the distant future, and strategies for producing the changes needed to achieve that vision
Organizing and Staffing – establishing some structure for accomplishing plan requirements, staffing that structure with individuals, delegating responsibility and authority for carrying out the plan, providing policies and procedures to help guide people, and creating methods or systems to monitor implementation	Aligning People – communicating the direction by words and deeds to all those whose cooperation may be needed so as to influence the creation of teams and coalitions that understand the vision and strategies, and accept their validity
Controlling and Problem Solving – monitoring results vs. plan in some detail, identifying deviations, and then planning and organizing to solve these problems	Motivating and Inspiring – energizing people to overcome major political, bureaucratic, and resource barriers to change by satisfying very basic, but often unfulfilled, human needs
Produces a degree of predictability and order, and has the potential of consistently producing key results expected by various stakeholders (e.g., for customers, always being on time; for stockholders, being on budget)	Produces change, often to a dramatic degree, and has the potential of producing extremely useful change (e.g., new products that customers want, new approaches to labor relations that help make a firm more competitive)

Source: John P. Kotter, *A Force for Change* (1990).

Mental or emotional health seems to be yet another important attribute. ... In a sense, emotional health is probably a base upon which so-called interpersonal skills grow. When that base is missing or weak, those kind of skills seem to have difficulty emerging in later years. ...

Integrity seems to be another important attribute, for at least two reasons. Many people are remarkably capable in assessing whether a person values others and their well-being; they just watch what the person does and what impact that has. Someone whose integrity is questioned by others will, in particular, have great difficulty with alignment. People will not believe what he or she says, and they will be very reluctant to follow his or her lead.

JOHN ADAIR
From *Understanding Motivation* (1990).

It is perhaps best to work out a single list of leadership functions within the context of a given working situation, so that the sub-headings can have the stamp of reality upon them. But there is general agreement upon the essentials, and to illustrate some of these major functions meeting the three interacting areas of need, I give here a list originally worked out at the Royal Military Academy, Sandhurst, which has been the basis for numerous adaptations in industry and other fields:

- *Planning*: e.g. Seeking all available information.
Defining a group task, purpose or goal.
Making a workable plan (in right decision-making framework).
- *Initiating*: e.g. Briefing group on the aims and the plan.
Explaining why aim or plan is necessary.
Allocating tasks to group members.
Setting group standards.
- *Controlling*: e.g. Maintaining group standards.
Influencing tempo.
Ensuring all actions are taken towards objectives.
Keeping discussion relevant.

Prodding group to action/decision.
- *Supporting*: e.g. Expressing acceptance of persons and their contribution.

Encouraging group/individuals.
Disciplining group/individuals.
Creating team spirit.
Relieving tension with humour.
Reconciling disagreements or getting others to explore them.
- *Informing*: e.g. Clarifying task and plan.

Giving new information to the group, i.e. keeping them 'in the picture'.
Receiving information from group.
Summarizing suggestions and ideas coherently.
- *Evaluating*: e.g. Checking feasibility of an idea.

Testing the consequences of a proposed solution.
Evaluating the group performance.
Helping the group to evaluate its own performance against standards.

PETER M. SENGE
From *The Fifth Discipline* (1990).

Our traditional views of leaders – as special people who set the direction, make the key decisions, and energize the troops – are deeply rooted in an individualistic and non-systemic worldview. Especially in the West, leaders are *heroes* – great men (and occasionally women) who 'rise to the fore' in times of crises. Our prevailing leadership myths are still captured by the image of the captain of the cavalry leading the charge to rescue the settlers from the attacking Indians. So long as such myths prevail, they re-inforce a focus on short-term events and charismatic heroes rather than on systemic forces and collective learning. At its heart, the traditional view of leadership is based on assumptions of people's powerlessness, their lack of personal vision and inability to master the forces of change, deficits which can be remedied only by a few great leaders.

The new view of leadership in learning organizations centers on subtler and more important tasks. In a learning organization, leaders are designers, stewards, and teachers. They are responsible for *building organizations* where people continually expand their capabilities to understand complexity, clarify vision, and improve shared mental models – that is, they are responsible for learning.

But leaders of learning organizations must do more than just formulate strategies to exploit emerging trends. They must be able to help people understand the systemic forces that shape change. It is not enough to intuitively grasp these forces. Many 'visionary strategists' have rich intuitions about the causes of change, intuitions that they cannot explain. They end up being authoritarian leaders, imposing their strategies and policies or continually intervening in decisions. They fall into this fate even if their values are contrary to authoritarian leadership – because *only* they see the decisions that need to be made. Leaders in learning organizations have the ability to conceptualize their strategic insights so that they become public knowledge, open to challenge and further improvement.

'Leader as teacher' is not about 'teaching' people how to achieve their vision. It is about fostering learning, for everyone. Such leaders help people throughout the organization develop systemic understandings. Accepting this responsibility is the antidote to one of the most common downfalls of otherwise gifted leaders – losing their commitment to the truth.

Leaders who are designers, stewards, and teachers come to see their core task very simply. 'Just as Socrates felt that it was necessary to create a tension in the mind,' said Martin Luther King, Jr., 'so that individuals could rise from the bondage of myths and half truths . . . so must we . . . create the kind of tension in society that will help men rise from the dark depths of prejudice and racism.' The tension of which King spoke is the *creative tension* of personal mastery. This tension is generated by holding a vision and concurrently telling the truth about current reality relative to that vision – 'to dramatize the issue so that it can no longer be ignored,' as King put it.

The leader's creative tension is not anxiety: that is psychological tension. A leader's story, sense of purpose, values and vision establish the direction and target. His relentless commitment to the truth and to inquiry into the forces underlying current reality continually highlight the gaps between reality and the vision. Leaders generate and manage this creative tension – not just in themselves but in an entire organization. This is how they energize an organization. That is their basic job. That is why they exist.

NOW READ ON . . .

Adair, John, *Understanding Motivation*, Guildford: Talbot Adair (1990)

Bennis, Warren, *On Becoming a Leader*, London: Hutchinson (1989)

Drucker, Peter F., *The Practice of Management*, New York: Harper & Row (1954); London: Heinemann (1955)

Drucker, Peter F., *Managing the Non-Profit Organization*, Oxford: Butterworth-Heinemann (1990). Quoted in *The Frontiers of Leadership*, ed. Michel Syrett and Clare Hogg, Oxford: Blackwell (1992)

Harvey-Jones, John, *Making it Happen*, Glasgow: William Collins (1988)

Kotter, John P., *A Force for Change*, New York: The Free Press (1990)

McGregor, Douglas, *The Human Side of Enterprise*, New York: McGraw-Hill (1960)

Peters, Tom and Waterman, Robert H. Jr., *In Search of Excellence*, New York and London: Harper & Row (1982)

Peters, Tom, *Thriving on Chaos*, New York: Alfred A. Knopf (1987); London: Macmillan (1988)

Senge, Peter M., *The Fifth Discipline*, New York: Doubleday (1990); London: Century (1992)

Chapter 8

Strategy and Strategic Thinking

The concept of strategy and strategic thinking applied to business was a legacy of World War II, in particular the strategic studies carried out by the US Army Air Force. The methodology was adapted to US industry in the late 1940s; leading practitioners included Robert McNamara, president of Ford Motor Company, who became US Secretary of Defense under President John F. Kennedy. But the 'bridge to business usage', wrote H. Igor Ansoff, the first great theorist of management strategy, was a 1953 publication by two Princeton academics, J. von Neumann and O. Morgenstern, called *Theory of Games and Economic Behavior*. It attempted to formulate methods of resolving conflict in politics, war and business, and in it, wrote Ansoff, the concept of strategy was interpreted in two ways: pure strategy, a move or series of moves by a firm in a specific area such as product development, and grand (or mixed) strategy, a statistical rule by which the firm could decide what pure strategy it should adopt in any given situation.

Before Ansoff established strategy in management studies in the mid-1960s, the subject had been put on the academic map by Alfred D. Chandler of Harvard Business School. His studies of US corporations and their historical development, published as *Strategy and Structure* in 1962, demonstrated convincingly that the structure of an organization was determined by its strategic goals and the actions and resources employed to achieve them. The organization's function, he argued, was to implement strategy, and all its varied management structures and hierarchies developed from that objective. The dictum has remained a foundation stone of strategy studies ever since.

Chandler, a business historian rather than a management theorist, traced the roots of the modern managerial system to the origins of the US railroad business in the mid-nineteenth century. The nature of the railways dictated a need for central scheduling but local management of track operations – the basic principle of decentralization. It took another century, however, for decentralization to be widely adopted in business organizations, a development in which Chandler's book and Alfred P. Sloan's *My Years With General Motors*, published in 1963, were hugely influential.

The 1960s saw the first flowering of management theory devoted to the subject of corporate strategy. The trail-blazer, and the most influential academic in the field, was H. Igor Ansoff, whose *Corporate Strategy* (1965) set out to be 'a practical method for strategic decision-making within a business firm', and provided a series of detailed processes and checklists for accomplishing it. Henry Mintzberg, the Canadian authority on managerial and strategic decision-making, called it 'the most elaborate model of strategic planning in the literature', and Sir John Harvey-Jones, Britain's celebrated business troubleshooter, described the revised version in 1987 as 'one of the best business books of all time'.

Ansoff later felt that his original approach had been too prescriptive and spent the best part of two decades refining his concepts and building more flexibility into the planning process to accommodate the increasingly turbulent and unpredictable pace of business change. The result, *Implanting Strategic Management*, was first published in 1984 and introduced Ansoff's 'strategic success formula', based on the premise that a company performs best when its external strategy and internal capabilities are both matched to the turbulence of the business environment. The book put forward methods of creating a dual system for managing both long-term strategic change and daily business targets.

Corporate Strategy in its 1987 edition provides a first-rate analysis of how strategic decision-making interacts with that in the administrative and operational fields, explaining the key questions to be addressed when forming strategy:

- what are the firm's objectives and goals?
- should it seek to diversify, and if so, in what areas?
- how should it develop and exploit its current market position?

Ansoff stresses that most strategic decisions are made within a restricting framework of resources and are therefore limited to a choice of alternatives. 'The object is to produce a resource-allocation pattern which will offer the best potential for meeting the firm's objectives.'

Corporate Strategy was also years ahead of Michael Porter's influential work in identifying 'competitive advantage' in strategic planning, and in providing a checklist for profiling competitors.

By the early 1970s, strategy technique was a flourishing discipline at Harvard. Kenneth R. Andrews in *The Concept of Corporate Strategy* (1971) defined corporate strategy (which he treats separately from business strategy) as 'the pattern of decisions in a company that determines and reveals its objectives, purposes or goals, produces the principal policies and plans for achieving those goals, and defines the range of business the company is to pursue, the kind of economic and human organization it is or intends to be, and the nature of the economic and non-economic contribution it intends to make to its shareholders, employees, customers and communities.'

In line with Chandler, Andrews wrote that corporate strategy is 'an organization process, in many ways inseparable from the structure, behaviour and culture of the company.' Business strategy, in Andrews' definition, deals more narrowly with how a company positions itself in a given business.

Andrews identified four components of strategy, well ahead of his time in acknowledging the wider responsibilities of a business enterprise: market opportunity; corporate competence and resources; personal values and aspirations; and acknowledged obligations to people in society other than shareholders. In evaluating a strategic approach, he suggested ten key questions (quoted in *Writers on Strategy and Strategic Management*, by J.I. Moore):

1. Is the strategy identifiable, and has it been made clear either in words or in practice?
2. Is the strategy in some way unique?
3. Does the strategy fully exploit domestic and international environmental opportunity?
4. Is the strategy consistent with corporate competence and resources, both present and projected?
5. Are the major provisions of the strategy and the programme of major policies of which it is comprised internally consistent?
6. Is the chosen level of risk feasible in economic and personal terms?
7. Is the strategy appropriate to the personal values and aspirations of the key managers?
8. Is the strategy appropriate to the desired level of contribution to society?
9. Does the strategy constitute a clear stimulus to organizational effort and commitment?
10. Are there early indications of the responsiveness of markets and market segments to the strategy?

In evaluating strategy, Andrews warns against overusing financial ratios such as debt/equity, return on investment or earnings per share, because of the risk that they may encourage short-term solutions at the expense of long-term planning.

Harvard's third great authority on strategy was and is Michael Porter, now one of the world's best-known and highest-earning management gurus. By the 1980s, as he noted in the introduction to *Competitive Strategy*, the increased attention to formal strategic planning in American industry had highlighted such questions as:

- What is driving competition in my industry, or in industries I am thinking of entering?
- What actions are competitors likely to take, and what is the best way to respond?
- How will my industry evolve?
- How can my firm be best positioned to compete in the long run?

Competitive Strategy set out to answer these. Porter took corporate strategy out into the marketplace and in doing so, began a process by which he successfully 'branded' the subject of competitive strategy as his own. (The principles Porter laid out in this book and in *The Competitive Advantage of Nations* are further explored in Chapter 14.)

The early 1980s, before Porter established his towering reputation, was a period of growing American angst over Japan's rising power in global markets. Kenichi Ohmae's *The Mind of the Strategist* (1982) offered penetrating insights into Japanese competitive strategy and how it was instinctively practised by business leaders who often lacked any formal intellectual training in the techniques. For students of the art and craft of strategic thinking, it continues to be a valuable handbook, explaining in fascinating detail how techniques can be developed to become an effective strategist.

Henry Mintzberg also wrote illuminatingly about 'crafting strategy' as part of his work on analysing the processes of managerial decision-making, and a useful and stimulating short book in the same genre is Peter Schwartz's *The Art of the Long View* (1991), a lucid and enjoyable exposition of scenario-planning by a former Shell executive who was involved in the oil giant's consistently successful use of scenarios in plotting future strategy.

Mintzberg has since turned a sceptical eye on the planning industry in *The Rise and Fall of Strategic Planning* (1994), which pokes gentle fun at planners for overemphasizing the post-1960s as an era of exceptional turbulence. When, he asks, was any age not one of change and turbulence to those going through it, with the possible exception of the 1950s and 1960s? Ask anyone who had to run a business in the Depression, or in the aftermath of World War I, when inflation in Europe ran out of control. Like the chicken in the Russian folk tale which shrieked that the sky was falling because an acorn hit it on the head, planners cry that the environment has become turbulent, whereas it is only their own plans that are being proved fallible. Mintzberg does concede a role for strategic planning, but in a broader, more flexible concept than the earlier 'one best way' approach; with planners acting as teachers and catalysts for opening up strategic thinking:

'Planning never was any 'one best way'. But reconceived as strategic programming, it can sometimes be a good way. It does have an important role to play in organizations, as do plans and planners, when matched with the appropriate contexts. Too much planning may lead us to chaos, but so too would too little, and more directly. . . . Several decades of experience with strategic planning have taught us about the need to loosen up the process of strategy formation rather than try to seal it off through arbitrary formalization.'

KEY TEXTS

H. IGOR ANSOFF
From *Implanting Strategic Management* (1990).

A strategy has several distinguishing characteristics:

1. The process of strategy formulation results in *no immediate action*. Rather, it sets the general directions in which the firm's position will grow and develop.
2. Therefore, strategy must next be used to generate strategic projects through a *search process*. The role of strategy in search is first to focus on areas defined by the strategy, and, second to filter out and uncover possibilities which are inconsistent with the strategy.
3. Thus, strategy becomes *unnecessary whenever the historical dynamics of an organization will take it where it wants to go*. This is to say, when the search process is already focussed on the preferred areas.
4. At the time of strategy formulation it is not possible to enumerate all the project possibilities which will be uncovered. Therefore, strategy formulation must be based on *highly aggregated, incomplete and uncertain information* about classes of alternatives.
5. When search uncovers specific alternatives, the more precise, less aggregated information which becomes available may cast doubts on the wisdom of the original strategy choice. Thus, successful use of strategy requires *strategic feedback*.

6. Since both strategy and objectives are used to filter projects, they appear similar. Yet they are distinct. Objectives represent the ends which the firm is seeking to attain, while the *strategy is the means to these ends.* The objectives are higher-level decision rules. A strategy which is valid under one set of objectives may lose its validity when the objectives of the organization are changed.

7. Strategy and objectives are interchangeable; both at different points in time and at different levels of organization. Thus, some attributes of performance (such as market share) can be an objective of the firm at one time and its strategy at another. Further, as objectives and strategy are elaborated throughout an organization, a typical hierarchical relationship results: *elements of strategy at a higher managerial level become objectives at a lower one.*

KENICHI OHMAE
From *The Mind of the Strategist* (1982).

The strategist's weapons are strategic thinking, consistency, and coherence. With them, and relying on staff to provide the relevant knowledge or information, the strategist sets out to devise a method to clear away confusion and break the bottlenecks that have put the company into its current difficulties. No dramatic leap or stroke of genius is involved. The object of the quest is to come up with ideas or innovations that will introduce new life into the company's market situation, its resource allocation system, or anywhere else its existing practices have become rigid, thus enabling it to move forward in a specific direction.

The strategist's method is very simply to challenge the prevailing assumptions with a single question: Why? and to put the same question relentlessly to those responsible for the current way of doing things until they are sick of it. This way bottlenecks to fundamental improvement are identified, and major breakthroughs in achieving the objectives of the business become possible.

Strategic thinking in business . . . must be backed by the daily use of imagination and by constant training in logical thought processes. Success must be summoned; it will not come unbidden and unplanned. Top management and its corporate planners cannot sensibly base their day-to-day work on blind optimism and apply strategic thinking only when confronted by unexpected obstacles. They must develop the habit of thinking strategically, and they must do it as a matter of course. Ideally, they should approach it with real enthusiasm as a stimulating mental exercise.

To become an effective strategist requires constant practice in strategic thinking. It is a daily discipline, not a resource that can be left dormant in normal times and tapped at will in an emergency.

In the construction of any business strategy, three main players must be taken into account: the corporation itself, the customer, and the competition. Each of these 'strategic three C's' is a living entity with its own interests and objectives. We shall call them, collectively, the 'strategic triangle'.

Seen in the context of the strategic triangle, the job of the strategist is to achieve superior performance, relative to competition, in the key factors for success of the business. At the same time, the strategist must be sure that his strategy properly matches the strengths of the corporation with the needs of a clearly defined market. Positive matching of the needs and objectives of the two parties involved is required for a lasting good relationship; without it, the corporation's long-term viability may be at stake.

A key aspect of Japanese corporate strategy, again prompted by the awareness of resource limitations, is the tendency to look for a different battleground on which to compete with the Western giants. For example, it was to capitalize on emission-control regulations that Honda entered four-wheel-vehicle manufacturing in the early 1970s, designing plant and car (the Civic) simultaneously so that they would be competitive in productivity with such experienced automakers as Toyota and Nissan. This

approach, known as value design and zero-based production, has been one of the biggest single factors
contributing to the success of assembly-oriented Japanese
manufacturers.

Choosing the battleground so that they would not have
to fight head-on against large Western enterprises has been
the key to their success. They have sought out markets,
functions, and product ranges where they could initially
avoid head-to-head competition. As a result, Japanese production styles, design and engineering approaches, and
personnel management philosophies are so different today
that Western companies find it extremely difficult to fight
back or catch up with their Japanese competitors.

Doing as the Japanese do, even if it were possible,
would not be the answer. But Japanese strategic
approaches, properly understood, can be a valuable source
of insight for any thoughtful corporate strategist.

HENRY MINTZBERG
From *Mintzberg on Management* (1989).

To manage strategy is in the first place mostly to manage
stability, not change. Indeed, most of the time senior
managers should not be formulating strategy at all; they
should be getting on with making their organizations as
effective as possible in pursuing the strategies they already
have. Like distinguished craftsmen, organizations become
distinguished because they master the details.

To manage strategy, then, at least in the first instance, is
not so much to promote change as to know *when* to do so.
Advocates of strategic planning often urge managers to
plan for perpetual instability in the environment (for
example, by rolling over five-year plans annually). But
this obsession with change is dysfunctional. Organizations
that reassess their strategies continuously are like individuals who reassess their jobs or their marriages
continuously – in both cases, they can drive themselves
crazy, or else reduce themselves to inaction. The formal
planning process repeats itself so often and so mechanically

that it can desensitize organizations to real change, programming them more and more deeply into set patterns, and thereby encouraging them to make only minor adaptations.

So-called strategic planning must be recognized for what it is: a means, not to create strategy, but to program a strategy already created – to work out its implications formally. It is essentially analytic in nature, based on decomposition, while strategy creation is essentially a process of synthesis. That is why trying to create strategies through formal planning most often leads to the extrapolation of existing strategies or to the copying of the strategies of competitors. . . .

The real challenge in crafting strategy lies in detecting the subtle discontinuities that may undermine an organization in the future. And for that, there is no technique, no program, just a sharp mind in touch with the situation. Such discontinuities are unexpected and irregular, essentially unprecedented. They can be dealt with only by minds that are attuned to existing patterns yet able to perceive important breaks in them.

PETER SCHWARTZ
From *The Art of the Long View* (1991).

Without driving forces, there is no way to begin thinking through a scenario. They are a device for honing your initial judgement, for helping you decide which factors will be significant and which factors will not.

As a business executive thinking about the future of your company, you know that interest rates, energy prices, new technology, the behaviour of the markets, and your competitors' actions all come from the outside to affect your business. But how do you find the significant driving forces among them, and the forces which underlie them? You start by taking another look at the decision you have to make.

You will quickly see that some driving forces are critical to that decision, while others don't require much attention. . . .

Driving forces often seem obvious to one person and hidden to another. That is why I almost always compose scenarios in teams. Often, we begin this stage (after we have individually done our research) by standing before a large sheet of white paper, and brainstorming together. . . .

Whenever I look for driving forces I first run through a familiar litany of categories:

- Society
- Technology
- Economics
- Politics
- Environment

In nearly every situation, I find forces from each of these arenas which make a difference in the story.

NOW READ ON . . .

Ansoff, H. Igor, *Corporate Strategy*, New York: McGraw-Hill (1965); London: Sidgwick & Jackson (1986)

Ansoff, H. Igor, *Implanting Strategic Management*, New Jersey: Prentice-Hall (1984, 1990)

Mintzberg, Henry, *Mintzberg on Management*, New York: The Free Press; London: Collier Macmillan (1989)

Mintzberg, Henry, *The Rise and Fall of Strategic Planning*, Hemel Hempstead: Prentice-Hall International (1994)

Moore, J.I., *Writers on Strategy and Strategic Management*, London: Penguin (1992)

Ohmae, Kenichi, *The Mind of the Strategist*, New York: McGraw-Hill (1982); London: Penguin Business Library (1983)

Porter, Michael, *Competitive Strategy: Techniques for Analysing Industries and Competitors*, New York: The Free Press (1980)

Schwartz, Peter, *The Art of the Long View*, New York: Doubleday (1991); London: Century Business (1992)

Chapter 9

Decision-making

Making decisions is ultimately what managers are paid for. 'The first managerial skill,' wrote Peter Drucker in 1973, 'is . . . the making of effective decisions.' (*Management: Tasks, Responsibilities, Practices.*)

Managers make decisions every day, most of them routine and low-risk, but every decision, however small, requires an assessment of objectives, alternatives and potential risks. As Charles H. Kepner and Benjamin B. Tregoe described it in their 'Decision Analysis' system, the choice may involve a thousand criteria and the deliberation of a hundred or more people, or five criteria and ten minutes of deliberation by one person. 'The dimensions are immaterial because the basic process is always the same. And the final judgment is always: "This is what ought to be done".' (*The New Rational Manager*, 1981.)

The principles of decision-making, as Drucker pointed out in an earlier book, *The Practice of Management*, have been known for thousands of years, but in the 1950s a number of new tools were introduced – mathematical analysis, modern symbolical logic, mathematical information theory, the 'Theory of Games' and mathematical probability – all part of Operations Research, a legacy of World War II military planning. These, wrote Drucker in 1954, could not assist the most important phases in decision-making – determining the right question, setting objectives for the solution, setting the rules, or making a decision effective – though they were useful in analysing the problems and developing alternatives.

Since then, technology has taken a hand: Herbert Simon,

Professor of Computer Science at Carnegie Mellon University, Pittsburgh, and a 1978 Nobel laureate for economics, has used computer techniques to analyse and simulate the decision-making process. In his book *The New Science of Management Decision*, first published in 1960 and revised in 1977, he suggested that finding the solution to any problem could be divided into four stages:

- Perception of decision need or opportunity, the 'intelligence phase'
- Formulation of alternative courses of action
- Evaluation of the alternatives for their respective contributions
- Choice of one or more alternatives for implementation.

Simon also differentiated between 'programmed' and 'unprogrammed' decisions; the first being those capable of processing to an established pattern, the second embracing new or complex situations for which there exists no precedent.

In the 1970s, when fashion rolled round again to scientific management with such techniques as learning curves and the Boston Consulting Group's 'Boston Box', a matrix for deciding investment strategies, there was a vogue for 'decision trees' and similar systems for eliminating options until one core choice was reached. But the problem with such superficially attractive methodologies, like computer-generated analysis, is that they cannot provide a properly holistic assessment because they fail to take in 'soft' data or values.

Henry Mintzberg, recording his own growing disagreement with Simon's book since its first publication in 1960, concluded that technological analysis could never be seen in the same uncritical light after the Vietnam War when, in Mintzberg's words, 'America's finest analytic talent, drawn from the centres of liberal intelligentsia, applied the modern techniques to the White House's non-programmed decisions, and the result was a war effort both ill-conceived and fundamentally immoral.'

What went wrong? Analysis, Mintzberg suggested, could not handle the soft data – the will of the enemy, for example

– as opposed to hard data such as the number of bombs needed to lay waste a jungle. 'Facts become impregnated with value when they consistently line up behind a single set of goals,' wrote Mintzberg. 'In Vietnam they supported the military goals; the humanitarian goals, supported only by soft data, were driven out of the analysis. We see the same thing in corporations when the hard data line up behind the economic goals – cost reduction, profit increase, growth in market share – leaving the social goals – product quality, employee satisfaction, protection of the environment – to fend for themselves.' (*Mintzberg on Management*, 1989.)

The Japanese rarely make the mistake of leaving soft data out of a decision process because of their lengthy system of achieving consensus through debate at a number of organizational levels. This ensures that the eventual decision, though itself made by a small group and therefore not participative, is already 'pre-sold' to everyone who will be affected by it.

Peter Drucker delves deeper into the Japanese process to find that there is a key difference between East and West in 'making a decision'. Whereas in the West the emphasis is on the answer to the question, to the Japanese the vital element is defining the question. 'The important and crucial steps are to decide whether there is a need for a decision and what the decision is about,' writes Drucker in *Management: Tasks, Responsibilities, Practices*. 'And it is in this step that the Japanese aim at attaining consensus. . . . The answer to the question (what the West considers the decision) follows from its definition.'

During the consensus-seeking process, people are not forced to take sides on the ultimate answer. So the result, says Drucker, is 'a meeting of minds that there is (or is not) a need for a change in behaviour.' Once this stage is reached, the way is clear for top management to refer the final decision-making to a chosen group of 'appropriate people'.

The length of time all this takes is often infuriating for non-Japanese negotiators working on quite different premises, and it is only of value for big decisions, with the result that many small decisions are never made at all. But it does have the merit of making for very effective decisions, with great organizational clout behind them.

'It almost guarantees that all the alternatives will be considered,' says Drucker. 'It rivets management attention to essentials. . . . Japanese managers may come up with the wrong answer to the problem (as was the decision to go to war against the United States in 1941) but they rarely come up with the right answer to the wrong problem. And that, as all decision-makers learn, is the most dangerous course, the irretrievably wrong decision.'

Decision-making, as Drucker sums up, is not a mechanical job. 'It is risk-taking and a challenge to judgment.' And there is always the danger that decision-making in groups runs up against conscious or unconscious defences among individuals that deter them from a fully open approach to risk-taking, as the Harvard organizational psychologist Chris Argyris discovered. He analysed 265 decision-making meetings in six companies and found that the actual behaviour of the executives – defensive, distrustful, inhibited in groups – ran counter to their declared beliefs that trust and innovation were essential to good decision-making.

'During the study of the decision-making processes of the president and the nine vice-presidents of a firm with nearly 3,000 employees, I concluded that the members unknowingly behaved in such a way as not to encourage risk-taking, openness, expression of feelings and cohesive, trusting relationships.' ('Interpersonal Barriers to Decision-Making', *Harvard Business Review*, 1966.) Yet later, interviewing them as individuals, Argyris became aware that part of the problem was a reluctance to express dissent and negative feelings 'because we trust each other and respect each other'. Issues of conflict were ignored because it was felt 'we should not air our dirty linen'.

By the late 1980s, management theorists such as Richard Pascale were encouraging the positive uses of conflict in an organization. But wise old practitioners like Alfred P. Sloan of General Motors had long known that. Sloan once told one of his top GM committees: 'Gentlemen, I take it we are all in complete agreement on the decision here.' Everyone nodded. 'Then,' said Sloan, 'I propose we postpone further discussion of this matter until the next meeting to give ourselves time to develop disagreement, and perhaps gain some understanding of what the decision is all about.'

KEY TEXTS

PETER F. DRUCKER
From *The Practice of Management* (1954).

The importance of decision-making in management is generally recognized. But a good deal of the discussion tends to centre on problem-solving, that is, on giving answers. And that is the wrong focus. Indeed, the most common source of mistakes in management decisions is the emphasis on finding the right answer rather than the right question.

The only kind of decision that really centres in problem-solving is the unimportant, the routine, the tactical decision. If both the conditions of the situation and the requirements that the answer has to satisfy, are known and simple, problem-solving is indeed the only thing necessary. In this case the job is merely to choose between a few obvious alternatives. And the criterion is usually one of economy: the decision shall accomplish the desired end with the minimum of effort and disturbance. . . .

But the important decisions, the decisions that really matter, are strategic. They involve either finding out what the situation is, or changing it, either finding out what the resources are or what they should be. These are the specifically managerial decisions. Anyone who is a manager has to make such strategic decisions, and the higher his level in the management hierarchy, the more of them he must make.

Among these are all decisions on business objectives and on the means to reach them. All decisions affecting productivity belong here: they always aim at changing the total situation. Here also belong all organization decisions and all major capital-expenditure decisions. But most of the decisions that are considered operating decisions are also strategic in character: arrangement of sales districts or training of salesmen; plant layout or raw-materials inventory; preventive maintenance or the flow of payroll vouchers through an office.

Strategic decisions – whatever their magnitude, complexity or importance – should never be taken through problem-solving. Indeed, in these specifically managerial decisions, the important and difficult job is never to find the right answer, it is to find the right question. For there are few things as useless – if not as dangerous – as the right answer to the wrong question.

Nor is it enough to *find* the right answer. More important and more difficult is to make effective the course of action decided upon. Management is not concerned with knowledge for its own sake; it is concerned with performance. . . . And one of the most crucial jobs in the entire decision-making process is to ensure that decisions reached in various parts of the business and on various levels of management are compatible with each other, and consonant with the goals of the whole business.

Decision-making has five distinct phases: Defining the problem; analysing the problem; developing alternate solutions; deciding upon the best solution; converting the decision into effective action. Each phase has several steps.

Making decisions can either be time-wasting or it can be the manager's best means for solving the problem of time utilization. Time should be spent on defining the problem. Time is well spent on analysing the problem and developing alternate solutions. Time is necessary to make the solution effective. But much less time should be spent on finding the right solution. And any time spent on selling a solution after it has been reached is sheer waste and evidence of poor time utilization in the earlier phases.

The objectives should always reflect the objectives of the business, should always be focused ultimately on business performance and business results. They should always balance and harmonize the immediate and the long-range future. They should always take into account both the business as a whole and the activities needed to run it.

At the same time the rules that limit the solution must be thought through. What are the principles, policies and rules of conduct that have to be followed? It may be a rule of the company never to borrow more than half its capital needs. It may be a principle never to hire a man from the outside without first considering all inside managers carefully. It may be considered a requirement of good manager development not to create crown princes in the organization. It may be established policy that design changes must be submitted to manufacturing and marketing before being put into effect by the engineering department.

To spell out the rules is necessary because in many cases the right decision will require changing accepted policies or practices. Unless the manager thinks through clearly what he wants to change and why, he is in danger of trying at one and the same time both to alter and to preserve established practice.

There are four criteria for picking the best from among the possible solutions.
1. The risk. The manager has to weigh the risks of each course of action against the expected gains. There is no riskless action nor even riskless non-action. But what matters most is neither the expected gain nor the anticipated risk, but the ratio between them. Every alternative should therefore contain an appraisal of the odds it carries.
2. Economy of effort. Which of the possible lines of action will give the greatest results with the least effort, will obtain the needed change with the least necessary disturbance of the organization? . . .
3. Timing. If the situation has great urgency, the preferable course of action is one that dramatises the decision and serves notice on the organization that something important is happening. If, on the other hand, long, consistent effort is needed, a slow start that gathers momentum may be preferable. . . .
4. Limitations of resources. The most important resource whose limitations have to be considered are the human beings who will carry out the decision. No decision can be better than the people who have to carry it out. Their vision, competence, skill and understanding determine what they can and cannot do. . . .

The wrong decision must never be adopted because people and the competence to do what is right are lacking. The decision should always lie between genuine alternates, that is, between courses of action every one of which will adequately solve the problem. And if the problem can be solved only by demanding more of people than they are capable of giving, they must either learn to do more or be replaced by people who can.

M.J. CULLIGAN, C.S. DEAKINS, AND A.H. YOUNG
From *Back-to-Basics Management* (1983).

In implementing decisions you should gather as much information as possible about the circumstances surrounding the decision. You must:

- Decide whom the decision will affect, i.e., personnel, other departments and managers, etc.
- Decide if you need to include other personnel in the decision and get their reactions
- Decide whom you need to communicate the decision to
- Decide whether the equipment and resources can stand the extra load that will be added
- Decide if any equipment or other resources are needed
- Decide how the decision will affect the budget or monetary situation of the corporation, i.e., purchasing new equipment, adding sales personnel, offering an additional service or part
- Decide if you need to eliminate or change any previous decision
- Decide how long will you need before the decision goes into effect
- Decide whether to delegate the planning and to whom, or to do it yourself
- Decide how you implement the decision without higher authority

Once you have asked yourself these questions, and any others you feel are important, you are ready to begin your planning for implementation. To start your planning make a list of the following:

- All the surrounding elements of the decision needed in

134

order for it to work; i.e., personnel, budget, goal, possible results, ways of reversing decision, equipment needed, motivation communication, presentation, etc.
- Decide which elements must be done before others can be started. Can some elements be worked on at the same time?
- The number of work hours needed to complete each element.
- The name of the individual who will be responsible for seeing each aspect completed.

Look at the work hours and elements:

- Which element will take the longest time?
- Does it need any other elements to be complete?
- If 'yes', add up all the time needed to finish the longest element and you will have the approximate time in which you can start to implement the decision.

CHARLES H. KEPNER AND BENJAMIN B. TREGOE
From *The New Rational Manager* (1981).

Every decision we make requires us to think in terms of *objectives, alternatives*, and *potential risks*. . . . These decision situations fall into five categories:

- The complex decision that requires examination of a large amount of information, and involves the judgments of many people.
- The 'Yes/No' decision that involves only two alternatives: to take or reject a course of action; to do something in a different way or continue as before.
- The decision as to whether a single proposed course of action is sound enough to be implemented.
- The decision in which an original alternative must be developed by the decision-maker or team.
- The routine decision: hiring, purchase of equipment or services, development of personnel policies, and other everyday decisions.

Decision Analysis is a systematic procedure based on the thinking pattern we all use in making choices. Its techniques represent expansions and refinements of the elements in this thinking pattern:

- We appreciate the fact that a choice must be made.
- We consider the specific factors that must be satisfied if the choice is to succeed.
- We decide what kind of action will best satisfy these factors.
- We consider what risks may be attached to our final choice of action that could jeopardize its safety and success.

Good decision-making, like good problem-solving, depends heavily on experience and judgment. In both areas of managerial responsibility, however, it is within the framework of a *systematic procedure* that experience and judgment produce successful results and a reputation for managerial excellence.

In Decision Analysis, resolution will consist of an answer to the questions 'To what purpose?' 'Which?' and 'How?'

A decision statement provides the focus for everything that follows and sets the limit of the choice. The criteria to be developed will follow from it, describing in detail the requirements of the decision. The alternatives will be judged on their ability to meet these requirements. Because the decision statement sets all these activities in motion, it has another quality in common with the deviation statement: *the way it is worded deserves careful attention.*

A decision statement always indicates some kind of action and its intended result: 'Select a New Director of Quality Control' or 'Devise a New Personnel Evaluation System'. It also indicates the *level* at which the decision is to be made. . . .

Objectives, in our terminology, are the criteria for the decision – the specific details of what the decision is to accomplish. We establish these objectives once we state the purpose of the decision and agree upon the level at which it is to be made. We do this before discussing alternatives, sometimes even before identifying alternatives. Decision Analysis is the antithesis of identifying a course of action and then building a case to support it. Instead we are moving from what needs to be accomplished toward the alternative that can best accomplish it. For example, if we want to hire a new executive, we are more likely to make a good choice if we *first* identify the qualities of an ideal candidate and *then* begin the interviewing process. . . .

We divide the objectives into two categories: MUSTS and WANTS. The MUST objectives are mandatory: they *must* be achieved to guarantee a successful decision. When the time comes to assess alternatives against our objectives, any alternative that cannot fulfill a MUST objective will immediately drop out of the analysis. These objectives must be measurable because they function as a screen to eliminate failure-prone alternatives. We must be able to say, 'This alternative *absolutely* cannot fulfill this objective; it cannot meet a requirement that is mandatory for success.' For example, a typical MUST objective in a hiring decision is 'Two years' experience as supervisor in this industry.' If that length of experience is mandatory, then there is no point in considering any candidate who hasn't put in the two years. It is a measurable objective: A candidate either has it or doesn't have it. His or her *other* good qualities are irrelevant.

All other objectives are categorized as WANTS. The alternatives we generate will be judged on their *relative* performance against WANT objectives, not on whether or not they fulfill them. The function of these objectives is to give us a comparative picture of alternatives – *a sense of how the alternatives perform relative to each other*.

A WANT objective may be mandatory but cannot be classified as a MUST for one or two reasons. First, it may not be measurable. It cannot, therefore, give us an absolute Yes-or-No judgment about the performance of an alternative. Secondly, we may not want a Yes-or-No judgment. We may prefer to use that objective as a *relative* measure of performance.

An objective will be stated frequently as a MUST and

then be rephrased as a WANT so that it can perform both functions. For example, 'Two years' experience in this industry' (MUST) may be rephrased as 'Maximum experience in this industry' (WANT). Now, when we come to evaluate the alternatives, we can make two kinds of judgments: Candidates with less than two years' experience will be eliminated. The remaining candidates will be judged relative to each other on the basis of their experience. . . .

An ideal alternative perfectly fulfills every condition set for it without adding new difficulties. Unfortunately, ideal alternatives are rare. We must, therefore, evaluate each available alternative by measuring it against all of our objectives. It is the relative quality of that fit that concerns us.

If we must choose among several alternatives, we will have to decide which one will best fulfill our objectives with the smallest acceptable risk. . . .

If there is only one alternative, we must decide whether it is good enough to accept. In this case our evaluation will focus on its relative worth compared with a perfect but unobtainable alternative.

If we must choose between a current and a proposed course of action, then we consider both to be alternatives. We evaluate their performance against our objectives just as we would if both had been proposed. . . .

If, in the absence of *any* alternative, we must create something new, we can usually build an alternative from available components. We then choose the best and most feasible combinations, treat each as a separate alternative, and evaluate all of them against an ideal model of an alternative. . . .

The final step in Decision Analysis is the search for possible adverse consequences of all feasible alternatives. . . .

We must thoroughly explore and evaluate the possible adverse consequences of any alternative *before* we make a final decision. This is the only opportunity we will ever have to deal with such effects at no cost beyond a little intellectual effort.

JOHN ADAIR
From *Great Leaders* (1989).

In order to guide a group, organization or nation in the right direction a leader needs the ability to think and decide. It could be called the intellectual dimension of leadership. Practical reason, intuition and imagination are all included under that heading. But it is not only a matter of the leader having some or all of these attributes. He or she has to be able to guide a problem-solving or decision-making body, such as a board of directors, whose members may have different mental abilities as well as different personalities. . . .

The core activity is undoubtedly *thinking*. The Canadian entrepreneur Roy Thomson, who built up a vast publishing empire and owned *The Times*, insisted upon its importance. In *After I was Sixty* (1975), his autobiography, he wrote:

'Thinking is work. In the early stages of a man's career it is very hard work. When a difficult decision or problem arises, how easy it is, after looking at it superficially, to give up thinking about it. It is easy to put it from one's mind. It is easy to decide that it is insoluble, or that something will turn up to help us. Sloppy and inconclusive thinking becomes a habit. The more one does it the more one is unfitted to think a problem through to a proper conclusion.

If I have any advice to pass on, as a successful man, it is this: if one wants to be successful, one must think; one must think until it hurts. One must worry a problem in one's mind until it seems there cannot be another aspect of it that hasn't been considered. Believe me, that is hard work and, from my close observation, I can say that there are few people indeed who are prepared to perform this arduous and tiring work.'

NOW READ ON . . .

Adair, John, *Great Leaders*, Guildford: Talbot Adair (1989)
Culligan, M.J., Deakins, C.S., and Young, A.H., *Back-to-Basics Management*, New York: Facts on File (1983)
Drucker, Peter F., *The Practice of Management*, New York: Harper & Row (1954); London: Heinemann (1955)
Kepner, C.H. and Tregoe, B.B., *The New Rational Manager*, London: John Martin Publishing (1981); now published by Princeton Research Press, Princeton, N.J.

Chapter 10

Managing Time

Ruthlessly effective use of time is the factor that separates the exceptional manager from the herd. Without it, all the other qualities for which he or she is being handsomely paid – high skills of decision-making, leadership and motivation, strategic thinking, financial brilliance – will have far less impact on the business.

The great cautionary example here comes from Henry Mintzberg's famous study of how managers actually spend their time (*The Nature of Managerial Work*, 1973; 'The Manager's Job, Folklore and Fact', *Harvard Business Review*, 1975). In this he found that the work of senior managers was continually being disrupted by interruptions, which they did not necessarily resent, believing them to be a source of information. Half of the activities of the five CEOs studied lasted less than nine minutes, while an investigation of 160 British top and middle managers discovered that only once every two days were they able to work for half an hour or more without interruptions.

Although Mintzberg found that these fragmented days actually convinced managers they were doing a good job by responding to problems and covering a great many issues, however superficially, he pointed out that reflective planning was impossible. 'The manager is simply responding to the pressures of his or her job. . . . One president not only placed his desk so that he could look down a long hallway but also left his door open when he was alone – an invitation for subordinates to come in and interrupt him.

'Clearly, these managers wanted to encourage the flow of

141

current information. But, more significantly, they seemed to be conditioned by their own workloads. They appreciated the opportunity cost of their own time, and they were continually aware of their ever-present obligations – mail to be answered, callers to attend to, and so on. It seems that no matter what they are doing, managers are plagued by the possibilities of what they might do and what they must do.'

Big-league managers such as Sir Colin Marshall of British Airways, a man accustomed to managing his time across several international zones, are not at the mercy of events and interruptions. They are freeholders rather than leaseholders of their time; most arrive very early at their offices and use the quiet dawn of the business day to organize the hours ahead and assess likely problems. Marshall arrives at his office near Heathrow Airport at 7 a.m., and has received a digest of the day's press coverage by 7.30 a.m.

At this level of seniority, of course, it is easier to use 'dead' travelling time productively: chauffeured cars with telephones and in-car faxes, Concorde flights that lengthen the New York working day by more than six hours. But anyone can practise the other disciplines; reserving blocks of time for meetings and 'clustering' telephone calls, and rigorously limiting the time spent on both; putting reading matter into a file, as Sir John Harvey-Jones does, for catching up on long journeys by air, train or car.

Sir Denys Henderson, chairman of both ICI and its spin-off pharmaceutical sister company Zeneca, uses Sundays to plan the week ahead and to think strategically. He planned a great deal of Zeneca's strategy in a holiday deckchair in the south of France in 1992. Sir Alistair Grant, chairman of Argyll Group, which owns the Safeway supermarkets, does some of his best thinking on Sunday mornings, wrapped in a dressing-gown, eating ginger nut biscuits (*Director*, January 1994).

Mark McCormack, agent to sporting and media stars, is an obsessive time manager. He plots each week out into 168 hours for everything – tennis games, pleasure reading and dining out are all subject to the same discipline – and allocates activities to each hour or subdivision of an hour on American yellow legal pads with a line drawn down the middle. Things to do go on the right-hand side, people to call go on the left.

In *What They Don't Teach You At Harvard Business School*, he sets out his method in detail: 'In addition to my yellow pads, I always have a stack of 3 × 5 cards in any coat pocket. Some of them are marked with the names of employees or business associates with whom I am in regular contact. If I think of something in relation to one of these people, I will jot it down on the appropriate card. The next time I speak to that person I will have everything I want to talk about at my fingertips. I also carry a stack of blank cards that I fill up with miscellaneous notes during the day, and at the end of the day I transfer that information to the appropriate page of the appropriate yellow pad.

'I write down everything I intend to do and once I have written it down I forget about it. I know it will turn up at the appropriate time and place on the appropriate day. . . . I have never known a successful person in business who didn't operate from some personal organizational system.'

All such time-management systems are broadly similar, featuring 'to do' lists and priority listing of tasks, the blocking out of chunks of time; psychological tricks like meeting others in their own offices rather than yours (you can then leave while appearing considerate of their time), and calling people back rather than accepting calls, for the same reason. Yet, although all the books repeat the same formulae, the appetite for them remains insatiable: every business publisher is said to want a time-management book on the list.

Major management writers have curiously little to say on the subject. The magisterial Peter Drucker, in *The Practice of Management* (1954), approached it in 'macro' terms, identifying how a good time-user will, for example, appraise subordinates once a year, not continuously, and use planning to cut through the need to 'firefight' recurrent problems. Andrew Grove, president of Intel, recommended in *High Output Management* (1983) a system akin to good production principles – 'batching' similar tasks, for example.

Delegation is an essential part of managing time at a senior level, and a more difficult process than many books of advice make it seem. Losing control, even partially, is hard for a hands-on manager to do voluntarily. Included in the key texts to this chapter is an extract from an American publication, *Back-to-Basics Management* (1983), which sets out sensible guidelines on what and how to delegate without stress.

Time management is a relatively recent discipline in terms of books and courses – Time Management International is just one thriving company devoted to the business – though as a management technique it has been influential since the 1900s. F.W. Taylor's attempts to apply scientific methodology to manufacturing processes were ruled by time management, as evidenced by the 'time and motion' label that superseded 'scientific management'. One could argue that, as with so many other management aids and theories, it is all at bottom applied common sense, but it often takes uncommon discipline to realize it.

If time management remains basically a do-it-yourself exercise – everyone has to work out a system that suits his or her own temperament and workload – it is no less important for that. The first sign of managerial breakdown is often an abstracted shuffling of piles of paper and the inability to process any task to its conclusion. And time is the one resource which, though renewed each day, once lost is lost for ever.

KEY TEXTS

PETER F. DRUCKER
From *The Practice of Management* (1954).

Managers who know how to use time well achieve results by planning. They are willing to think before they act. They spend a great deal of time on thinking through the areas in which objectives should be set, a great deal more on thinking through systematically what to do with recurrent problems.

Most managers spend a large amount of time – in small driblets – on attempts to appraise the performance and quality of the men who work under them. Good time-users do not. Instead, they systematically appraise their men once a year. As the result of a few hours' work, they then have the answers for all the decisions – concerning a man's salary, for instance, or his promotion or work assignment – on which judgment is required.

Good time-users do not spend a great deal of time on the modification engineering of their products. They sit down once a year – for a few days perhaps – and work out with their sales and manufacturing departments the basic policy, the objectives and rules for the necessary modifications, determining then how much of it there should be – and assign engineering manpower in advance to the job. In their eyes it is no praise to say: 'This year we managed to get through this inventory crisis, thanks to the experience we had acquired last year.' If they have a recurrent crisis, they spend the time to find out what causes it, so as to prevent its repetition. This may take time, but in the long run it saves more.

The good time-users among managers spend many more hours on their communications up than on their communications down. They tend to have good communications down, but they seem to obtain these as an effortless by-product. They do not talk to their men about their own problems, but they know how to make the subordinates talk about theirs.

JOHN ADAIR
From *Effective Leadership* (1983).

Check yourself against this ten-point programme once a month for the next six months.

1. *Develop a new personal sense of time*
Do not rely on memory: record where your time goes.
2. *Plan ahead*
Make plans on how you are going to spend your time a day, a week, a month, a year head. Plan in terms of opportunities and results, priorities and deadlines.
3. *Make the most of your best time*
Programme important tasks for the time of day you function best. Have planned quiet periods for creative thinking.

4. *Capitalize on marginal time*
Squeeze activities into the minutes you spend waiting for a train or between meetings.
5. *Avoid clutter*
Try re-organizing your desk for effectiveness. Sort papers into categories according to action priorities. Generate as little paper as possible yourself.
6. *Do it now*
'Procrastination is the thief of time.'
'My object was always to do the business of the day in the day.' (Wellington)
7. *Learn to say No*
Do not let others misappropriate your time.
Decline tactfully but firmly to avoid over-commitment.
8. *Use the telephone as a time-saving tool*
Keep telephone calls down to a minimum length.
Screen telephone interruptions.
9. *Delegate*
Learn to delegate as much as possible.
10. *Meetings*
Keep them short.
Sharpen your skills as a chairman.
Cut out unnecessary meetings.

ANDREW GROVE
From *High Output Management* (1983).

The most common approach to increasing a manager's productivity – his output over time – has been time-management techniques, which try to reduce the denominator on both sides of this equation. Any number of consultants will tell a manager that the way to higher productivity is to handle a piece of paper only once, to hold only stand-up meetings (which will presumably be short), and to turn his desk so that he presents his back to the door.

These time-management suggestions can be improved upon, I think, by applying our production principles.

First, we must identify our *limiting step*. . . . If we determine what is immovable and manipulate the more
yielding activities around it, we can work more efficiently.

A second production principle we can apply to managerial work is *batching* similar tasks. Any manufacturing
operation requires a certain amount of set-up time. So for
managerial work to proceed efficiently, we should use the
same set-up effort to apply across a group of similar activities. . . .

Set-up time has many parallels in managerial work. For
example, once we have prepared a set of illustrations for a
training class, we will obviously increase our productivity
if we can use the same set over and over again with other
classes or groups. Similarly, if a manager has a number of
reports to read or a number of performance reviews to
approve, he should set aside a block of time and do a batch
of them together, one after the other, to maximize the use
of the *mental* set-up time needed for the task. . . .

From my experience a large portion of managerial work
can be forecasted. . . . Forecasting and planning your time
around key events are literally like running an efficient
factory.

What is the *medium* of a manager's forecast? It is something very simple: his *calendar*. Most people use their
calendars as a repository of 'orders' that come in. Someone
throws an order to a manager for his time, and it automatically shows up on his calendar. This is mindless
passivity. To gain better control of his time, the manager
should use his calendar as a 'production' planning tool,
taking a firm initiative to schedule work that is not time-
critical between those 'limiting steps' in the day.

Another production principle can be applied here.
Because manufacturing people trust their indicators, they
won't allow material to begin its journey through the
factory if they think it is already operating at capacity. If
they did, material might go halfway through and back up
behind a bottleneck. Instead, factory managers say 'no' at
the outset and keep the start level from overloading the
system. Other kinds of managers find this hard to apply
because their indicators of capacity are not as well established or not as believable. How much time do you need to

read your mail, to write your reports, to meet with a colleague? You may not know precisely, but you surely have a feel for the time required. And you should exploit that sense to schedule your work.

To use your calendar as a production-planning tool, you must accept responsibility for two things:

1. You should move toward the *active* use of your calendar, taking the initiative to fill the holes between the time-critical events with non–time–critical though necessary activities.
2. You should say 'no' at the outset to work beyond your capacity to handle.

It is important to say 'no' earlier rather than later because we've learned that to wait until something reaches a higher value stage and then abort due to lack of capacity means losing more money and time. You can obviously say 'no' either explicitly or implicitly, because by not delivering you end up saying what amounts to 'no'. Remember too that your time is your one finite resource, and when you say 'yes' to one thing you are inevitably saying 'no' to another. . . .

A manager should carry a raw material *inventory* in terms of projects. This is not to be confused with his work-in-process inventory, because that, like eggs in a continuous boiler, tends to spoil or become obsolete over time. Instead this inventory should consist of things you need to do but don't need to finish right away – discretionary projects, the kind the manager can work on to increase his group's productivity over the long term. Without such an inventory of projects, a manager will most probably use his free time *meddling* in his subordinates' work.

M.J. CULLIGAN, C.S. DEAKINS, AND A.H. YOUNG
From *Back-to-Basics Management* (1983).

Mastering the art of delegation, like the mastery of any art form, demands patience and earnest effort. But it's of prime importance if you are to succeed as a back-to-basics manager. Your job is to think, plan and supervise as much as possible. In practising the art of delegation you are: (1) freeing yourself from tasks that can be done by someone else, (2) concentrating your available energy on that which no one else can do better or be responsible for, (3) giving those under you a chance to develop and learn how to carry more of the load, (4) freeing time available for the development of your leadership abilities and thinking of innovative ideas which will keep your company ahead of the competition, (5) freeing your thinking from details which may keep you from obtaining an overview of the work situation you are managing, (6) finding out who can be trusted to carry out tasks. (This will be very useful in making both plans and decisions.)

Delegation is a five-step process . . .:
- *Policy must be stated clearly and explicitly.*
- *Tasks must be defined.*
- *Goals must be set.*
- *Ideas must be communicated.*
- *Controls must be established.*

Saying you need to delegate more is easy. But planning and deciding on what should be delegated becomes more difficult. As a rule of thumb those tasks which you do well and can train someone else to do should be considered. The first part of planning should be to list tasks that can be delegated. Here's how to go about it:

- List all the tasks you are responsible for
- Keep a running list of all you do during the day for two weeks (even answering the phone during lunch break)
- Keep a time sheet or estimate the time needed for each task
- Make a list of the qualities and/or skills needed for each task
- Review your personnel and their skills and attributes
- Place the name of a staff member by each task matching skills and attributes with the need of each task

- Make a list of all the details and instructions an employee will need to accomplish each task
- Decide on check points and balances for each task
- Decide on alternative time plans for each task (in case the job needs to be redone or is not finished)
- Review in your mind all tasks that you have previously delegated. Examine the causes of failures as well as successes.

The back-to-basics manager and leader

- Avoids trespassing on authority once it is given
- Periodically checks performance
- Encourages his people to make decisions
- Defines jobs for his people so they are provided with the greatest challenge and opportunity
- Inspires his people with the will to work towards objectives and goals
- Makes full use of the skills and abilities of his people
- Has his people participate in setting work objectives and schedules
- Gets group reaction before going ahead with projects
- Generates a sense of belonging
- Encourages cooperation with others
- Goes to bat for his people.

MARK McCORMACK
From *What They Don't Teach You At Harvard Business School* (1984).

Obviously, how you choose to organize your work life is the most personal of all aspects of time management. I know people who use a pocket calendar and a notebook the same way I use yellow pads and note cards. I have worked with people who seldom organize more than one week in advance. And I have seen people work quite efficiently simply from a 'to-do' list unrelated to time itself.

Yet I have never known a successful person in business

who didn't operate from some personal organizational system.

There are two points about the way I organize myself which have an almost universal application.

First, *write it down*. Write it down anywhere, shirt-sleeves if necessary, but write it down. This allows you to free your mind for other things. But more important, *it means you are going to do it*. Writing something down is a commitment. Once you have performed this physical act you have provided the momentum for getting something done. The agony of carrying over an item and the ecstasy that comes with crossing it off will provide further incentive.

Second, *organize for the next day at the end of the previous day*. This is what gives me peace of mind at night, a feeling that I am on top of things, and a real excitement about coming into work the next morning. Simply by arranging the next day – defining on paper what I want to accomplish – I feel that I have a head start.

I do the same thing periodically over longer time spans: weekly, monthly, bi-monthly, semi-annually, annually and bi-annually, on up to some general things I want to accomplish over the next five years.

Once you have made an itinerary or schedule it is worthless if you don't stick to it.

A large part of sticking to your schedule is an awareness that it is very rare that something is so important or a crisis is so imminent that it has to be attended to immediately. Treat interruptions or anything else that just comes up as you would any other time commitment. Don't respond immediately but programme time for dealing with these situations into your future schedule – that afternoon, tomorrow or next week – whenever you have a space to fit them in or can make a space to fit them in.

The other major aspect of sticking to your schedule is allocating the appropriate amount of time to the activities that will be filling it up.

It is probably worse to allocate too little time than it is to allocate too much. This puts you in a position of always having to catch up, which backs up through your schedule and usually gets worse as the day wears on.

I think most people can predict with reasonable accuracy how long their usual business activities will take them, but they will often deceive themselves.

To manage time well you have to *believe in your own knowledge.* If you know a weekly meeting takes thirty minutes, don't convince yourself that today it will only take fifteen minutes simply because today you have more to do. If you have to be somewhere in ten minutes and you have ten minutes to get there, don't make one more phone call simply because you want to get it out of the way. People who manage their time badly seem to want to be unrealistic and go out of their way to create out-of-control situations.

HENRY MINTZBERG
From *Mintzberg on Management* (1989).

The manager is challenged to gain control of his or her own time by turning obligations to advantage and by turning those things he or she wishes to do into obligations. The chief executives of my study initiated only 32 per cent of their own contacts (and another 5 per cent by mutual agreement). And yet to a considerable extent they seemed to control their time. There were two key factors that enabled them to do so.

First, managers have to spend so much time discharging obligations that if they were to view them as just that, they would leave no mark on their organizations. The unsuccessful manager blames failure on the obligations; the effective manager turns obligations to his or her own advantage. A speech is a chance to lobby for a cause; a meeting is a chance to reorganize a weak department; a visit to an important customer is a chance to extract trade information.

Second, managers free some of their time to do those things that they – perhaps no one else – think important by turning them into obligations. Free time is made, not found, in the manager's job; it is forced into the schedule. Hoping to leave some time open for contemplation or general planning is tantamount to hoping that the pressures of the job will go away. The manager who wants to innovate initiates a project and obligates others to report back to him or her; the manager who needs certain external information establishes channels that will automatically keep him or her informed; the manager who has to tour facilities commits him- or herself publicly to doing so.

PETER M. SENGE
From *The Fifth Discipline* (1990).

The management of time and attention is an area where top management has a significant influence, not by edict but by example. . . . In a well-designed organization, the *only* issues that should reach a senior manager's attention should be complex, dilemma-like 'divergent' issues. These are the issues that require the thought and experience of the most senior people, in addition to the input of less experienced people. If top managers are handling twenty problems in a workday, either they are spending too much time on 'convergent' problems that should be dealt with more locally in the organization, or they are giving insufficient time to complex problems. Either way, it is a sign that management work is being handled poorly. . . .

The principle is simple to say and understand, but it's not the way most organizations operate. Instead, people at the top continually make decisions on issues such as how to run a promotion – as opposed to why they need to run promotions at all. Or they discuss how to make a sale to a particular customer – instead of inquiring about how their products serve the customers' expressed and latent needs in general.

On the other hand, as the basic learning disciplines start to become assimilated into an organization, a different view of managerial work will develop. Action will still be critical, but incisive action will not be confused with incessant activity. There will be time for reflection, conceptualizing, and examining complex issues. . . .

One useful starting point for all managers is to look at their time for thinking. If it isn't adequate, why not? Are work pressures keeping us from taking the time, or, to some degree, are we doing it to ourselves? Either way, where is the leverage for change? For some people, it may involve changing personal habits. Others may need to soften or deflect the organization's demands for incessant 'busyness'. The way each of us and each of our close colleagues go about managing our own time will say a good deal about our commitment to learning.

NOW READ ON . . .

Adair, John, *Effective Leadership*, Aldershot: Gower (1983)

Culligan, M.J., Deakins, C.S., Young, A.H., *Back-to-Basics Management*, New York: Facts on File (1983)

Drucker, Peter F., *The Practice of Management*, New York: Harper & Row (1954); London: Heinemann (1955)

Grove, Andrew, *High Output Management*, New York: Random House (1983)

Harvey-Jones, John, *Making It Happen*, Glasgow: William Collins (1988)

McCormack, Mark, *What They Don't Teach You at Harvard Business School*, Glasgow: William Collins (1984)

Mintzberg, Henry, *The Nature of Managerial Work*, New York: Harper & Row (1973)

Mintzberg, Henry, *Mintzberg on Management*, New York: The Free Press; London: Collier Macmillan (1989)

Senge, Peter M., *The Fifth Discipline*, New York: Doubleday (1990); London: Century (1992)

Chapter 11

Corporate Mission and Culture

'Where there is no vision, the people perish': the Biblical proverb could also apply to business organizations. The 1980s saw many dazzling but hollow corporate stars flash across the sky, only to burn out leaving debt and unemployment in their wake, while companies that consistently perform well decade after decade are usually notable for powerfully rooted values and a steadfast vision or purpose beyond the purely commercial.

In the UK, retailers spring first to mind – Marks and Spencer, Sainsbury's, The Body Shop – while in the US the spread is wider, and not so obviously linked with the customer. Hewlett-Packard, 3M and Johnson and Johnson are three leading examples of high-esteem companies with strong corporate value systems: J&J ranks those who own its stock last among the 'stakeholders' to whom it owes a duty of good practice. IBM, for all its failures in anticipating the personal computer revolution, might well have been more seriously damaged without the founding ethos of Thomas Watson. Japanese corporations are famously strong on values and missions – Matsushita, the world's largest electronics company, cites its primary purpose as serving society, with profit as a by-product.

Konosuke Matsushita was one of three founders of the above businesses to write influential books stressing the value of a guiding corporate philosophy. Matsushita's was entitled *Not by Bread Alone*. Marcus Sieff's *Don't Ask the Price* eloquently expressed the value-for-money, customer-driven ethos of Marks and Spencer, while Thomas Watson Jr.'s

A Business and its Beliefs was virtually a book-length mission statement for IBM.

Mission and culture are a chicken-and-egg symbiosis, the one both originating and springing from the other, though crisp mission statements such as AT&T's 'Universal Service' were a part of American corporate awareness decades before anyone applied the term 'culture' to business organizations. Peter Drucker emphasized the importance of mission and philosophy in 1973, some years before management writers began using the phrase 'corporate culture'.

'Mission and philosophy is the key starting point in business,' Drucker wrote in *Management: Tasks, Responsibilities, Practices*. 'A business is not defined by its name, statutes, or articles of incorporation. It is defined by the business mission. Only a clear definition of the mission and purpose of the organization makes possible clear and realistic business objectives.' And he warned: 'The management that does not ask "What is our mission?" when the company is successful is, in effect, smug, lazy and arrogant. It will not be long before success will turn into failure.' Drucker pinned responsibility firmly at the top: it was the leader's first task, he stated, to define the mission.

The fact that mission was at that time largely ignored, except by firms with visionary founders like IBM or AT&T, was identified by Drucker as 'perhaps the most important single cause' of business failure. He put forward four key questions for managers in formulating mission and purpose:

- What is our business?
- Who is our customer?
- Where is our customer?
- What is our value to our customer?

Although founder-entrepreneurs such as Thomas Watson of IBM saw and implemented the value of implanting a moral dimension to their businesses, it was probably Chester Barnard, forty years with Bell Telephone and later president of New Jersey Bell, who first laid it down as a principle of executive responsibility. In his seminal 1938 book *The Functions of the Executive*, he expressed a view of business organizations as engines of social progress and stated that executive responsibility included the creation of a corporate philosophy or 'morality'.

Elaborating on this, he wrote: 'The distinguishing mark of the executive responsibility is that it requires not merely conformance to a complex code of morals but also the creation of moral codes for others. The most generally recognized aspect of this function is called securing, creating, inspiring of "morale" in an organization. This is the process of inculcating points of view, fundamental attitudes, loyalties, to the organization or cooperative system, and to the system of objective authority, that will result in subordinating individual interest and the minor dictates of personal codes to the good of the cooperative whole. This includes (also important) the establishment of the morality of standards of workmanship.'

For most companies in the US, however, understanding of the role of corporate mission arose out of the motivation studies of the 1950s and 1960s, such as those carried out by Abraham Maslow ('hierarchy of needs'), Frederick Herzberg (the intrinsic factors at work that enhance motivation and lead to 'job enrichment'), and Edgar Schein (the 'psychological contract' between a firm and its employees). Schein wrote that an employee's 'moral' commitment to the employer meant that 'the person intrinsically values the mission of the organization and his or her job, and is personally involved and identified with the organization.'

Mission statements, which can be as pithy as slogans (AT&T's original 'Universal Service', British Airways' 'Putting People First') or as long as 20,000 words (Thomas Watson's *A Business and its Beliefs*), are now perceived to spring from two main sources – business strategy and philosophy/ethics. Indeed, whole corporate cultures can be grown from these.

Theodore Levitt's famous article of 1960 in *Harvard Business Review*, 'Marketing Myopia', has been credited with originating the strategy-driven mission by pointing out that a company would focus its marketing strategy correctly (and probably survive longer) if it first defined the wider business it was in, e.g., not just railroads but transportation, not just oil but energy. Most of the UK's corporate turnrounds of the 1980s, especially the big privatizations, owed a large part of their success to this approach; for example British Airways, which moved from a technologically driven aviation culture with retired wing-commanders on its board to a service-driven culture based on the customer.

Johnson and Johnson exemplifies the ethical mission statement ('We believe our first responsibility is to the doctors, nurses, and patients, to mothers and all others who use our products and services'). Others put profitability into a context of quality and good corporate citizenship ('The purpose of Motorola is to honourably serve the needs of the community by providing products and services of superior quality at a fair price to our customers' and publisher McGraw-Hill's 'To serve the worldwide need for knowledge at a fair profit by gathering, evaluating, producing and distributing valuable information in a way that benefits our customers, employees, authors, investors, and our society').

Sainsbury's puts profit some way below its primary mission ('to discharge our responsibility as leaders in our trade by acting with complete integrity, by carrying out our work to the highest standards, and by contributing to the public good and to the quality of life in the community'). Like Matsushita, it treats profit as a means of further growth and improvement.

In Britain, most of the recent work on corporate mission has come out of Ashridge Management College, two of whose academics, Andrew Campbell and Kiran Tawadey, made a study of mission statements from nearly 200 companies around the world (*Mission and Business Philosophy*, 1990).

'A sense of mission is essentially an emotional feeling by the people in the organization,' write Campbell and Tawadey. 'An organization with a sense of mission has captured the emotional support of its people.'

Ashridge has evolved its own 'Mission Model' in the form of a diamond. At the top sits Purpose (why the company exists); at the left point of the diamond is Strategy (the commercial rationale), matched to the right by Company Values (what senior management believes in). The fourth point of the diamond is Standards and Behaviours (the policies and behaviour patterns that guide how the company operates). 'Purpose' can be pragmatic – a means of reconciling the interests of all a company's stakeholders, such as McGraw-Hill's mission statement expresses – or it may be some higher goal such as Matsushita's service to society or Body Shop's ethos about the environment and animal testing in the production of cosmetics.

Two questions are suggested by Campbell and Tawadey to help managers decide whether they have created a satisfactory mission:

1. Does the statement describe an inspiring purpose that avoids playing to the selfish interests of the stakeholders – shareholders, customers, employees, suppliers?
2. Does the statement describe the company's responsibility to its stakeholders? (What is the nature of its preferred relationship with each stakeholder?)

Culture in its widest anthropological sense has been defined by the Dutch management professor Geert Hofstede as 'the collective programming of the mind which distinguishes the members of one group or category of people from another'. The first published use of the term 'corporate culture' is uncertain, but one of the earliest references appeared in Stanley Davis's 1970 book *Comparative Management: Organizational and Cultural Perspectives*. Davis, who became a research professor at Boston University's School of Management, wrote of a company's 'guiding beliefs', both external – how to direct the business competitively – and internal – how to manage from within. By the late 1970s the term was in widespread use.

Britain's Charles Handy was one of the first to explore in depth the different characteristics of organizational cultures. In *Understanding Organizations*, first published in 1976, he wrote: 'All organizations . . . develop their own cultures [and] to work in them you have to join them, psychologically as well as physically.' He divided them into four main categories: the power culture, the role culture, the task culture and the person culture. In *Gods of Management* (1986), he elaborated on these with classical analogies, assigning the four cultures to Greek deities – Zeus (patriarchal power, a club culture, typical of the founder-entrepreneur); Apollo (ordered roles, reason, bureaucracy); Athena (knowledge for tasks, meritocracy); and Dionysus (individualism, the professional culture).

All writers on corporate culture use variations on these four categories: the Franco–Dutch professor Fons Trompenaars labels them the family culture (personal, paternal, hierarchical); the Eiffel Tower culture (hierarchical bureaucracy broad at the base, narrowing to the top); the guided missile culture (oriented to tasks); and the incubator culture (nurturing individual creativity).

Within each main culture lurk subcultures, often powerful in driving the business and usually revealing the dominant functions, whether managerial, marketing, production or financial. (In an accountant-driven business culture such as Britain's, it is usually the latter.) Philip Sadler, vice-president of Ashridge, believes that a true understanding of the subcultures in an organization is essential to those who direct it; otherwise the direction may prove skewed and ineffective.

Handy had studied at MIT's Sloan School of Management under several key American management thinkers, including Edgar Schein, a pioneer of organizational cultural studies. Schein, inventor of the 'psychological contract' and 'career anchor' concepts, perceived that the assumptions which individual employees develop about their organizations are largely shaped by the assumptions those organizations hold about themselves and 'the way we do things here' – a rough but generally accepted definition of corporate culture.

Schein defined an organization's culture as 'what it has learned as a total social unit over the course of its history'. He outlined five areas in which a consensus should operate on cultural landmarks:

- The mission – what business are we in, and why?
- The goals, which should include specific goals for all workers
- The means to accomplish the goals, including reward and incentives systems

- The means of measuring progress, including reporting and feedback
- The strategies for what to do when things go wrong.

Schein's works on organizational psychology and culture in the late 1970s and early 1980s were probably the first to address the problems of takeover or merger involving two companies with differing cultures. He designed a set of diagnostic principles to help identify and solve such problems, and has a good claim to be regarded as the father of corporate culture studies.

In 1980 the magazine *Business Week* ran a cover story on corporate culture and a year or two later best-sellers were pouring out on the subject. In 1981 McKinsey consultants Richard Pascale and Anthony Athos, in *The Art of Japanese Management*, analysed and pinned down the contrasting cultures and management styles of two multinational corporations, Matsushita of Japan and ITT of America. The 'Seven-S' framework which formed the conceptual basis for the book was worked out by four McKinsey high-flyers – Pascale, Athos, Tom Peters and Robert Waterman – and described as 'a simple but powerful insight into what makes enterprises succeed'. It separated the 'hard S' management levers (strategy, structure, systems) from the 'soft S' levers (style, staff, skills and superordinate goals). Whereas American management practice traditionally stressed the first three, Japanese business leaders regarded all seven as inter-dependent. Superordinate goals – the cultural touchstone – was the key differentiator.

The Seven-S system also formed the framework of Peters and Waterman's *In Search of Excellence* in 1982, which identi-fied Japanese-style superordinate goals and strong cultures in each of their excellent companies. (Significantly, IBM's Thomas Watson Jr. had visited Matsushita in the 1930s.) 'Without exception, the dominance and coherence of culture proved to be an essential quality of the excellent companies. . . . In these companies, people way down the line know what they are supposed to do in most situations, because the handful of guiding values is crystal clear,' wrote Peters and Waterman. Also in 1982, *Corporate Cultures: the Rites and*

Rituals of Corporate Life, by Terrence Deal and Allan Kennedy (another ex-McKinseyite), followed a Peters and Waterman pattern by analysing eighty companies and discovering that the eighteen which had clearly articulated values or beliefs were 'uniformly outstanding'.

Since those days of heady certainty and the apparent discovery of the grail of management excellence, everything has changed, including cultures in companies forced by circumstances to change direction. AT&T, a company with one of the most deeply rooted cultures in US business, went through corporate culture shock in the mid-1980s when deregulation forced it to change from a monolithic, proud public utility service to one of several communications groups fiercely competing for market share. Adapting a strong, old culture to new market conditions is one of the biggest tests of contemporary business leadership.

John Kotter, a leading authority on corporate culture, leadership and change management, has found that the 'vast majority' of companies do not have adaptive cultures, which poses a huge challenge of leadership to the current generation of top managers. 'Only with leadership does one get the boldness, the vision and the energy needed to create large and difficult changes – and cultural change certainly tends to be large and difficult,' Kotter wrote with James L. Heskett in *Corporate Culture and Performance* (1992). More of their conclusions will be found in Chapter 12.

KEY TEXTS

CHARLES HANDY
From *Understanding Organizations* (1976).

The power culture
A power culture is frequently found in small entrepreneurial organizations, traditionally in the robber-baron companies of nineteenth-century America, occasionally in today's trade unions, and in some property, trading and finance companies. Its structure is best pictured as a *web*:

If this culture had a patron god it would be Zeus, the all-powerful head of the Gods of Ancient Greece who ruled by whim and impulse, by thunderbolt and shower of gold from Mount Olympus.

This culture depends on a central power source, with rays of power and influence spreading out from that central figure. They are connected by functional or specialist strings but the power rings are the centres of activity and influence.

The organization depends on trust and empathy for its effectiveness and on telepathy and personal conversation for communication. If the centre chooses the right people, who can think in the same way as it thinks, they can be left to get on with the job. There are few rules and procedures, little bureaucracy. Control is exercised by the centre largely through the selection of key individuals, by occasional forays from the centre or summonses to the centre. It is a political organization in that decisions are taken very largely on the outcome of a balance of influence rather than on procedural or purely logical grounds.

These cultures, and organizations based on them, are proud and strong. They have the ability to move quickly and can react well to threat or danger. Whether they do move or whether they move in the right direction will, however, depend on the person or persons in the centre; for the quality of these individuals is of paramount importance in those organizations and the succession issue is the key to their continued success. Individuals employed in them will prosper and be satisfied to the extent that they are power-orientated, politically minded, risk-taking, and rate security as a minor element in their psychological contract. Resource power is the major power base in this culture with some elements of personal power in the centre.

The role culture

The role culture is often stereotyped as bureaucracy. But bureaucracy has come to acquire a pejorative note in common parlance, so 'role' will be used here. The accompanying structure to a role culture can be pictured as a *Greek temple.*

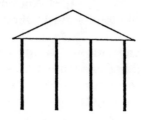

Its patron god is Apollo, the god of reason; for this culture works by logic and by rationality. The role organization rests its strength in its pillars, its functions or specialities. These pillars are strong in their own right; the finance department, the purchasing department, the production facility may be internationally renowned for their efficiency. The work of the pillars, and the interaction between the pillars, is controlled by:

Procedures for roles, e.g. job descriptions, authority definitions;
Procedures for communications, e.g. required sets of copies of memoranda;
Rules for settlement of disputes, e.g. appeal to the lowest crossover points.

They are coordinated at the top by a narrow band of senior management, the pediment. It is assumed that this should be the only personal coordination needed, for if the separate pillars do their job, as laid down by the rules and procedures, the ultimate result will be as planned.

In this culture the role, or job description, is often more important than the individual who fills it. Individuals are selected for satisfactory performance of a role, and the role is usually so described that a range of individuals could fill it. Performance over and above the role prescription is not required, and indeed can be disruptive at times. Position power is the major power source in this culture, personal power is frowned upon and expert power tolerated only in its proper place. Rules and procedures are the major methods of influence. The efficiency of this culture depends on the rationality of the allocation of work and responsibility rather than on the individual personalities.

The role organization will succeed as long as it can operate in a stable environment. . . .

But Greek temples are insecure when the ground shakes. Role cultures are slow to perceive the need for change and slow to change even if the need is seen. If the market, the product needs or the competitive environment changes, the role culture is likely to continue to forge straight ahead confident in its ability to shape the future in its own image. Then collapse, or replacement of the pediment by new management, or takeover, is usually necessary. Many large organizations found themselves in this position in the changing conditions of the 1960s.

Role cultures offer security and predictability to the individual. They offer a predictable rate of climb up a pillar. They offer the chance to acquire specialist expertise without risk. They tend to reward the satisfier, the man concerned with doing his job up to a standard. But come disaster – collapse or takeover – and the security of the role culture may be found to be built too much on the organization and too little on the individual's capacities.

The task culture
The task culture is job or project orientated. Its accompanying structure can be best represented as a *net*, with

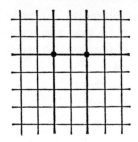

some of the strands of the net thicker and stronger than the others. Much of the power and influence lies at the interstices of the net, at the knots. The so-called 'matrix organization' is one structural form of the task culture.

The task culture has no totally appropriate presiding deity, perhaps because the Ancients were more interested in style and principle and power than in performance, for the whole emphasis of the task culture is on getting the job done. To this end the culture seeks to bring together the appropriate resources, the right people at the right level of the organization, and to let them get on with it. Influence is based more on expert power than on position or personal power, although these sources have their effect. Influence is also more widely dispersed than in other cultures, and each individual tends to think he has more of it. It is a team culture, where the outcome, the result, the product, of the team's work tends to be the common enemy obliterating individual objectives and most status and style differences. The task culture utilizes the unifying power of the group to improve efficiency and to identify the individual with the objective of the organization.

This culture is extremely adaptable. Groups, project teams, or task forces are formed for a specific purpose and can be reformed, abandoned or continued. The net organization works quickly since each group ideally contains within it all the decision-making powers required. Individuals find in this culture a high degree of control over their work, judgement by results, easy working relationships within the group with mutual respect based upon capacity rather than age or status.

The task culture therefore is appropriate where flexibility and sensitivity to the market or environment are important. You will find the task culture where the market is competitive, where the product life is short, where speed of reaction is important. . . .

Control in these organizations is difficult. Essentially control is retained by the top management by means of allocation of projects, people and resources. Vital projects are given to good people with no restrictions on time, space or materials. But little day-to-day control can be exerted over the methods of working or the procedures without violating the norms of the culture. These cultures therefore tend to flourish when the climate is agreeable, when the product is all-important and the customer always right, and when resources are available for all who can justify using them. Top management then feels able to relax day-to-day control on resource allocation decisions and the hiring and placing of key people.

However, when resources are not available to all who can justify their needs for them, when money and people have to be rationed, top management begins to feel the need to control methods as well as results. Alternatively team leaders begin to compete, using political influence, for available resources. In either case, morale in the work-groups declines and the job becomes less satisfying in itself, so that individuals begin to change their psychological contract and to reveal their individual objectives. This new state of affairs necessitates rules and procedures or exchange methods of influence, and the use of position or resource power by the managers to get the work done. In short, the task culture tends to change to a role or power culture when resources are limited or the total organization is unsuccessful. It is a difficult culture to control and inherently unstable by itself.

The person culture
The fourth culture is an unusual one. It will not be found pervading many organizations, yet many individuals will cling to some of its values. In this culture the individual is the central point. If there is a structure or an organization it

exists only to serve and assist the individuals within it. If a group of individuals decide that it is in their own interests to band together in order the better to follow their own bents, to do their own thing, and that an office, a space, some equipment or even clerical and secretarial assistance would help, then the resulting organization would have a person culture. It would exist only for the people in it without any superordinate objective. Barristers' chambers, architects' partnerships, hippy communes, social groups, families, some small consultancy firms, often have this 'person' orientation. Its structure is as minimal as possible, a *cluster* is the best word for it, or perhaps a galaxy of individual stars:

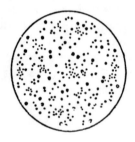

Dionysus is its patron deity, the god of the self-oriented individual, the first existentialist.

Clearly, not many organizations can exist with this sort of culture, since organizations tend to have objectives over and above the collective objectives of those who comprise them. Furthermore control mechanisms, or even management hierarchies, are impossible in these cultures except by mutual consent. The psychological contract states that the organization is subordinate to the individual and depends on the individual for its existence. The individual can leave the organization but the organization seldom has the power to evict the individual. Influence is shared and the power-base, if needed, is usually expert; that is, individuals do what they are good at and are listened to on appropriate topics.

RICHARD PASCALE AND ANTHONY ATHOS
From *The Art of Japanese Management* (1981).

In management, as in music, there is a bass clef as well as a treble. The treble generally carries the melody in music, and melody's equivalent in management is the manager's style. A manager's style – the way he focuses his attention and interacts with people – sets the 'tune' for his subordinates and communicates at the *operational* level what his expectations are and how he wants business conducted. Beneath these messages is a deeper rhythm that communicates more fundamentally. The bass in music – whether hard rock or a classical symphony – often contains much of what moves the listener. So, too, the 'bass' of management conveys meanings at a deeper level and communicates what management *really* cares about. These messages can influence an organization profoundly. In Japanese organizations, a great deal of managerial attention is devoted to ensuring the continuity and consistency of these 'bass clef' messages.

TOM PETERS
From *Thriving on Chaos* (1987).

Visions are aesthetic and moral – as well as strategically sound. Visions come from within – as well as from outside. They are personal – and group-centered. Developing a vision and values is a messy, artistic process. Living it convincingly is a passionate one, beyond any doubt. Posters and wallet-sized cards declaring the vision and corporate values may be helpful, but they may not be. In fact, they can hinder and make a mockery of the process if the visions and values are merely proclaimed, but not lived convincingly.

1. Effective visions are inspiring.
2. Effective visions are clear and challenging – and about excellence.
3. Effective visions make sense in the marketplace, and, by

stressing flexibility and execution, stand the test of time in a turbulent world.

4. Effective visions must be stable but constantly challenged – and changed at the margin.

5. Effective visions are beacons and controls when all else is up for grabs.

6. Effective visions are aimed at empowering our own people first, customers second.

7. Effective visions prepare for the future, but honor the past.

8. Effective visions are lived in details, not broad strokes.

ROBERT H. WATERMAN, Jr.
From *The Renewal Factor* (1987).

One of the most difficult challenges in management is developing a sense of value and vision. Stanford's Hal Leavitt calls this part of the manager's job 'pathfinding', and he distinguishes the thought process it requires from the way a manager thinks when he is making decisions or carrying them out. 'The pathfinding part of managing is the homeland of the visionary, the dreamer, the innovator, the creator, the entrepreneur. . . . The central questions are very difficult and often unaddressed: How do I decide what I want to be when I grow up? What should this organization try to become if it could become anything imaginable? What do we really want to do with this company?'

How do leaders do the pathfinding that leads to vision, value, and stability? By finding a way to give the organization a sense of pride. The questions that seem most helpful in translating the need for vision and values into specific statements are: (1) Looking back on the history of our organization, what have we done that gives us the most pride? (2) Looking back on our history, what ought we to be ashamed of? (3) What could we do now that would make us all proud? (4) Ten years from now, looking back, what will we have done that will have made us most proud?

GEERT HOFSTEDE
From *Cultures and Organizations* (1991).

Key Steps and considerations regarding organizational culture

MANAGING (WITH) ORGANIZATIONAL CULTURE

Is a task of top management which cannot be delegated

Demands both power and expertise

Should start with a cultural map of the organization
    Demands a culture diagnosis

Demands strategic choices:
    Is present culture matched with strategy?
    If not, can strategy be adapted?
    If not, what change of culture is needed?
    Is this change feasible – do we have the people?
    What will be the costs in terms of management attention and money?
    Do the expected benefits outweigh these costs?
    What is a realistic time span for the changes?
    If in doubt, better change strategy anyway
    Different subcultures may demand different approaches

Create a network of change agents in the organization
    Some key people at all levels
    If key people start, others will follow
    Can resisters be circumvented?

Design necessary structural changes
    Opening or closing departments
    Merging or splitting departments or tasks
    Moving groups or individuals?
    Are tasks matched with talents?

Design necessary process changes
    Eliminating or establishing controls
    Automation or disautomation
    Establishing or cutting communication links
    Replace control of inputs by control of outputs?

Revise personnel policies
    Reconsider criteria for hiring
    Reconsider criteria for promotion

Is personnel management up to its new task?
Design timely job rotation
Be suspicious of plans to train others; need for training
has to be felt by trainees themselves
Continue monitoring development of organizational culture
Sustained attention, persistence
Periodically repeat culture diagnosis

JOHN P. KOTTER
From *A Force for Change* (1990).

The right kind of culture can foster both leadership and
management, despite differences in function, process, and
structure that create a potential for conflict. It can help
hundreds of people to create the short-term results expected by an organization's constituencies and the
long-term changes needed to adapt to a shifting environment.

Developing a culture that creates strong leadership and
management is probably difficult under any circumstances. In large, older organizations, creating the right
vision and values, if they do not already exist, can be an
awesome task. Institutionalizing such a culture, so that it
does not disintegrate after the creator has left, is even
tougher. Doing this demands great skill, perseverance,
and not a small amount of courage. But for those who are
successful, the payoff is gigantic: in terms of long-term
economic results, the quality of life offered to employees
over the length of their careers, the overall package of
goods and services offered to customers over a decade or
more, and the general benefits to society.

Nowhere is this clearer than in a time of crisis, the ultimate example of an unstable and changing environment
demanding competent leadership. Many corporations
today look inept, if not just plain evil, when a major crisis
erupts. Lacking a broad vision of their responsibilities, the
alignment of their employees to such a vision, or the capacity to motivate people to execute all that, these firms

freeze under the pressure of a crisis or take actions that ultimately hurt both themselves and others.

JOHN P. KOTTER AND JAMES L. HESKETT
From *Corporate Culture and Performance* (1992).

The single most visible factor that distinguishes major cultural changes that succeed from those that fail is competent
leadership at the top. In all ten of the cases we studied,
major change began after an individual who already had a
track record for leadership was appointed to head an
organization. Each of these individuals had previously
shown the capacity to do more than manage well; they
knew how to produce change and were willing to do just
that. In their new jobs, they did this again, albeit on a
grander scale. Each new leader created a team that established a new vision and set of strategies for achieving that
vision. Each new leader succeeded in persuading important groups and individuals in the firm to commit
themselves to that new direction and then energized the
personnel sufficiently to make it happen, despite all the obstacles. Ultimately, hundreds (or even thousands) of
people helped make all the changes in strategies, products,
structures, policies, personnel, and (eventually) culture.
But often, just one or two people seem to have been essential in getting the process started. . . .

Visions and strategies were communicated with words –
spoken simply, directly, and often – and with deeds. In
some cases (British Airways, Nissan, SAS, Xerox), these
top managers spent far more time communicating with
their employees than their predecessors had. In most cases,
they encouraged people to engage in a dialogue with them,
not allowing the communication to flow in one direction
only. In almost all cases, the leaders became living em-
bodiments of the cultures they desired. The values and
practices they wanted infused into their firms were usually
on display in their daily behavior: in the questions they
asked at meetings, in how they spent their time, in the decisions they made. These actions seem to have given

critical credibility to their words. The behavior made it clear to others that their speeches were serious. And successes, which seemed to result from that behavior, made it clear that the speeches were sensible.

ANDREW CAMPBELL, MARION DEVINE AND DAVID YOUNG
From *A Sense of Mission* (1990).

Mission planning goes beyond strategic planning in three ways: it involves an analysis of employee values and organization behaviour to assess the changes needed; it focuses on identifying behaviour standards that are central to the implementation of strategy and symbolic of the new value system; and it encourages a discussion of the organization's commitment to its stakeholders and to some higher-level purpose. Mission planning forces managers to think through the behavioural implications of their plans; it prompts them to articulate an inspirational reason for any new plans; and it prevents them from side-stepping the issue of whether existing managers and employees are capable of responding to the challenge. Mission planning is where strategy, organization and human resource issues come together. It asks managers to take a holistic view of their organization and its environment before developing a plan of action.

If you are in charge of a business, whether it is a small family business, a large focused business or a business unit in a larger company, start to think about how you can make your business into a cause. Thomas Watson Jr. had a saying that captures this: 'Don't just put your heart into the business. Put the business into your heart.' By doing this, managers can create a cause for themselves and for their employees.

Many managers feel this is unrealistic. They strive to win the diligent and creative involvement of employees and no more. Some even question the morality of seeking to engage the emotional interest, let alone the spiritual interest, of employees. We side with Watson. Managers who don't aim to persuade employees to take the business into their hearts are aiming for second best. They are missing the opportunity to help their employees find greater fulfilment from work and they are running less effective organizations. These passionless managers will find that their companies start to lose ground to those companies with leaders prepared to engage the emotions of their people.

NOW READ ON . . .

Campbell, A., Devine, M. and Young, D., *A Sense of Mission*, London: The Economist Books (1990)

Campbell, A. and Tawadey, K., *Mission and Business Philosophy*, Oxford: Heinemann Professional Publishing (1990)

Drucker, Peter F., *Management: Tasks, Responsibilities, Practices*, London: Heinemann; New York: Harper & Row (1973)

Handy, Charles, *Understanding Organizations*, London: Penguin (1976)

Hofstede, Geert, *Cultures and Organizations*, Maidenhead: McGraw-Hill (1991)

Kotter, J.P., *A Force for Change*, New York: The Free Press (1990)

Kotter, J.P. and Heskett, J.L., *Corporate Culture and Performance*, New York: The Free Press (1992)

Pascale, R.T. and Athos, A.G., *The Art of Japanese Management*, New York: Simon & Schuster (1981); London: Allen Lane (1982); Penguin (1986)

Peters, Tom, *Thriving on Chaos*, New York: Alfred A. Knopf (1987); London: Macmillan (1988)

Waterman, R.H. Jr., *The Renewal Factor*, New York: Bantam (1987)

Chapter 12

Corporate Performance

When Peter Drucker published *The Practice of Management* in 1954, measuring a company's performance against its objectives was a 'brand new' subject. 'It is one of the most active frontiers of thought, research and invention in American business today,' he wrote. 'Company after company is working on the definition of the key areas, on thinking through what should be measured and on fashioning the tools of measurement.'

In fact, in the early 1950s Drucker was a consultant on just such a programme, General Electric's 'Measurement Project', and the eight areas which his book suggests for objectives of performance and results were broadly those commended to GE by its task force: market standing; innovation; productivity; physical and financial resources; profitability; manager performance and development; worker performance and responsibility; public responsibility. The last three 'intangibles' were somewhat ahead of their time, but Drucker argued that neglect of these areas 'soon results in the most practical and tangible loss of market standing, technological leadership, productivity and profit – and ultimately in the loss of business life.'

Forty years on, there is wide acceptance of such intangible factors in corporate performance – though Drucker himself reduced his guidelines to the first five in *Managing for the Future* (1992) – and much of this is due to the pursuit of 'excellence' that grew out of American managers' reaction to Japan's assault on their markets, both local and global, in the late 1970s. What made Peters and Waterman's *In Search of Excellence* the wildfire seller it became in 1982 – and for years afterwards – was the assurance it gave that not all US companies were lagging behind the Japanese, that superior performance could be home-grown too and could be learned by applying the lessons practised in America's 'excellent companies'.

The two McKinsey's consultants – each to become, on the strength of their joint book, an international management guru – selected six criteria over a twenty-year period to measure long-term excellent performance, prior to analysing what made each company excellent. Three were measures of growth and wealth-creation: compound asset growth; compound equity growth; and the average ratio of market value to book value, taking market value as the closing share price multiplied by the number of ordinary shares, divided by ordinary book-value shares at year-end over a twenty-year period.

The other three were measures of return on capital and sales: average return on total capital (net income divided by total invested capital, consisting of ordinary shares, long-term debt, non-redeemable preferred stock and minority interest); average return on equity; and average return on sales, all over the period 1961 through 1980.

To qualify as a top performer, each of Peters and Waterman's excellent companies had to have been in the top half of its industry in at least four of those six measures over the twenty-year period. As a final test, the authors asked a number of businessmen in the appropriate sectors to assess each company's record of innovation over twenty years, judged on its flow of innovatory products and how quickly it was perceived to respond to changing markets and external circumstances.

They ended with forty-three companies, half of which were studied in depth, half less intensively, using as one of their tools the McKinsey 'Seven-S' framework, in which the 'soft S' levers such as superordinate goals outnumbered the 'hard S' factors such as structure. The attributes they found in common, which could reasonably be assumed to contribute to the companies' consistently superior performance, each formed the subject of a chapter in the book:

- A bias for action

- Close to the customer
- Autonomy and entrepreneurship
- Productivity through people
- Hands-on, value-driven
- Stick to the knitting
- Simple form, lean staff
- Simultaneous loose-tight properties

All of these, still sound guidelines to good management, are presumably the reason that *In Search of Excellence* continues to sell in huge numbers, unrevised, although a good half of its excellent companies fell from stock-market favour within five years of the book's publication. In several of these key success factors, Peters and Waterman blazed a trail that continues to point the way to superior performance.

The 'action' principle, for example, included a willingness to work through small project teams of five to twenty-five people as a way of speeding up innovation and bringing new products to market. Such self-directed teams were to become a dominant feature of successful corporate culture in the 1990s.

'Close to the customer' laid down a principle that every board now acknowledges, in theory at least: listen to your customers and learn from them. By doing so, Peters and Waterman found, their excellent companies provided 'unparalleled quality, service and reliability – things that work and last. They succeed in differentiating . . . the most commodity-like products.'

'Autonomy and entrepreneurship' meant championing the innovator, tolerating failure in pursuit of innovation and 'empowering' employees, as the fashionable buzzword now has it, to take action where it was needed.

'Productivity through people' meant treating employees as the company's core asset, again stressing the value of small-scale organizational units. Peters and Waterman quoted a chairman of Texas Instruments who spoke of every worker being 'seen as a source of ideas, not just acting as a pair of hands'.

'Hands-on, value-driven' expressed an early awareness, before corporate culture had been much written about, of the importance of the chief executive embodying the clear values and mission of the company. MBWA, or 'managing by wandering around' in the Hewlett–Packard tradition, was one recommended outward and visible sign of this committed leadership.

'Stick to the knitting', while not ruling out diversified conglomerates, advocated concentrating on core businesses and competencies, building on known strengths and market advantages.

'Simple form, lean staff' has gone on to prove its worth even more strongly in the 1990s, when a massive global conglomerate like ABB, for example, is run with a head office of fewer than 100 people. (ABB's chief executive, Percy Barnevik, is famous for saying that the staff of any head office can be cut by 90 per cent.) Again, the principle of small units and teams – 'adhocracy' rather than bureaucracy – reflected the inherent flexibility found in top-performing companies.

Peters and Waterman's final attribute, 'simultaneous loose-tight properties', was another early pointer to the team-based organization, while acknowledging the need for tightly held common values and a certain amount of central control.

Some management commentators subsequently noted that many of Peters and Waterman's chosen companies were in high technology or project-based businesses, and that characteristics shared by such companies would not necessarily be found in high-performing businesses in more traditional industries. There was also criticism that some of these attributes could be found in less successful companies, but since these were excluded from the research, it was impossible to prove that such attributes were in themselves keys to excellence.

In *Controversies in Management* (1993), Alan Berkeley Thomas writes: 'In short, Peters and Waterman, like their classical predecessors, had generalized from the experience of particular types of firms in particular contexts to all firms in all contexts. Just as the classical mechanistic/military model of organization did not amount to the "one best way" to manage, neither could the "excellence" model. It was not so much wrong as incomplete and therefore inadequate as a valid and reliable guide to management practice.'

Bob Waterman, however, with one or two caveats about the chosen companies, thinks that the criteria have stood up pretty well. Certainly, a company such as ABB, based on heavy engineering and therefore unlike most of the Excellence 43, shares enough of the eight attributes to support their validity.

In Search of Excellence unleashed a spate of imitators, books with similar titles claiming to identify shared critical success factors in high-performance companies. Most of their authors, like Peters and Waterman, used predominantly financial measures as a preliminary judge of performance, but as the quality movement gathered pace in the early 1980s, allied to a growing emphasis on customer satisfaction, these too were becoming measures of performance, certainly among end users.

In January 1991 Professor Robert Eccles of Harvard Business School published an article in the *Harvard Business Review* questioning profit-based measurements on the grounds that they often distort the realities of a business and that they are necessarily lagging indicators of success rather than leading ones. He later developed the theme of this article, 'The Performance Measurement Manifesto', into a chapter of his 1992 book *Beyond the Hype*, written in conjunction with Nitin Nohria, also of Harvard.

In his book, Eccles argues that there is no universal consensus on how best to measure financial performance – even on so basic a matter as how earnings should be calculated. Citing the growing belief that sustainable long-term success is more likely to be attained when financial indicators are not the sole arbiter, Eccles quotes the example of Sealed Air Corporation, a speciality packaging company that changed its performance measurement criteria following a leveraged recapitalization.

From using earnings per share as its primary performance measurement, the company developed a five-category ranking: (1) customer satisfaction, (2) cash flow, (3) world-class manufacturing, (4) innovation, and (5) earnings per share. It came to believe so strongly in its new approach that its chief financial officer planned to introduce monthly statements of mainly non-financial measures, with financial statements relegated to quarterly publication.

180

Motorola, another example, had focused largely on financial measurements until the adoption of its 'Six Sigma Quality' programme in the early 1980s. This, aimed at achieving 99.99966 per cent defect-free products by 1992, won the company a Baldrige Award (the US national quality prize) in 1988, and by the 1990s had changed Motorola's whole definition of performance.

Such switches to non-financial indicators have the benefit, Eccles argues, of forcing managers to think freshly and hard about 'the trade-offs between objectives and how to achieve an appropriate balance among the different performance measures being employed.'

John Kotter, the Harvard guru of corporate culture and change management, believes that a company's culture can have a significant impact on its long-term economic performance and that it will probably be even more important in years to come. Cultures can be made 'more performance enhancing' through leadership and vision, he argues. His book *Corporate Culture and Performance*, written with James L. Heskett, publishes ten cases of 'major cultural change' under dynamic leadership, including British Airways, General Electric, ICI and Nissan, all of which have shown dramatic growth by a variety of performance measurements.

As global competition intensifies and more companies are forced to train for what Rosabeth Moss Kanter calls the 'corporate Olympics', techniques for raising performance and measuring competitors will continue to proliferate. Even by 1986, a survey by Kanter and her research team of nearly 100 large corporations found that 83 had already been engaged for an average 2.2 years on some form of improvement campaign; whether excellence, quality, entrepreneurship or innovation. Fully 70 per cent of UK companies are now said to practise benchmarking, a technique usually interpreted as measuring a company against the best of its competitors. Lucas Industries was doing it in the mid-1980s as part of its forward-thinking 'Competitiveness Achievement Plan', which still forms the core of the Lucas re-engineering programme.

The winning posts are moving farther away all the time, and performance measurements need to keep pace.

KEY TEXTS

ROBERT H. WATERMAN JR.
From *The Renewal Factor* (1987).

There are people who *do* do it right and they seem to have a common vision. They are the renewers, and while their lessons can be organized in many ways, the eight themes that emerge as most important are:

1. INFORMED OPPORTUNISM

The renewing companies treat information as their main strategic advantage, and flexibility as their main strategic weapon. . . .

2. DIRECTION AND EMPOWERMENT

The renewing companies treat *everyone* as a source of creative input. . . . Their managers define the boundaries, and their people figure out the best way to do the job within those boundaries. . . .

They give up a measure of control in order to gain control over what counts: results. . . .

3. FRIENDLY FACTS, CONGENIAL CONTROLS

. . . Renewing companies have a voracious hunger for facts. They see information where others see only data. They love comparisons, rankings, measurements, anything that provides context and removes decision-making from the realm of mere opinion. Meanwhile, the renewers maintain tight, accurate, real-time financial controls. . . .

4. A DIFFERENT MIRROR

. . . . leaders of renewing organizations seem to get their determination from their singular ability to anticipate crisis. That stems from their continuing willingness to look into 'a different mirror'.

IBM looks at 'best of breed'. The Ford Taurus team

looked at 'best of class'. . . . They get ideas from customers, suppliers, front-line employees, competitors, politicians – almost anyone outside the hierarchy. . . .

5. TEAMWORK, TRUST, POLITICS, AND POWER

. . .Renewers . . . are relentless in fighting office politics and power contests, and in breaking down the we/they barriers that paralyse action. . . .

6. STABILITY IN MOTION

The renewing companies know how to keep things moving. If they share a habit pattern, it's the habit of habit breaking. . . . Renewing companies are deliberate bureaucracy-busters. But they do that against a base of underlying stability. . . .

Renewal requires a constant interplay between stability and change. . . . Most of the good companies look for the best people, enforce high performance standards, and then hold a very large safety net under them. They offer security of employment, not position. . . .

7. ATTITUDES AND ATTENTION

. . . Attention makes a difference, and so do attitudes and expectations. If I expect you to do well, you probably will do well, and if I expect the reverse, you probably won't do as well. Psychologists call it the Pygmalion effect. Managers who renew companies seem to understand it. . . .

8. CAUSES AND COMMITMENT

. . . Renewing organizations seem to run on causes. Quality is the most prevalent cause, even for longtime champs like Maytag and Hewlett-Packard. At Ford, it's employee involvement *and* quality *and* the customer. . . . Renewing companies constantly review their causes in light of the issues: the major problems and opportunities that shift with time. . . .

Causes are one thing; commitment is another. . . . It re-sults from extensive communication and management's ability to turn grand causes into small actions so that people throughout the organization can contribute to the central purpose. . . .

A company, even one with a long history of good perform-ance, needs to introduce fresh management energy into its system to stave off the inexorable forces of decay. One way to think about renewal, then, is as the antidote for corporate entropy. . . .

Renewal, after all, is about builders. Many people can introduce change for change's sake and call it renewal. That is illusory. A builder, on the other hand, leads an organization toward renewal that outlives the presence of any single individual and revitalizes even as it changes.

ROSABETH MOSS KANTER
The Corporate Olympics. From *When Giants Learn to Dance* (1989).

THE CORPORATE OLYMPICS
The global economy in which American business now oper-ates is like a corporate Olympics – a series of games played all over the world with international as well as domestic com-petitors. The Olympic contests determine not just which business team wins but which nation wins overall. . . .

In the corporate Olympics, there are many different games to be entered, requiring specialized abilities and with widely varying competitive conditions. But there are common overall characteristics in those teams that can compete and win again and again – the strength, skill, and discipline of the athlete, focused on individual excellence, coupled with the ability to work well within a well-organized team. . . .

The necessities for winning the new game are pushing American corporations in ever-less-bureaucratic and ever-more-entrepreneurial directions. Across the nation, com-panies are attempting to unravel red tape, cut out unnecessary layers of the hierarchy, and set up new ventures in their midst that resemble small companies in order to move into new areas quickly, without having to start from scratch. They are forging closer ties with employees, suppliers, and customers, to fortify their ability to compete. They are reconsidering how they dole out rewards. And as they do all this, they are piling up the demands on their people.

The new game brings with it new challenges. The mad rush to improve performance and to pursue excellence has multiplied the number of demands on executives and managers. These demands come from every part of business and personal life, and they increasingly seem incompatible and impossible:

- Think strategically and invest in the future – but keep the numbers up today.
- Be entrepreneurial and take risks – but don't cost the business anything by failing.
- Continue to do everything you're currently doing even better – and spend more time communicating with employees, serving on teams, and launching new projects.
- Know every detail of your business – but delegate more responsibility to others.
- Become passionately dedicated to 'visions' and fanatically committed to carrying them out – but be flexible, responsive, and able to change direction quickly.
- Speak up, be a leader, set the direction – but be participative, listen well, cooperate.
- Throw yourself wholeheartedly into the entrepreneurial game and the long hours it takes – and stay fit.
- Succeed, succeed, succeed – and raise terrific children.

Corporations, too, face escalating and seemingly incompatible demands:

- Get 'lean and mean' through restructuring – while being a great company to work for and offering employee-centered policies, such as job security.
- Encourage creativity and innovation to take you in new directions – and 'stick to your knitting'.

- Communicate a sense of urgency and push for faster execution, faster results – but take more time to deliberately plan for the future.
- Decentralize to delegate profit and planning responsibilities to small, autonomous business units. But centralize to capture efficiencies and combine resources in innovative ways.

RICHARD J. SCHONBERGER
From *Building a Chain of Customers* (1990).

Principles of World-Class, Customer-Driven Performance:
General
1. Get to know the next and final customer
2. Get to know the competition
3. Dedicate to continual, rapid improvement in quality, cost, response time, and flexibility
Design and Organization
4. Cut the numbers of components or operations and number of suppliers to a few good ones.
5. Cut the number of flow paths (where the work goes next)
6. Organize product- or customer-focused linkages of resources
Operations
7. Cut flow time, flow distance, inventory, and space along the chain of customers.
8. Cut setup, changeover, get-ready, and start-up time
9. Operate at the customer's rate of use (or a smoothed representation of it)
Human Resource Development
10. Develop human resources through cross-training (for mastery), continual education, job switching, and multi-year cross-career reassignments
11. Develop operator/team-owners of products, processes, and outcomes
Quality and Problem-Solving
12. Make it easier to produce or provide the product without error (total quality)

13. Record and retain quality, process, and problem data at the workplace
14. Assure that line people get first crack at problem-solving – before staff experts
Accounting and Control
15. Cut transactions and reporting; control causes not costs
Capacity
16. Maintain and improve present resources and human work before thinking about new equipment and automation
17. Automate incrementally when process variability cannot otherwise be reduced
18. Seek to have plural instead of singular workstations, machines, and cells or flow lines for each product or customer family
Marketing
19. Market and sell your firm's capability and competence

PETER F. DRUCKER
From *Managing for the Future* (1992).

How, then, do the institutional owners of German or Japanese industry define performance and results? Though they manage quite differently, they define them in the same way. . . . They do not 'balance' anything. They maximize. But they do not attempt to maximize shareholder value or the short-term interest of any one of the enterprise's 'stakeholders'. Rather, they *maximize the wealth-producing capacity of the enterprise*. It is this objective that integrates short-term and long-term results and that ties the operational dimensions of business performance – market standing, innovation, productivity, and people and their development – with financial needs and financial results. It is also this objective on which all constituencies depend for the satisfaction of their expectations and objectives, whether shareholders, customers, or employees. . . .

The first step toward a clear definition of the concept was probably taken in my 1954 book, *The Practice of Management*, which outlined eight key objective areas for a business. These areas (or some variations thereof) are still the starting point for business planning in the large Japanese company. Since then, management analysts have done an enormous amount of work on the strategy needed to convert objectives into performance.

Financial objectives are needed to tie all this together. Indeed, financial accountability is the key to the performance of management and enterprise. Without financial accountability, there is no accountability at all. And without financial accountability, there will also be no results in any other area. It is commonly believed in the United States that the Japanese are not profit conscious. This is simply not true. In fact, their profitability goals as measured against the cost of capital tend to be a good deal higher than those of most American companies. Only the Japanese do not start with profitability; they end with it.

The first true measurement of a company is its standing in its markets. Is market standing going up or going down? And is the improvement in the right markets? . . .

The second 'dial' on a company's 'instrument board' measures innovative performance. Is the company's achievement as a successful innovator in its markets equal to its market standing? Or does it lag behind it? There is altogether no more reliable early warning of a company's imminent decline than a sharp and persistent drop in its standing as a successful innovator. And equally dangerous is a deterioration in innovative lead time, that is, in the time between the inception of an innovation and its introduction as a successful product or service in the market. . . .

The third set of measurements on the executive control panel measures productivity. It relates the input of all major factors of production – money, materials, people – to the 'value added' they produce, that is, to the (inflation-adjusted) value of total output of goods or services minus whatever is spent on buying supplies, parts, or services from the outside. Each factor has to be measured separately. Indeed, in the large organization – whether a business, a hospital, or a university – the productivity of different segments within each factor needs to be measured, e.g., blue-collar labour, clerical labour, managers, and service staffs.

Ideally, the productivity of each factor should increase steadily. At the very least, however, increased productivity of one factor, e.g., people, should not be achieved at the expense of the productivity of another factor, e.g., capital – something that American industry has been guilty of far too often. Such a 'tradeoff' usually damages the company's break-even point of operations. Increased productivity in good times is then paid for by decreased productivity when a company needs productivity the most – in poor or depressed times. . . .

The fourth 'dial' shows liquidity and cash flows. It is old wisdom that a business can run without profits for long years provided it has adequate cash flow. The opposite is not true, however. There are far too many businesses around – and by no means only small ones – that have to abandon the most profitable developments because they run out of cash. And increased profits, e.g., through rapid expansion of sales volume, which weakens rather than strengthens liquidity and cash position, is always a danger signal. It commonly means the company 'buys' rather than 'earns' its additional sales – through overly generous financing of its customers, for instance. And 'bought' markets don't last. . . .

The final 'dial' should measure a business's profitability – which is both more and less than conventional profit. Profitability measures show the capacity of a company's resources to produce a profit. They thus exclude profits or losses from nonrecurring transactions such as the sale or abandonment of a division, a plant, a product line. They also do not include overhead-cost allocations. But they also do not try to measure the profit in any given time period, focusing instead on the profitability of the going concern.

The easiest way to do this is probably to show operating profits on a 36 months' rolling basis – adjusted, if needed, for inflation or for fluctuations in foreign-exchange rates. . . . And the profitability trend is then projected three ways to test its adequacy: (a) cost of capital; (b) new ventures, new products, and new services (is profitability going up at these margins, or is it declining?); and (c) the need for profitability to be tested in respect to its composition.

JOHN P. KOTTER AND JAMES L. HESKETT
From *Corporate Culture and Performance* (1992).

1. *Corporate culture can have a significant impact on a firm's long-term economic performance.* We found that firms with cultures that emphasized all the key managerial constituencies (customers, stockholders, and employees) and leadership from managers at all levels outnumbered firms that did not have those cultural traits by a huge margin. . . .

2. *Corporate culture will probably be an even more important factor in determining the success or failure of firms in the next decade.* . . . In a world that is changing at an increasing rate, one would predict that unadaptive cultures will have an even larger negative financial impact in the coming decade.

3. *Corporate cultures that inhibit strong long-term financial performance are not rare; they develop easily, even in firms that are full of reasonable and intelligent people.* . . .

4. *Although tough to change, corporate cultures can be made more performance-enhancing.* Such change is complex, takes time, and requires leadership, which is something quite different from even excellent management. That leadership must be guided by a realistic vision of what kinds of cultures enhance performance – a vision that is currently hard to find in either the business community or the literature on culture.

ROBERT G. ECCLES AND NITIN NOHRIA
From *Beyond the Hype* (1992).

Unfortunately, there is no universal consensus on how best to measure something even as seemingly objective as

TEN CASES OF MAJOR CULTURAL CHANGE
From *Corporate Culture and Performance*, by J. P. Kotter and J. L. Heskett

Company	Period of Cultural Change	Long-Term Economic Performance
Bankers Trust	1977–1985	Annual growth in return on assets rose from − 8.71% in 1967-1976 to + 14.09% in 1977-1988
British Airways	1982–1985	Firm turned around from losses of £520 million in 1977-1982 to profits of £1,059 million in 1984-1989
ConAgra	1974–1978	Stock grew in value fiftyfold over fourteen years
First Chicago	Since 1981	Profits grew from $200 million in 1979-80 to nearly $900 million in 1988-89. This trend is ongoing
General Electric	Since 1980	Market value has grown from $12 billion to $60 billion in ten years. This trend is ongoing
ICI	1982–1987	Net income rose 500% from 1982 to 1987
Nissan	Since 1985	After a fifteen-year decline, domestic market share rose in 1988-89. Net income rose from $165 million in 1987 to $939 million in 1990. This trend is ongoing
SAS	1980–1983	Net income grew from SKr 450 million in 1974-1981 to SKr 12 billion in 1982-1989
American Express TRS	1978–1983	Profits have risen 18% annually for a decade despite an onslaught of new competition
Xerox	1983–1989	Return on assets rose from 5% to 12.4% and revenue from $8.5 billion to $17.5 billion between 1983 and 1989. Copier market share rose from 8.6% in the early 1980s to 16% in 1991. In 1991 Xerox won the Malcolm Baldrige National Quality Award

financial performance. For example, currently there is a great deal of debate about the relative virtues of using earnings as calculated by the techniques of accrual accounting versus using cash flow analysis – with the trend now favoring the latter. Such debates are connected to broader, often highly rhetorical debates, such as the one over whether 'shareholder value' serves as a company's ultimate economic objective. Once set in the context of these broader debates, questions of what makes the 'better' measure can be phrased in almost limitless ways: Is the market which determines a company's stock price more interested in earnings or in cash flow? Which is a more accurate measure of the economic value of the firm? Which is least likely to create perverse incentives for sacrificing the long-term viability of the company in the interest of short-term objectives?

Since sound arguments can be marshalled for each position, the earnings versus cash flow debate is a complicated one that is unlikely to be completely resolved. But it illustrates an important point, which is that no measure by itself is going to suffice as an adequate snapshot of an organization's performance. To the contrary, exclusive attention to a single method of measurement will result in some things being optimized at the expense of others.

What can the manager do? One obvious solution is to use a variety of financial measures (e.g., revenues, cost variances, gross margin, net income before taxes, return on investment, and return on assets) in concert with nonfinancial measures (e.g., market share, quality, customer satisfaction, employee morale, safety, and innovativeness). Although we will see that the idea itself is an old one, this solution has been growing in popularity as companies become more frenzied in their search for ways to deal with competitive challenges. While sustained long-term financial performance is still the objective, those who advocate this solution argue that such long-term success is most likely to be obtained when financial numbers alone are *not* the sole focus of performance measurement.

When used properly, multiple measures are a central

ingredient of robust managerial action. Taking robust action means that first one thing and then another needs to be emphasized as conditions change and as the consequences of action unfold. Having multiple measures, including nonfinancial ones, gives the manager a larger rhetorical vocabulary to mobilize action. It legitimizes discussion about actions that affect a range of outcomes in a way that simply focusing on the bottom line does not.

ROBERT H. WATERMAN Jr.
From *The Frontiers of Excellence* (1994).

What makes top performing companies different, I would urge, is their organizational arrangements. Specifically:

- They are better organized to meet the needs of their *people*, so that they attract better people than their competitors do and their people are more greatly motivated to do a superior job, whatever it is they do.
- They are better organized to meet the needs of *customers* so that they are either more innovative in anticipating customer needs, more reliable in meeting customer expectations, better able to deliver their product or service more cheaply, or some combination of the above.

Organizing to meet your own people's needs seems a simple enough idea. It isn't. It means understanding what motivates people and aligning culture, systems, structure, people, and leadership attention toward things that are inherently motivating. It's a radical departure from management convention. The old (and still very pervasive) dictum says that the job of the manager is to tell people what to do. My research says that the manager's job is to lead.

Recent research coming from the business schools strongly supports this theme. For example, over an eleven-year period, from 1977 to 1988, Harvard business professors John P. Kotter and James L. Heskett studied the

193

nature of corporate values and culture as they related to company success. As they dug, they found one type of strong-culture company that outperforms all the rest. This is the company that values all *constituent groups* – employees, customers, shareholders. Kotter and Heskett found that companies which, perversely, *don't* put shareholders first did do better for their shareholders than organizations that *only* put shareholders first.

Specifically, their sample of big, established companies that fit this category did 4 times better in revenue growth, almost 8 times better in job creation, 12 times better on stock prices, and an astounding 756 times better in net income growth. Kotter and Heskett's work, similar research conducted years ago at Johnson & Johnson, and research conducted by Jerry Porras, Jim Collins, and Kirk Hansen at the Stanford Business School all support this book's hypothesis. Organizing around the needs of people – your own and your customer's – pays off big.

NOW READ ON . . .

Drucker, Peter, F., *The Practice of Management*, New York: Harper & Row (1954); London: Heinemann (1955)

Drucker, Peter, F., *Managing for the Future*, Oxford: Butterworth-Heinemann (1992)

Eccles, Robert G. and Nohria, Nitin, *Beyond the Hype*, Boston: Harvard Business School Press (1992)

Kanter, Rosabeth M., *When Giants Learn to Dance*, New York and London: Simon & Schuster (1989)

Kotter, John P. and Heskett, James L., *Corporate Culture and Performance*, New York: The Free Press (1992)

Peters, Tom and Waterman, Robert H. Jr., *In Search of Excellence*, New York and London: Harper & Row (1982)

Schonberger, Richard J., *Building a Chain of Customers*, New York: The Free Press; London: Business Books (1990)

Waterman, Robert H. Jr., *The Renewal Factor*, New York: Bantam (1987)

Waterman, Robert H. Jr., *The Frontiers of Excellence*, London: Nicholas Brealey Publishing (1994)

Chapter 13

Marketing

If 1963, for the poet Philip Larkin, was 'the year that sexual intercourse began', then in management theory 1960 was the year that marketing began. It began with a single article in *Harvard Business Review* entitled 'Marketing Myopia'. The author was a German-born lecturer at Harvard Business School called Theodore Levitt, who subsequently edited the *Review* from 1986 to 1990. 'Marketing Myopia' has since sold hundreds of thousands of reprints and Levitt has published five books on the subject.

Levitt's message – that 'industry is a customer-satisfying process, not a goods-producing process' – seems obvious to managers nurtured ever since Peters and Waterman's *In Search of Excellence* on the necessity of staying 'close to the customer'. But it was not so in 1960, when industry was probably at its apogee of postwar growth. Production was what counted: customers were still queueing up for goods, with money to spend in an era of relatively novel affluence. The idea of having to woo customers, find out what they wanted and make it, rather than confidently expecting them to buy what was put in front of them, would have struck chief executives (particularly in the Detroit car industry) as ludicrous.

Levitt was prescient enough even in 1960 to see that Detroit was heading for a fall. It never researched the customer's wants, he wrote, only 'the kind of things which it had already decided to offer him'. It took the Japanese challenge, some twenty years later, to shake the motor megaliths into realizing that their taken-for-granted customer base had changed for ever.

In every case, Levitt argued, where growth in an industry is slowed or stopped, it is not because the market itself is saturated; 'it is because there has been a failure of management'. Taking America's railroads as a fundamental example, his article pointed out that the railway companies let the car, truck and aircraft industries take business away from them because they saw themselves as in the railroad business rather than the transportation business.

A thoroughly customer-oriented management could keep a growth industry growing even after the first obvious opportunities had been exhausted, wrote Levitt. While no amount of improvement could save a product whose time of obsolescence had come, sensitivity to customers' needs could always suggest a diversification. Levitt's famous example was the buggy whip industry, doomed by the coming of the automobile. 'Had the industry defined itself as being in the transportation business rather than the buggy whip business, it might have survived . . . by becoming a manufacturer of, say, fanbelts or air cleaners.'

(As it happens, America's oldest surviving company, J.E. Rhoads and Sons, started in 1702 tanning leather for buggy whips but in the 1860s switched to conveyor belts, a business it is still in today.)

In 1960, Levitt made the business world realize that marketing suffered from a 'stepchild' status. 'Basic questions about customers and markets seldom get asked. . . . They are recognized as existing, as having to be taken care of, but not worth very much real thought or dedicated attention.'

Selling was not ignored, but selling was not marketing. 'Selling concerns itself with the tricks and techniques of getting people to exchange their cash for your product. It is not concerned with the values that the exchange is all about. And it does not, as marketing invariably does, view the entire business process as consisting of a tightly integrated effort to discover, create, arouse and satisfy customer needs.'

Commenting retrospectively on his 1960 article fifteen years later, Levitt noted that some companies had gone to the other extreme and become 'obsessively responsive to every fleeting whim of the customer'. Managements had expanded product lines and added new ones without first establishing proper control systems for these more complex operations. Marketing budgets had suddenly been expanded without the organizational support to make them work, and some functionally organized companies had converted overnight to being marketing- or brand-based organizations 'with the expectation of instant and miraculous results. The outcome has been ambiguity, frustration, confusion, corporate infighting, losses, and finally a reversion to functional arrangements that only worsened the situation.'

Before Levitt, there had been one prophet crying in the wilderness – and, as usual, it was Peter Drucker, who has been ahead of the pack in virtually every management theory of the past half-century. In *The Practice of Management* (1954) he pointed out that marketing is 'the distinguishing, the unique function of the business. A business is set aside from all other human organizations by the fact that it markets a product or service. . . . Any organization in which marketing is either absent or incidental is not a business and should never be run as if it were one.'

Drucker paid tribute to Cyrus McCormick, inventor of the mechanical harvester, as the unsung inventor of 'the basic tools of modern marketing: market research and market analysis, the concept of market standing, modern pricing policies, the modern service-salesman, parts and service supply to the customer and instalment credit. He is truly the father of business management. And he had done all this by 1850. It was not until fifty years later, however, that he was widely imitated even in his own country.'

Drucker added: 'Fifty years ago the typical attitude of the American businessman towards marketing was still: "The sales department will sell whatever the plant produces".' Drucker was writing of the 1900s. In Europe – certainly in Britain – that attitude was to persist for the best part of the twentieth century. Marketing has proverbially been the downfall of British innovators who have seen, time and again, their breakthroughs developed and marketed by more commercially alert companies, frequently overseas.

Curiously, today's fashionable management writers are in danger of ignoring marketing again. There is not a single index entry for the subject in Tom Peters' *Liberation Management*, though the whole theme of the book is geared to the flexible, fast-moving business able to respond to markets that change like the wind.

Perhaps it is now taken for granted that managers have marketing in their bloodstreams. But that could be a rash assumption.

KEY TEXTS

PETER F. DRUCKER
From *The Practice of Management* (1954).

There is only one valid definition of business purpose: to create a customer.

Markets are not created by God, nature or economic forces, but by businessmen. The want they satisfy may have been felt by the customer before he was offered the means of satisfying it. It may indeed, like the want of food in a famine, have dominated the customer's life and filled all his waking moments. But it was a theoretical want before; only when the action of businessmen makes it an effective demand is there a customer, a market. It may have been an unfelt want. There may have been no want at all until business action created it – by advertising, by salesmanship, or by inventing something new. In every case it is business action that creates the customer.

It is the customer who determines what a business is.

Because it is its purpose to create a customer, any business enterprise has two – and only these two – basic functions: marketing and innovation. They are the entrepreneurial functions.

Marketing is the distinguishing, the unique function of the business. A business is set apart from all other human organizations by the fact that it markets a product or a service. Neither Church, nor Army, nor School, nor State does that. Any organization that fulfils itself through marketing a product or a service, is a business. Any organization in which marketing is either absent or incidental is not a business and should never be run as if it were one. . . .

Actually marketing is so basic that it is just not enough to have a strong sales department and to entrust marketing to it. Marketing is not only much broader than selling, it is not a specialized activity at all. It encompasses the entire business. It is the whole business seen from the point of view of its final result, that is, from the customer's point of view. Concern and responsibility for marketing must therefore permeate all areas of the enterprise.

THEODORE LEVITT
From 'Marketing Myopia' (*Harvard Business Review*, 1960).

The difference between marketing and selling is more than semantic. Selling focuses on the needs of the seller, marketing on the needs of the buyer. Selling is preoccupied with the seller's need to convert his product into cash, marketing with the idea of satisfying the needs of the customer by means of the product and the whole cluster of things associated with creating, delivering, and finally consuming it.

In some industries the enticements of full mass production have been so powerful that for many years top management in effect has told the sales departments, 'You get rid of it; we'll worry about profits.' By contrast, a truly marketing-minded firm tries to create value-satisfying goods and services that consumers will want to buy. What it offers for sale includes not only the generic product or service, but also how it is made available to the customer, in what form, when, under what conditions, and at what terms of trade. Most important, what it offers for sale is determined not by the seller but by the buyer. The seller takes his cues from the buyer in such a way that the product becomes a consequence of the marketing effort, not vice versa.

The view that an industry is a customer-satisfying process, not a goods-producing process, is vital for all businessmen to understand. An industry begins with the customer and his needs, not with a patent, a raw material, or a selling skill. Given the customer's needs, the industry develops backwards, first concerning itself with the physical *delivery* of customer satisfactions. Then it moves back further to *creating* the things by which these satisfactions are in part achieved. How these materials are created is a matter of indifference to the customer, hence the particular form of manufacturing, processing, or what-have-you cannot be considered as a vital aspect of the industry. Finally, the industry moves back still further to *finding* the raw materials necessary for making its products.

The irony of some industries oriented toward technical research and development is that the scientists who occupy the high executive positions are totally unscientific when it comes to defining their companies' overall needs and purposes. They violate the first two rules of the scientific method – being aware of and defining their companies' problems, and then developing testable hypotheses about solving them. They are scientific only about the convenient things, such as laboratory and product experiments.

The reason that the customer (and the satisfaction of his deepest needs) is not considered as being 'the problem' is not because there is any certain belief that no such problem exists, but because an organizational lifetime has conditioned management to look in the opposite direction. Marketing is a stepchild.

I do not mean that selling is ignored. Far from it. But selling, again, is not marketing. As already pointed out, selling concerns itself with the tricks and techniques of getting people to exchange their cash for your product. It is not concerned with the values that the exchange is all about. And it does not, as marketing invariably does, view the entire business process as consisting of a tightly integrated effort to discover, create, arouse, and satisfy customer needs. The customer is somebody 'out there' who, with proper cunning, can be separated from his loose change.

Actually, not even selling gets much attention in some technologically minded firms. Because there is a virtually guaranteed market for the abundant flow of their new products, they do not actually know what a real market is. It is as if they lived in a planned economy, moving their products routinely from factory to retail outlet. Their successful concentration on products tends to convince them of the soundness of what they have been doing, and they fail to see the gathering clouds over the market.

No organization can achieve greatness without a vigorous leader who is driven onward by his own pulsating *will to succeed*. He has to have a vision of grandeur, a vision that can produce eager followers in vast numbers. In business, the followers are the customers.

In order to produce these customers, the entire corporation must be viewed as a customer-creating and customer-satisfying organism. Management must think of itself not as producing products but as providing customer-creating value satisfactions. It must push this idea (and everything it means and requires) into every nook and cranny of the organization. It has to do this continuously and with the kind of flair that excites and stimulates the people in it. Otherwise, the company will be merely a series of pigeonholed parts, with no consolidating sense of purpose or direction.

In short, the organization must learn to think of itself not as producing goods or services but as *buying customers*, as doing the things that will make people *want* to do business with it. And the chief executive himself has the inescapable responsibility for creating this environment, this viewpoint, this attitude, this aspiration. He himself must set the company's style, its direction, and its goals. This means he has to know precisely where he himself wants to go, and to make sure the whole organization is enthusiastically aware of where that is.

PETER F. DRUCKER
From *Managing for Results* (1987).

A good deal of what is called 'marketing' today is at best organized, systematic selling in which the major jobs – from sales forecasting to warehousing and advertising – are brought together and co-ordinated. This is all to the good. But its starting point is still *our* products, *our* customers, *our* technology. The starting point is still the inside. . . .

1. What the people in the business think they know about customer and market is more likely to be wrong than right. There is only one person who really knows: the customer. Only by asking the customer, by watching him, by trying to understand his behaviour, can one find out who he is, what he does, how he buys, how he uses what he buys, what he expects, what he values, and so on.

2. The customer rarely buys what the business thinks it sells him. One reason for this is, of course, that nobody pays for a 'product'. What is paid for is satisfactions. But nobody can make or supply satisfactions as such – at best, only the means to attaining them can be sold and delivered.

Not 'who pays' but 'who determines the buying decision' is the 'customer'. . . .

The minimum number of customers with decisive impact on the buying decision is always two: the ultimate buyer and the distributive channel.

A manufacturer of processed canned foods, for instance, has two main customers: the housewife and the grocery store.

All the standard questions of a market study should, of course, be asked: Who is the customer? Where is the customer? How does he buy? What does he consider value? What purposes of the customer do our products satisfy? What role in the customer's life and work does our particular product play? How important is it to him? Under what circumstances – age, for instance, or structure of the family – is this purpose most important to the customer? Under what circumstances is it least important to him? Who are the direct and the indirect competitors? What are they doing? What might they be doing tomorrow?

But the emphasis might be on different questions that are rarely asked. They are the questions that force us to see the unexpected.

1. Who is the non-customer, the man who does not buy our products even though he is (or might be) in the market? And can we find out why he is a non-customer? . . .
2. Equally important may be the question: What does the customer buy altogether? What does he do with his money and with his time? . . . This leads in turn to two questions that are not asked in the ordinary market survey or customer study:
3. What do customers – and non-customers – buy from others? And what value do these purchases have for them? What satisfactions do they give? Do they, indeed, actually or potentially compete with the satisfactions our products or services are offering? Or do they give satisfactions our products or services – or products or services we could render – could provide too, perhaps even better? . . .
4. This is, of course, very close to the crucial question: What product or service would fulfil the satisfaction areas of real importance – both those we now serve and those we might serve? . . .

Four additional areas demand investigation.

First: What would enable the customer to do without our product or services? What would force them to do without? On what in the customer's world – economy, business, market – do we, in other words, depend? Is it economics? Is it such trends as the constant shifts from goods into services, and from low price into high convenience in an affluent society? What is the outlook? And are we geared to take advantage of the factors favourable to us?

Second: What are the meaningful aggregates in the customer's mind and in his economy? What makes them aggregates? . . .

Another searchlight on the unexpected is the third question: Who are our non-competitors – and why? . . .

The question: Who is our non-competitor? logically leads to the fourth question: Whose non-competitor are we? Where are there opportunities we neither see nor exploit – because we do not consider them part of our industry at all?

Finally, one should always ask the question: What in the

customer's behaviour appears to me totally irrational? And what therefore is it in *his* reality that I fail to see? . . .

Forcing oneself to respect what looks like irrationality on the customer's part, forcing oneself to find the realities of the customer's situation that make it rational behaviour, may well be the most effective approach to seeing one's entire business from the point of view of market and customer. It is usually the quickest way to get outside one's own business and into market-focused action.

Marketing analysis is a good deal more than ordinary market research or customer research. It first tries to look at the entire business. And second, it tries to look not at our customer, our market, our products, but at the market, the customer, his purchases, his satisfactions, his values, his buying and spending patterns, his rationality.

THEODORE LEVITT
From *Thinking About Management* (1991).

In a competitive world, getting and keeping customers requires innovation. Because somebody will always try to serve people better in order to merit their custom, you have to try better yourself. That requires innovating attitudes in all things – making products better, more suitable, more versatile, more easily operable and reparable; manufacturing them better and cheaper; improving dealings with customers and suppliers; improving effectiveness in the office, the sales force, the distribution system, and the trade. The marketing view of the business process requires that all innovations be thought of as intended to help get and keep customers, in short, to make the firm more competitive.

Also much neglected is cultivation of the marketing imagination – the ability to make insightful leaps into the minds, emotions, and practices of customers, and into the vulnerabilities of competitors; leaps that help you to get and keep more customers. The marketing imagination is not terribly unique or elusive. It is not a talent, but a skill.

It can be developed, cultivated, and enhanced. The problem is the false presumption that 'you either have it or you don't'.

Some of the biggest opportunities for the cultivation and exercise of the marketing imagination, and therefore for the practice of product differentiation, exist in intangible products – what are usually but not very helpfully called 'services'. Intangible products have certain unique properties. They can usually be more easily and quickly redesigned and less expensively customized and remanufactured than can processed or manufactured tangible products. Think only of how much insurance programs are customized and modified to suit particular people and situations, and similarly investment or commercial banking, industrial cleaning, travel, entertainment, legal services.

NOW READ ON . . .

Drucker, Peter F., *The Practice of Management*, New York: Harper & Row (1954); London: Heinemann (1955)
Drucker, Peter F., *Managing for Results*, Oxford: Heinemann (1964, 1989)
Levitt, Theodore, 'Marketing Myopia', *Harvard Business Review*, Cambridge, Mass. (1960)
Levitt, Theodore, *Thinking About Management*, New York: The Free Press (1991)

Chapter 14

Competitive Advantage

When Michael Porter was appointed in the mid-1980s to President Ronald Reagan's Commission on Industrial Competitiveness, he found himself among a group of business and labour leaders, academics and former government officials, none of whom could agree on a definition of competitiveness. To business, it largely meant the ability to compete in world markets; to many Congressmen, it meant a favourable balance of trade.

'An even more serious problem has been that there is no generally accepted theory to explain it [competitiveness],' Porter wrote in the book that came out of his work on the commission, *The Competitive Advantage of Nations* (1990), which set out to provide such a theory in a national and international context.

If Porter could not enlighten his peers on the presidential commission, perhaps no one in the US could. Since 1980, when he published *Competitive Strategy*, the youthful Harvard business professor has been the acknowledged world authority on how companies – and, by extension, nations – position themselves with a competitive edge over their rivals. Boiled down to its basics, his argument is that competitive advantage arises from the value a firm is able to create for its buyers, whether that value is based on lower costs or on unique benefits (differentiation) that offset a premium price for the product or service provided.

The basic tool Porter offers managers in both *Competitive Strategy* and *Competitive Advantage* (1985) is his rule of the Five Forces that drive competition in any industry. The central element is the rivalry of existing competitors in the field, while orbiting around it are: potential entrants, the threat of substitutes for the product or service offered, and the bargaining power of suppliers and buyers. 'The significance of any strength or weakness a firm possesses is ultimately a function of its impact on relative cost or differentiation [which] in turn stem from industry structure. They result from a firm's ability to cope with the five forces better than its rivals.'

Arising from these two basic types of competitive advantage, Porter spells out in *Competitive Advantage* three alternative 'generic strategies' which a firm can follow: cost leadership (where it sets out to become the low-cost leader in its industry); differentiation (where it seeks to be unique in some way that customers will value); or focus (in which it targets niche markets within its industry).

As a mechanism for analysing the competitive position of a firm's internal operations, Porter introduced the concept of the 'value chain', by which every single activity within a firm's cycle of production, marketing, delivery and support of its product or service can be broken down to reveal how it interacts with the rest. The process is claimed to reveal the potential for improving both cost and differentiation at an early stage. 'A firm gains competitive advantage by performing these strategically important activities more cheaply or better than its competitors.'

The value chain links into those of its suppliers 'upstream' and its buyers 'downstream', and each needs to be understood as part of the competitive process, as do the value chains of competitors. 'Differences among competitor value chains are a key source of competitive advantage.'

Ten major 'cost drivers' in the value chain determine a firm's cost advantages, and these can be applied to competitors' activities and how they are performed. Similarly, in differentiation, 'virtually any value activity is a potential source of uniqueness', such as a brewing company's emphasis on the quality and purity of its raw ingredients. *Competitive Advantage* offers a detailed methodology to analyse 'drivers of uniqueness' and select policies accordingly, and to demonstrate how both these and cost drivers are affected by technological change.

Porter's final message in *Competitive Advantage* was one he carried through to *The Competitive Advantage of Nations*: that the right competitors in an industry can strengthen rather than weaken a firm's sustainable competitive advantage. In a national/international context, he argued, one key factor determining why countries succeed in particular industries is the strength and quality of domestic rivals in those industries. 'Tough domestic rivalry breeds international success.'

This is one of the four points in the 'Porter diamond'; the other self-reinforcing determinants being the sophistication and demanding nature of the customer base, the country's resources and infrastructure (including the educational quality of its workforce) and the 'cluster' phenomenon, where related and supplier industries tend to cluster in certain geographical areas, and by doing so, mutually support each other's performance (as in the healthcare industries in Switzerland and certain regions of the US). In the 'diamond', these elements are described, respectively, as 'Firm strategy, structure and rivalry', 'Demand conditions', 'Factor conditions' and 'Related and supporting industries'.

'Ultimately,' says Porter, 'nations succeed in particular industries because their home environment is the most forward-looking, dynamic and challenging.' These conclusions, he noted in a *Harvard Business Review* article in 1990, contradicted beliefs about international competitiveness, which largely turned on labour costs, interest rates, exchange rates, economies of scale and supranational globalization.

While Porter remains the leading authority on competitive strategies, two vice-presidents of the influential Boston Consulting Group, George Stalk Jr. and Thomas M. Hout, produced in 1990 what is likely to remain one of the most original books of the decade, *Competing Against Time*. This argues that the ways in which leading companies manage and compress time in all their activities – new product development, production, sales and marketing – are the most powerful sources of competitive advantage.

Responsiveness, giving customers what they want when they want it, is the key to success in today's markets, contend Stalk and Hout, a message shared by most of today's leading management gurus. They claim that 'time compression' is the fundamental advantage behind Japanese success in a number of highly competitive markets, enabling them to increase the variety and technological sophistication of their products and services.

'Time is the secret weapon of business because advantages in response time lever up all other differences that are basic to overall competitive advantage. Some Western managements know this, others are learning, and the rest will be victims. . . . Providing the most value for the lowest cost in the least amount of time is the new pattern for corporate success.'

As time cycles are compressed, the book points out, productivity increases, costs are lowered (but prices can be increased, for premium service), risks are reduced and market share is increased. Most beneficial of all, new products and services can be brought to market much more quickly, establishing a valuable lead over competitors and raising the innovating company's margins.

Fast innovations, the authors observe, can enable managements to change the whole nature of a business in order to adapt to changing market conditions. The list of companies that have successfully done this is mostly Japanese, including Fujitsu (from machine tool control mechanisms to computers); Honda (from small motors to motorcycles to cars), and Brother (from sewing machines to typewriters, then printers, then small computers). Canon responded to changes in its initially successful camera market by diversifying into copiers and, more recently, into high-growth fax machines and laser printers.

In order to compress the time cycles throughout an organization, it is first necessary to understand that organization's systems, and to analyse where time delays occur. This is, of course, an integral part of business process redesign or 're-engineering', and not a million miles removed from F.W. Taylor's pioneer ventures in time-and-motion study. (In management theory, as in every other field of human thought, there are only so many original ideas.) Nor is it new as an overarching principle of competitiveness: Stalk and Hout quote J.W. Forrester of Massachusetts Institute of Technology, writing in 1958 in *Harvard Business Review*, with his theory of 'industrial dynamics' to illustrate how time delays at different points built up a cumulative impact on a firm's performance.

As long ago as 1921, Henry Ford, who built his assembly lines on Taylorist principles, was stressing the importance of time as a competitive resource, noting memorably that 'time waste differs from material waste in that there can be no salvage'.

Competing Against Time examines the characteristics of a time-based company under three main headings: how work is structured, how information is created and shared, and how performance is measured. Much of it links in with the concepts of Porter's value chain and Richard Schonberger's 'chain of customers', and, like those, the ultimate goal is gaining and retaining satisfied customers.

'The ultimate purpose of the time-based competitor is not maximizing speed and variety, but owning the customer. Speed and variety are just tools allowing one to do more for the customer, to solve his problems, to reduce his costs – in short, to help him compete and make money.'

KEY TEXTS

MICHAEL E. PORTER
From *Competitive Advantage* (1985).

In any industry, whether it is domestic or international or produces a product or a service, the rules of competition are embodied in five competitive forces: the entry of new competitors, the threat of substitutes, the bargaining power of buyers, the bargaining power of suppliers, and the rivalry among the existing competitors.

The collective strength of these five competitive forces determines the ability of firms in an industry to earn, on average, rates of return on investment in excess of the cost of capital. The strength of the five forces varies from industry to industry, and can change as an industry evolves. The result is that all industries are not alike from the standpoint of inherent profitability. In industries where the five forces are favorable, such as pharmaceuticals, soft drinks, and data base publishing, many competitors earn attractive returns. But in industries where pressure from one or more of the forces is intense, such as rubber, steel, and video games, few firms command attractive returns despite the best efforts of management. Industry profitability is not a function of what the product looks like or whether it embodies high or low technology, but of industry structure. Some very mundane industries such as postage meters and grain trading are extremely profitable, while some more glamorous, high-technology industries such as personal computers and cable television are not profitable for many participants.

The five forces determine industry profitability because they influence the prices, costs, and required investment of firms in an industry – the elements of return on investment. Buyer power influences the prices that firms can charge, for example, as does the threat of substitution. The power of buyers can also influence cost and investment,

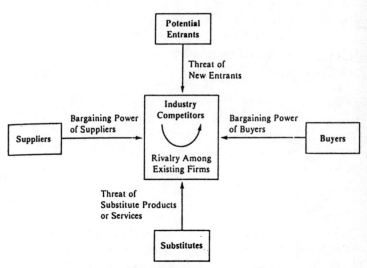

The Five Competitive Forces that Determine Industry Profitability

because powerful buyers demand costly service. The bargaining power of suppliers determines the costs of raw materials and other inputs. The intensity of rivalry influences prices as well as the costs of competing in areas such as plant, product development, advertising, and sales force. The threat of entry places a limit on prices, and shapes the investment required to deter entrants.

Technological change by a firm will lead to sustainable competitive advantage under the following circumstances:

The technological change itself lowers cost or enhances differentiation and the firm's technological lead is sustainable. A technological change enhances competitive advantage if it leads to lower cost or differentiation and can be protected from imitation. . . .

The technological change shifts cost or uniqueness drivers in favor of a firm. Changing the technology of a value activity, or changing the product in ways that affect a value activity, can influence the drivers of cost or uniqueness in that activity. Even if the technological change is imitated, therefore, it will lead to a competitive advantage for a firm if it skews drivers in the firm's favor. For example, a new assembly process that is more scale-sensitive than the previous process will benefit a large-share firm that pioneers it even if competitors eventually adopt the technology.

Pioneering the technological change translates into first-mover advantages besides those inherent in the technology itself. Even if an innovator is imitated, pioneering may lead to a variety of potential first-mover advantages in cost or differentiation that remain after its technological lead is gone. . . .

The technological change improves overall industry structure. . . .

Technological change that fails these tests will not improve a firm's competitive position, though it may represent a substantial technological accomplishment.

GEORGE STALK Jr. AND THOMAS M. HOUT
From *Competing Against Time* (1990).

To become a time-based competitor, three tasks must be

accomplished by the management of a company's management.

1. Make the value–delivery systems of the company two to three times more flexible and faster than the value–delivery systems of competitors
2. Determine how its customers value variety and responsiveness, focus on those customers with the greatest sensitivity, and price accordingly
3. Have a strategy for surprising its competitors with the company's time–based advantage

Time–based competitors are more productive. When time consumption in a value–delivery system is reduced by half, or even more, costs decrease substantially. If an order for a semi–custom–made product can be processed in 35 instead of 70 days with the same number of people, then the cost per order processed is reduced by half. In actuality, though, the number of man–hours needed in the faster processing system is probably less than half the number needed in the slower one. In many manufacturing–based businesses, this additional reduction in the costs of goods sold can be expected to be at least 20 to 25 per cent as time consumption is reduced by 50 to 75 per cent. And for people–intensive businesses such as the processing of insurance claims, the additional cost reduction can be even higher – between 35 and 50 per cent.

Time–based competitors also get more bang for their product development buck. The cost productivities of their development resources can be at least twice as great as those of slow innovators, and their time productivities, more than twice as fast. In fact, while the improvements in time productivities (or the previous time required to perform a specific task divided by the improved time required to perform the task) can be two to three times, the improvement in engineering time productivities can range even beyond this.

Seldom do time–based competitors allow all of their cost productivities to flow to their bottom lines, however. Almost always, time–based competitors invest the savings in more new products and services. As a result, they typically introduce new products at rates three to four times greater than those of slower innovators.

Time is a more useful management tool than cost. Cost is by and large a lagging indicator, a symptom, a set of control accounts after the fact. Cost is tracked through a set of accounts corresponding to what money is spent on – payroll, amortization of fixed assets, holding inventory, and so on. Cost is a financial calculation that includes some arbitrary allocations and deferrals. There are price level adjustments and variances of several kinds. It is sometimes hard to say what cost is really measuring – better real performance or just better utilization of sunk costs? . . .

Managing time, on the other hand, opens up the company for analysis. Time is an objectively measurable current flow, not a calculation shaped by accounting conventions. A manager can measure and quantify the flow of activities directly and ask with respect to each whether it is adding real value. For example, inventories are idle materials, just as in-baskets contain idle information. Reworking is doing something twice. Holding up a decision because the necessary data is late in arriving is response time lost. Time is a common, direct measure.

Time's major advantage as a management tool is that it forces analysis down to a physical level. Putting together a time line of activity – a chart that says what happened every hour or every day to an order, or to a project, or to whatever you want to track – tells you what actually goes on in your company. Once physical activity is laid bare, the right questions can be asked: Why do we do this step twice? Why are these tasks done serially and not in parallel? Why does this process work only half the time? Why do we invest to speed this up and then let its output sit and wait for the next process? Answers to these questions lead managers to where the cost and quality problems of the company actually are.

NOW READ ON ...

Porter, Michael E., *Competitive Strategy*, New York: The Free Press (1980)
Porter, Michael E., *Competitive Advantage*, New York: The Free Press (1985)
Porter, Michael E., *The Competitive Advantage of Nations*, London: The Macmillan Press (1990)
Stalk, George Jr., and Hout, Thomas M., *Competing Against Time*, New York: The Free Press; London: Collier Macmillan (1990)

Chapter 15

Managing Quality

The astonishing fact about the quality revolution is how recent it is. In 1980, almost nobody in senior management in Western countries considered quality to be a management issue. Quality was regarded as a matter of inspection and of correcting discovered faults, rather than of managing the production process so as to eliminate faults. Today, total quality management (TQM) has a strong claim to be the most influential management theory of our time, with its objectives enshrined in government quality audits such as ISO9000 and BS5750.

What caused the change was the Japanese assault on world markets in the late 1970s, particularly those markets long dominated by the US, such as copiers, cameras and cars. American industry discovered to its amazement that Japan, once a byword for shoddy goods and devastated by two atomic bombs in 1945, had managed to build a world-beating industrial base largely on the wisdom – ignored in his homeland – of an American statistician, W. Edwards Deming. Since 1951, Japanese companies had been competing for a quality award known as the Deming Prize, an event of national importance shown on prime-time television. (Not until 1987 did the US introduce the Malcolm Baldrige National Award for Quality, a prize of similar prestige.)

It was William E. Conway, president and later CEO of the Nashua Corporation, the office products company, who discovered the impact Deming was making in 1979, when the statistician was already 78 years old. Conway engaged him as a consultant after Deming had insisted he would only take the job if Conway, as CEO, agreed to become the change leader for a quality programme at Nashua. Nashua went on to achieve astounding improvements in its lead times (eight days cut to one hour) and in customer claims (a 70 per cent reduction).

In 1980, NBC Television showed a documentary called *If Japan Can, Why Can't We?* The producer could not believe that no one in the US government knew about Deming and what he had achieved in Japan. The day after the documentary was shown in June 1980, the telephone never stopped ringing in Deming's basement office in Washington. Later that year, Deming began to give four-day management seminars, a practice he continued at the rate of twenty a year almost to his death at the end of 1993.

US corporations that have implemented and paid tribute to Deming's principles include Ford (an early convert), Honeywell, AT&T, Campbell's Soups, Kimberly-Clark, Procter & Gamble, Velcro and Florida Power and Light – the first non-Japanese company to receive Japan's Deming Prize (in 1989).

Deming was not the sole progenitor of statistical quality control (SQC) or statistical process control (SPC), as the techniques became known. The principles were worked out in the 1920s by Dr Walter Shewhart, a Bell Laboratories physicist, at Western Electricity's Hawthorne Plant in Chicago, where both Deming and his later rival Joseph Juran were employed. (Hawthorne in the late 1920s was a crucible of influential management research, going down in industrial history as the source of industrial sociology with Elton Mayo's studies into motivation and worker-management relations.)

Shewhart pioneered the study of variables, both controlled (by the process itself, how it was designed and how its workers were trained) and uncontrolled (by factors outside the process). The techniques he worked out, and published in 1931 in a book called *Economic Control of Quality of Manufactured Product*, were designed for the zero-defect mass production of telephone handsets and exchanges. They also, excitingly, demonstrated that productivity as well as quality improves as variation is reduced.

Deming extended Shewhart's principles from production-line processes to non-manufacturing processes, including administration, and urged managers to focus on the causes of variability. When he applied the concept to his work on the 1940 US Census, productivity in some of the processes involved, such as coding and card-punching, increased up to six times. In 1942 Deming set up courses to teach Shewhart's methods to industrialists and others involved in the war effort, and the American Society for Quality Control was set up in 1946.

The message, however, failed to spread in the complacent world of postwar manufacturing where customers starved of goods were uncritically happy to accept abundance again. (Quality circles were also in use in American industry during World War II but failed to take hold after the war because proper statistical feedback was lacking.) Deming, the classic prophet without honour in his own country, was obliged to wait until he was invited to Japan in the summer of 1950 to lecture on American quality control methods used in the war. Earlier, in the late 1940s, a team from Bell Labs had visited Japan under the assistance programme for reconstruction to share their own expertise in the field. By the time Deming arrived, Japanese managers were already alert to the message that quality follows reduction in variability, and that productivity follows in its wake.

Deming's reception by middle managers was overwhelming, but he soon realized that if he were going to help change working practices, he had to address the message to the top. He asked his hosts, the Japanese Union of Scientists and Engineers (JUSE), to arrange meetings with members of the Keidanren, the association of Japanese chief executives, and the first was held in July 1950. By December of that year, the JUSE had instituted the Deming Prize.

Deming told his top-level audiences that if they followed his 'Management for Quality' philosophy they could be so competitive that in five years 'manufacturers the world over would be screaming for protection'. In the 1980s he reflected wryly: 'It took four years.' The core of his message was to think of the consumer as the most important part of the production line, a concept that is still being interpreted as new management thinking in the West, forty years on.

Deming's now famous 'Fourteen Points' were developed over a period of more than twenty years. There have been many variations on them, reflecting their originator's own refinements over the years. The version included here is taken from *The Deming Dimension* by Henry Neave, a British colleague of Deming's, but the words, says Neave, are 'virtually all Deming's'.

The Fourteen Points, it should be stressed, are not intended as a recipe or checklist for achieving quality. They are the outline of a philosophy designed to open the minds of top management to improving the performance of their companies, and, in the best Japanese tradition of 'kaizen', to creating a programme for continuous improvement.

The job of management, said Deming, is 'to accomplish the change required'. By the mid-1980s he had come to believe that management was accountable for as much as 94 per cent of the potential improvement in quality control. Similar emphasis is found in the work of Joseph M. Juran, a close contemporary of Deming's (born 1904) and fellow quality mentor during Japan's postwar reconstruction.

Juran's approach, which he calls Company-Wide Quality Management (CWQM), is less statistically driven than Deming's. It is based on a structured approach to quality planning across the company and is most easily assimilable in his 1988 book *Juran on Planning for Quality*. At the core of his teaching is a trilogy of techniques – quality planning, control and improvement. The keys to strategic quality planning are seen as identifying customer requirements, establishing quality goals and measurements to achieve them, setting up planning processes to meet quality goals under actual operating conditions and producing continuous improvement in market share, premium positioning and reduction of error.

Juran believes in a root-and-branch approach, as opposed to project-by-project quality management. He has likened it to the choice facing someone up to his waist in alligators: the project approach would kill the alligators one by one, but more will always come out of the swamp. The only enduring solution is 'to drain the swamp'. Like Deming, he assigns management the overwhelming responsibility for quality. In his view, over 80 per cent of quality problems are attributable to defects controllable by management.

As he approached his nineties, Juran remained unimpressed by the mass of tributes heaped on him and Deming. 'If neither I nor Deming had gone to Japan in the early 1950s, the Japanese would still have achieved world quality leadership,' he said in 1993.

By the late 1950s, the Japanese had begun to develop their own quality methodology, in which mass education and the use of teamwork and simple techniques played a key part. Three important Japanese gurus were, and are, Dr Kaoru Ishikawa (1915-89), a pioneer of the quality circle in Japan in the early 1960s; Dr Genichi Toguchi (b. 1924), who believes that quality starts before manufacture, at the design stage, and Shigeo Shingo (1909-90), who developed a source inspection system to prevent errors from becoming defects.

A third influential figure among the early quality gurus is Armand V. Feigenbaum, whose work on Total Quality Control (the title of his first book while still a doctoral student at MIT) was also studied by the Japanese in the 1950s. Feigenbaum, who headed quality control at General Electric for many years, argued for a systematic approach, building in quality from the start rather than as a result of inspection and control. His principal message is that quality is the single most important factor leading to the success and growth of business organizations. In 1977 he calculated that anything from 15 to 40 per cent of the manufacturer's cost in most US products represented waste embedded in the manufacturing process.

The leading name in the current generation of US quality gurus is Philip Crosby, former corporate vice-president of ITT. Crosby is famous for the slogan 'Quality is Free', the title of his best-known book (1979). So successful was the book that he left ITT to set up his own consultancy and established a Quality College in Florida to teach his principles.

Far from costing money to introduce a quality programme, Crosby explains, the savings that can be made by eliminating defects at source represent pure additional profit for the company. So persuasive and simple is his message, reinforced by irrefutable numbers, that Crosby has a good claim to be regarded as even more influential than the great philosophers of the quality movement, Deming and Juran.

The twin pillars of his philosophy are 'Do It Right First Time' and 'Zero Defects' – by which he means that the company does not start from a position of expecting mistakes to be made and then corrected. Crosby's definition of quality is conforming to the company's own requirements, which in turn are based on its customers' requirements.

His 'Four Absolutes' of quality management are:

1. Quality is conformance to requirements, not 'goodness' or 'elegance'.
2. The system for causing quality is prevention, not appraisal.
3. The performance standard must be Zero Defects, not 'that's close enough'.
4. The measurement of quality is the price of non-conformance, not indices.

Like Deming, he also has a fourteen-point programme, in Crosby's case called 'The Fourteen Steps to Quality Improvement'. They begin with the precept 'Make it clear that management is committed to quality' and end with the exhortation 'Do it all over again to emphasize that the quality improvement programme never ends.' (Crosby's Fourteen Steps are set out in full in *The Quality Gurus*, one of a series of 'Managing into the 90s' booklets published by the Department of Trade and Industry.)

Crosby is critical of what he calls 'the quality profession' for not grasping the opportunity to develop true cost measurements. At their most basic, the costs of failing to implement quality from the start include such items as inspection, testing, warranty, rework and scrap. In *Quality is Free* he lists the expenses of setting up a Cost of Quality (COQ) programme under three main headings: prevention costs, appraisal costs and failure costs.

Prevention cost specifics include design reviews, product qualification, supplier evaluations, supplier quality seminars, process capability studies, operation training, zero defects programme, quality audits and preventive maintenance. Appraisal costs include inspection and surveillance programmes, while failure costs embrace redesign, rework, product liability and occasionally lost credibility with the customer.

Once a finance department has calculated the COQ package, targets can be set for reducing costs as quality improves. Soon, reductions equal pure pretax profit. Case studies bear this out, often dramatically: a total quality drive at Motorola between 1987 and 1992 added a staggering $3.2 billion to the company's bottom line.

Richard Schonberger, author of *Building a Chain of Customers*, says that the cost of bad quality in many companies runs as high as 15–30 per cent of sales; cash down the drain in internal costs (scrap, rework, rescheduling, overtime) and external costs (warranties, returns, time spent placating irate customers).

Perhaps Crosby's most influential contribution to management thinking, along with Schonberger and others, has been to identify the supplier–customer relationship at all stages in an industrial production process. By treating each operator in the line as a customer with expectations of quality and performance, much waste and error could be removed, thus benefiting the real customer at the end of the chain. This principle has become a key component in cross-functional 're-engineering' of business processes.

The British Standards Institute's quality audit BS5750, introduced to a largely indifferent world in 1979, became the model for the worldwide standard ISO9000 and Europe's EN29000.

Quality is now recognized as a continually moving target: when low defect rates become the norm in an industry, the target changes to achieving top quality at lower cost.

Richard Schonberger observes in *Building a Chain of Customers* that, since generally accepted concepts of quality have progressed up four levels in less than a decade – from corrective to preventive to cost-based to customer-serving – another 'generational' progression may be expected before long. He suggests that the next leap forward will provide new techniques for 'getting all employees to become "owners" of the continual improvement effort. If all employees assume that ownership – creating a large army of customer-serving quality improvers – the goal of rapid improvement is assured.'

KEY TEXTS

PHILIP CROSBY
From *Quality is Free* (1979).

All you really need is enough information to show your management that reducing the cost of quality (COQ) is in fact an opportunity to increase profits without raising sales, buying new equipment, or hiring new people. The first step is to put together the fully loaded costs of (1) all efforts involved in doing work over, including clerical work; (2) all scrap; (3) warranty (including in-plant handling of returns); (4) after-service warranty; (5) complaint handling; (6) inspection and test; and (7) other costs of error, such as engineering change notices, purchasing change orders, etc. It is normal to obtain only one-third of the real cost the first time you try it.

Many quality management people start out with the thought that it is a good thing for them personally if the company has a very low figure for cost of quality. They tend to come up with readings like 1.3 per cent of sales. Then they run to the boss for applause. A few years later their successor finds that it is really 12.6 per cent of sales and embarks on a well-rewarded campaign to reduce this needless waste. The first person just refused to understand that the cost of quality has little to do with the operation of the quality department.

To make the total calculation more understandable to other managements it is a good idea to relate it to a significant base. Most people use a per cent of sales. However, if you are in a company where there are unusually high costs of distribution like the food industry, you may want to measure COQ as a percentage of cost of sales, or just plain manufacturing costs. In insurance, banks, hotels, and similar businesses the cost of operations makes a good base. What is really important is that the number be something that quality management can use to communicate the importance of the concept. That is what the whole business of COQ is all about.

Many managers wait, and fiddle, and never really do get

a workable COQ system installed. They collect endless lists and classifications of things that should be considered. They are too concerned with trying to obtain an exact cost figure, and don't really understand the reason for doing the calculation in the first place. . . .

Once an operation knows its COQ, or a good approximation, goals for reducing that cost can be set. Ten per cent a year is a good, attainable goal that people can relate to.

JOSEPH M. JURAN
From *Juran on Planning for Quality* (1988).

THE QUALITY PLANNING ROAD MAP

In broad terms, quality planning consists of developing the products and processes required to meet customers' needs. More specifically, quality planning comprises the following basic activities:

Identify the customers and their needs

Develop a product that responds to those needs

Develop a process able to produce that product

When we look more closely, it turns out that we can generalize *a road map for quality planning* – an invariable sequence of steps, as follows:

Identify who are the customers

Determine the needs of those customers

Translate those needs into our language

Develop a product that can respond to those needs

Optimize the product features so as to meet our needs as well as customers' needs

Develop a process which is able to produce the product

Optimize the process

Prove that the process can produce the product under operating conditions

Transfer the process to the operating forces

RICHARD J. SCHONBERGER
From *Building a Chain of Customers* (1990).

TQ is a world movement. Regardless of country or industry, the laggards are at risk; conversely, the leaders acquire insulation against failure. A good promoter can still sell junk, but it's tougher when another firm down the street, across the country, or beyond the sea sells quality at the same price.

The jobholders of the world have a nose for quality, too – a quality organization in which to work. Attractions include better safety conditions, job security, and chances for monetary gain. The poor-quality organization fails on each of these counts – and more. What is so demoralizing as a job designed to allow shoddiness and to block one's ideas for improvement? What is so sterile as one that obstructs contact with and chance to serve the customer. The antidote is continual improvement and employee involvement, which are TQ's backbone; they can become a force for sustaining the TQ effort, even if champions depart and leaders fumble.

A vital role of the organization's managers is to lead the effort to create this stem–to–stern sustaining force. Their ultimate success is when all jobholders become champions and leaders of the TQ effort in their own arena.

When our thinking about quality expands to consider losses to *society* and quality audits of everything from nuts to soup in the cafeteria, we are on the right track. Professor David Garvin has helped us broaden our thinking in another way. He's told us that conformance to specs is only one of eight ways that customers judge quality.

Multiple Dimensions of Quality
In that spirit, others are not content to stop at just eight items. My own expanded list numbers twelve dimensions of quality (Garvin's eight are starred):

*1. *Conformance to specifications*. Can be numeric specs, for example, package weight no less than 395 and no more than 405 grams; or yes-no specs, for example, bulb lights or does not.

*2. *Performance*. This refers to *grade* of service or product: degree of 'home-baked chewiness' in a commercial cookie; clarity of TV picture; expertness of advice. When people are willing to pay more, it is often for better performance. Surveys reveal that performance is the number one way that consumers think about quality.

3. *Quick response*. Often measured in delay or elapsed time: time wasted standing in a ticket line or clamping the phone to one's ear while on hold; delay in getting an order produced, filled, or delivered or a case heard in court; time-to-market for a new product or service.

4. *Quick-change expertise*. Costume changes in the theater, can size changes in a cannery, model-to-model changes in an auto assembly plant.

*5. *Features*. Automatic focus in a camera, free coffee while you shop, airbag safety device in an automobile.

*6. *Reliability*. Car starts every time, keeps running for whole trip. In other words, reliability is failure-free operation *over time*.

*7. *Durability*. How tough it is or how long it lasts: a premium windbreaker jacket that can be crammed into a fist-sized bag and that will take 20 years of wearing, an antismoking cure that lasts a lifetime.

*8. *Serviceability*. Ease of providing a service or of servicing goods. An easy-to-clean oven, a typewriter with easy-to-access-and-change cartridge-style ribbons, a free complaint phone line.

*9. *Aesthetics*. Beauty, elegance, schmaltz, and other factors that appeal to the eye or other senses: an engine's full-throated roar, a greeting-card phrase that 'tugs at the heartstrings'.

*10. *Perceived quality*. Impression of quality based on things other than here-and-now evidence: loyalty to a brand of clothing, reputation of a judge for fairness.

11. *Humanity*. Providing services or goods with the right degree of friendliness, attentiveness, humility, honesty: service with a smile, machines that talk, waiters who know just when and when not to interrupt table talk.

12. *Value*. How much of any of the above dimensions of quality we get for the cost or price. In their ratings of the quality of life in a certain community, sociologists find out the cost of a kilowatt-hour of electricity, of police protection, of getting a tire fixed.

The four unstarred items are not just variations on some of the eight starred ones. They are basic and vital in their own right. For example, quick response and quick changes (items 3 and 4) are so important to customers that we should not permit them to be buried in the *performance* dimension (item 2). Moreover, *managing* for quick response and managing for fast changes each have their own sizable, still fast-growing bodies of knowledge – which are out of the traditional mainstream of thinking in quality management.

Humanity, item 11, is a necessary addition to quality concepts that in the past have tended toward the mechanistic.

Value, item 12, is always on the final paying customer's mind. The world-class company makes value a vital issue throughout the chain of customers. That is, each of us may continually improve service to the next process by wiping out costly waste and improving all the other dimensions of quality.

DEMING'S FOURTEEN POINTS
From *The Deming Dimension* by Henry Neave (1990).

1. Create constancy of purpose for continual improvement of products and service.
2. Adopt the new philosophy created in Japan.
3. Cease dependence on mass inspection: build quality into the product in the first place.
4. End lowest-tender contracts; instead, require meaningful measures of quality along with price.
5. Improve constantly and forever every process for planning, production and service.
6. Institute modern methods of training on the job for all, including management.

7. Adopt and institute leadership aimed at helping people to do a better job.

8. Drive out fear, encourage effective two-way communication.

9. Break down barriers between departments and staff areas.

10. Eliminate exhortations for the workforce – they only create adversarial relationships.

11. Eliminate quotas and numerical targets. Substitute aid and helpful leadership.

12. Remove barriers to pride of workmanship, including annual appraisals and Management by Objectives.

13. Encourage education and self-improvement for everyone.

14. Define top management's permanent commitment to ever-improving quality and productivity, and their obligation to implement all these principles.

ROBERT H. WATERMAN, Jr.
From *The Frontiers of Excellence* (1994).

An effective total-quality program doesn't just benefit customers. Run right, total quality is one of those rare management ideas that, like self-direction, can really benefit most middle managers and employees as well. One reason: Such a program is typically organized in a way that shoves challenge, control, and learning way down the line in organizations. Another: It quite naturally fosters pride in work. People are craftsmen at heart. They want to produce products and give service they can be proud of. They also like being part of a team that strives to be the best at what it does.

Most firms organize total-quality programs in a broadly similar way. First, the whole organization divides itself into small, say, two- to seven-person teams. Armed with a big goal for improvement and trained both in quality techniques and team skills, each team identifies the main products it produces or services it provides. There may be only one or several.

Second, teams identify the customer or customers for their products and services. They talk to them. They find out what customers consider important. Significantly, this way of approaching quality forces people to define quality in the way that the customer sees quality. This is crucial and explains why total quality and total customer satisfaction are so closely linked at Motorola. In the old days of quality control, quality was usually defined by the engineers or manufacturing people. That's when quality gets expensive. Companies add all sorts of bells and whistles that the customer doesn't care about, while entirely overlooking what the customer does want. (Note that for many activities performed by a unit, the customer will be internal – one department of an organization serving another. Thus, quality buffs talk about both *internal customers* and *external customers*.)

Third, the team members analyse the way work currently gets done. They figure out how it might be dramatically improved. They start by analysing the major sources of customer complaints. Then they move on to the smaller ones. Often they uncover work that's completely unnecessary, a common source of almost immediate cost savings.

NOW READ ON...

Crosby, Philip B., *Quality is Free*, New York: McGraw-Hill (1979)

Deming, W.E., *Out of the Crisis*, Cambridge, Mass: MIT Center for Advanced Engineering Study (1982); Cambridge, England: Cambridge University Press (1986)

Feigenbaum, A.V., *Total Quality Control*, New York: McGraw-Hill (1983)

Juran, J.R., *Juran on Planning for Quality*, New York: The Free Press (1988)

Neave, Henry, *The Deming Dimension*, Knoxville, Tenn.: SPC Press Inc. (1990)

Schonberger, Richard J., *Building a Chain of Customers*, New York: The Free Press; London: Hutchinson (1990)

Chapter 16

Customer Care

'Industry is a customer-satisfying process, not a goods-producing process.' In 1960, when Harvard's Theodore Levitt made that statement in his ground-breaking article 'Marketing Myopia' for *Harvard Business Review*, it would have been greeted with baffled incomprehension in large swathes of industry and commerce; not because they disagreed with the first part of the proposition, but because customer satisfaction was presumed in those days to follow the provision of goods that people wanted to buy. Fifteen years after the end of World War II, industry was still geared to a philosophy of quantity before quality, of filling the shelves after years of shortages. Unless a customer actually complained or sent the goods back, he or she was deemed to be satisfied.

Today, customer care and satisfaction is seen as a proactive, not reactive process. It has been an integral part of the quality revolution ever since Peters and Waterman noted in their brushfire seller, *In Search of Excellence* (1982) that virtually all forty-three of their excellent companies had 'defined themselves as *de facto* service businesses.

'Customers reign supreme. They are not treated as untested technology or unnecessary gold-plating. They are the recipients of products that last, service delivered promptly.'

Peters and Waterman's chapter heading 'Close to the Customer', one of their eight rubrics of proven excellence in companies, has become part of business culture.

Like quality, the expected standards of customer care have progressed in less than ten years through several step-changes; from simply ensuring that customers were satisfied with the quality, price, delivery and service provided to encouraging active feedback from customers, to anticipating the future wants of customers, to achieving an entire 'customer-driven company'.

Along the way, the theory of the 'internal customer' has been influential in improving end products and services. It is a central theme in the work of quality guru Philip Crosby and industrial engineer Richard Schonberger, who also claims to have introduced Just-in-Time to US industry, and plays an important part in business process redesign, or 're-engineering'.

The internal customer is every operator in a business process to whom another operator supplies components, products or services in the course of the value chain that ultimately supplies the real, external customer. If each internal customer is treated as meticulously – and behaves as demandingly – as the external customer, quality and satisfaction to the real buyer should follow automatically, producing many cost savings along the way.

Customer feedback, managed through techniques such as questionnaires and toll-free telephone numbers, has spun off a host of improvements to products and services that could have been generated in no other way because they emerge from a market that is waiting for them. Examples cited by Peters and Waterman include pre-faded jeans, an idea that came to manufacturers Levi Strauss from the New York department store Bloomingdales, one of their leading primary customers. The concept became a worldwide craze that shows no signs of abating.

Nearly all IBM's early innovations were developed with its chief customer at the time, the Census Bureau, and when Procter & Gamble printed a toll-free number on all its packaging, inviting calls, the hundreds of thousands of ideas and complaints proved a rich source of product innovation. Every call received a response, and calls were logged and summarised for P&G's monthly board meeting – a telling reminder that listening to the customer must begin at the top.

With the exception of Richard Whiteley's *The Customer-Driven Company*, there are few books devoted entirely to the subject, though management books abound with case studies of customer care led by the chief executive. The Marriott hotel group is a prime exemplar: until well into his eighties, founder J. Willard Marriott Sr. read every customer complaint card, and his son Bill Marriott, so *Fortune* reported in 1988, still personally reads 10 per cent of the thousands of letters and 2 per cent of the 750,000 questionnaires each month.

Marriott also surveys its guests on their opinions of services offered by competitors. 'If Holiday Inn offers a free continental breakfast, Marriott will know within weeks whether its customers would like one too,' writes Richard Whiteley, whose company acts as a consultant to the hotel group. Marriott knows precisely how each segment of its market – business travellers, delegates to conferences and leisure travellers – will react to any innovation such as a change of practice at the concierge desk.

'Smart companies like Marriott are always listening,' says Whiteley. 'They realize that this is a struggle that never stops.' The results at Marriott speak for themselves, with occupancy rates averaging in the late eighties about 10 per cent above the industry norm, and a return on equity of more than 20 per cent over a decade. 'Not a bad reward for an attentive ear,' observes Whiteley.

Marriott was one of the excellent companies that survived the collapse in fortunes which overtook around half of Peters and Waterman's famous list in the mid-1980s. In *Thriving on Chaos* (1987), Tom Peters urges managements to implement ten measurements of customer satisfaction, involving formal surveys by a third party every 60 to 90 days, informal surveys monthly, informal focus groups at all levels of seniority, incentives and rewards linked to the satisfaction measurement. He also recommends that indirect as well as direct customers be included – every member of the distribution channel, for example, as well as the ultimate customer. Key customer satisfaction measures should be publicly posted everywhere in an organization, says Peters, and job descriptions and appraisals be devised to include the 'customer connection' for employees and their 'degree of customer orientation'.

Peters takes the message a stage further in *Liberation*

Management (1992), stressing the need for ever more rapid and flexible management responses to a marketplace that is changing and evolving at bewildering speed, accelerated by technology and globalization. Capturing and retaining the loyalty of customers made increasingly fickle by proliferating choice and competition is now the name of everybody's game. The key, says Peters, is to go beyond 'satisfied' customers to 'committed' customers, and he quotes a business academic who recommends that personnel management needs to be recast as a function to 'induce customer engagement with the firm' through its employees.

Deming, the godfather of the quality movement, foresaw this years ago when he wrote and spoke of the need to stay ahead of the customer. 'The customer does not know what he will need in one, three, five years from now. If you, as just one of his potential suppliers, wait until then to find out, you will hardly be ready to serve him.' (Quoted in *The Deming Dimension*, by Henry R. Neave.)

KEY TEXTS

PETER F. DRUCKER
From *Management: Tasks, Responsibilities, Practices* (1973).

A business is not defined by the company's name, statutes, or articles of incorporation. It is defined by the want the customer satisfies when he buys a product or a service. To satisfy the customer is the mission and purpose of every business. The question 'What is our business?' can, therefore, be answered only by looking at the business from the outside, from the point of view of customer and market. What the customer sees, thinks, believes, and wants, at any given time, must be accepted by management as an objective fact and must be taken as seriously as the reports of the salesman, the tests of the engineer, or the figures of the accountant. And management must make a conscious effort to get answers from the customer himself rather than attempt to read his mind.

Management always, and understandably, considers its

product or its service to be important. If it did not, it could not do a good job. Yet to the customer, no product or service, and certainly no company, is of much importance. The executives of a company always tend to believe that the customer spends hours discussing their products. But how many housewives, for instance, ever talk to each other about the whiteness of their laundry? If there is something badly wrong with one brand of detergent they switch to another. The customer only wants to know what the product or service will do for him tomorrow. All he is interested in are his own values, his own wants, his own reality. For this reason alone, any serious attempt to state 'what our business is' must start with the customer, his realities, his situation, his behavior, his expectations, and his values.

TOM PETERS AND ROBERT H. WATERMAN, Jr.
From *In Search of Excellence* (1982).

So the excellent companies are not only better on service, quality, reliability and finding a niche. They are also better listeners. That is the other half of the close-to-the-customer equation. The fact that these companies are so strong on quality, service and the rest comes in large measure from paying attention to what customers want. From listening. From inviting the customer into the company. The customer is truly in partnership with the effective companies, and vice versa.

W. EDWARDS DEMING
From *Out of the Crisis* (1982).

It will not suffice to have customers that are merely satisfied. An unhappy customer will switch. Unfortunately, a satisfied customer may also switch, on the theory that he could not lose much, and might gain. Profit in business comes from repeat customers, customers that boast about your product and service, and that bring friends with them.

TOM PETERS
From *Thriving on Chaos* (1987).

First, estimate the ten-year or lifelong value of a customer, based upon the size and frequency of a good customer's average transaction. Then multiply that number by two, to take into account the word-of-mouth factor. Finally, multiply the new total by the average number of customers served per day by the sales, service, dispatch, or other front-line person or group. The result is the lifelong value of the 'customer portfolio' that that individual or group deals with each day.

The implication is clear: *If you look at customers in this or a related way, you are likely to take a new view of hiring, training, compensating, and spending on tools to aid the customer-serving process.* Take that waiter, managing $750,000 of your future each night. Are you still sure you want to brag about the low average wages you pay? Are you certain that skimping on uniform quality makes sense? Does the investment in a small computer system to support order taking still look as expensive as it did? . . . When you build a plant, it starts depreciating the day it opens. The well-served customer, on the other hand, is an appreciating asset. Every small act on her or his behalf ups the odds for repeat business, add-on business, and priceless word-of-mouth referral.

RICHARD C. WHITELEY
From *The Customer-Driven Company* (1991).

Anybody can saturate a company with the voice of the customer. The key is that everyone throughout the organization, starting with the leader, must gauge every action against customers' needs, expectations, and wants. If an action isn't adding value for a customer, simply eliminate it.

You can achieve this kind of customer-driven behavior if you accomplish three things. They're difficult, but they're not unachievable for anyone.

- First, carefully target whom you want to be your customers. For the company as a whole, this is generally a top-management decision. And based on the company's vision and top management's understanding of who the company's customers are, individual work groups have to identify their internal customers, the people in the organization to whom they pass the results of their work and whom they have to satisfy so that the organization can satisfy its external customers.
- Second, get to know those customers better than they know themselves. Your entire organization must work to identify what customers need and expect, now and in the future.
- Third, inspire everyone in the organization to measure every action against customers' needs and expectations, and to strive constantly to exceed those expectations.

Most people in business serve three kinds of customers:

- **Final customers.** People who will use your product or service in daily life and, you hope, be delighted. They're also known as end users.
- **Intermediate customers.** These are often distributors or dealers who make your products and services available to the final customer.
- **Internal customers.** People within your organization who take your work after you've finished with it and carry out the next function on the way toward serving the intermediate and final customers. For an assembler, the internal customer may be the next person on the assembly line. But if you're a corporate leader, the internal customer is often someone who ranks lower than you do. A CEO's internal customer is often his or her secretary, and if the leader fails to prepare directions clearly enough to satisfy the secretary, they're not likely to be executed properly.

A market-share-building enterprise constantly challenges itself to answer four questions:

1. What *are* our customers' needs and expectations, and which of these needs and expectations matter most to them?
2. How well are we meeting those needs and expectations?
3. How well are our competitors meeting them?
4. How can we go beyond the minimum that will satisfy our customers, to truly delight them?

The most basic step is simple: Ask them how well you're currently serving them. Give them a chance to tell you what they want, where you're failing, where you're succeeding. The companies that do so consistently and act upon their findings reap massive benefits.

Because quality of service is hard to quantify, companies often fail to learn their customers' opinions about it. But a good guide is a structure developed by researchers at Texas A&M University. They determined that a customer's experience of service quality could be described in five dimensions which can be summarized with the acronym RATER:

- **Reliability**, the ability to provide what was promised, dependably and accurately.
- **Assurance**, the knowledge and courtesy of employees, and their ability to convey trust and confidence.
- **Tangibles**, the physical facilities and equipment, and the appearance of personnel.
- **Empathy**, the degree of caring and individual attention provided to customers.
- **Responsiveness**, the willingness to help customers and provide prompt service.

Becoming a customer-driven company means moving:

from motivation through fear and loyalty	*to*	motivation through shared vision.

from an attitude that says 'it's their problem'	*to*	ownership of every problem that affects the customer.
from 'the way we've always done it'	*to*	continuous improvement.
from making decisions based on assumptions and judgment calls	*to*	doing it with data and fact-based decisions.
from everything begins and ends with management	*to*	everything begins and ends with customers.
from functional 'stovepipes' where departments base decisions solely on their own criteria	*to*	cross-functional cooperation.
from being good at crisis management and recovery	*to*	doing it right the first time.
from depending on heroics	*to*	driving variability out of the process.
from a choice between participative *or* scientific management	*to*	participative *and* scientific management.

TOM PETERS
From *Liberation Management* (1992).

How customers perceive their relationship with your company determines whether or not you'll have a customer for life. That's almost obvious, if almost always ignored. To keep the 'lifetime customer idea' before you, I urge you to: forget unit product or service price and religiously substitute prospective lifetime value. Experience suggests that you would automatically turn your business practices upside down if primary emphasis were placed on the lifetime value concept.

NOW READ ON . . .

Deming, W.E., *Out of the Crisis*, Cambridge, Mass: MIT Center for Advanced Engineering Studies (1982); Cambridge, England: Cambridge University Press (1986)

Drucker, Peter F., *Management: Tasks, Responsibilities, Practices*, London: Heinemann (1973)

Peters, Tom and Waterman, Robert H. Jr., *In Search of Excellence*, New York: Harper & Row (1982)

Peters, Tom, *Thriving on Chaos*, New York: Alfred A. Knopf (1987); London: Macmillan (1988)

Peters, Tom, *Liberation Management*, New York: Alfred A. Knopf; London: Macmillan (1992)

Whitely, Richard C., *The Customer-Driven Company*, New York: Addison–Wesley; London: Business Books (1991)

Chapter 17

Managing Information

In the forty-odd years that they have been in commercial use, computers have revolutionized the business world, but like most revolutions, they have brought their share of trauma as well as triumph. The transformation of business operations has been stupendous: information technology, a term which expresses the combined power of computers and telecommunications to process, store and communicate information, is one of the most important forces shaping the economy.

We live in the information age, the knowledge economy, and it is the liberating force of technology that will enable information to become the currency of business success. Peter Drucker, who first outlined the rise of the post-industrial knowledge economy in *The Age of Discontinuity* (1969), was writing twenty years later in *The New Realities* of the information-based company as the model for the future.

The breakneck improvements in the price-performance ratio of information technology continues to fire expectations of ever-advancing business performance. In banking, airlines and the newly emerging information-based services, information technology is the backbone of their operations, and other sectors have become more dependent on computers for a vast range of functions, from word-processing and spreadsheet analysis through to computer-aided design and manufacturing (CAD/CAM).

In the early days of computerization, the focus was on automating back-office functions such as payroll, accounting and other administrative routines. The development of database systems capable of analysing large volumes of information opened the door to more sophisticated applications which reached into new areas of the organization such as inventory, sales and personnel records. Opportunities for revolutionizing the way organizations are run and work is performed have proliferated with the rapid spread of personal computers and developments in networking and outside communications. Business process redesign, or 're-engineering', could not be implemented without IT systems.

Yet many of the early expectations of productivity improvements from the automation of white-collar work have not been widely realized. For most organizations, the successful exploitation of IT has remained tantalizingly elusive, despite growing investments. Most companies are still struggling to make the balance sheet come out on the right side. Why this should be still perplexes many managers.

From the late 1970s on, however, ideas for applying information technology effectively began to coalesce. They set out to explain how IT can make a difference to performance, and where it merely adds to a company's problems.

In the early 1980s, when awareness of competition was intensifying under the Japanese onslaught, Michael Porter's Five Forces model (see Chapter 14) was instrumental in helping companies assess how IT could contribute to achieving competitive advantage. In 'How Information Gives You Competitive Advantage', a *Harvard Business Review* article in 1985, Porter and Victor Millar, a senior partner in consultancy Arthur Andersen, wrote that the information revolution was affecting competition in three vital ways.

- It changes industry structure and, in so doing, alters the rules of competition
- It creates competitive advantage by giving companies new ways to outperform their rivals
- It spawns whole new businesses, often from within a company's existing operations.

Porter's and Millar's ideas on modifying the value chain through the application of IT provided clues as to where and how management could influence performance by focusing IT on specific areas, such as production or distribution, or in improving external links with suppliers and customers.

Opportunities for applying IT differ not only according to an individual company's circumstances but also according to sector, some of which are by nature far more information-intensive than others. Porter's and Millar's 'information intensity' matrix provides a simple method of positioning a firm against two axes: the information intensity of the value chain and the information content of the product.

Other frameworks have enabled managers to relate IT to their own corporate circumstances. Warren MacFarlan and J.L. McKenney in 1983 proposed a matrix for establishing the changing strategic importance of IT to a given business (*Corporate Information Systems Management: The Issues Facing Senior Executives*). The two–by–two grid they devised can be used by managers to determine the scale of investment and the degree of attention IT should merit in their business.

In the first, 'support', quadrant of the matrix, information technology provides a support role and computers are needed only to promote greater efficiency in administration. Investment levels and management attention are therefore both minimal. Next come businesses where computers are critical to operations; these are sited in the 'factory' quadrant. Companies such as financial services, which are dependent on information technology, occupy the 'strategic' quadrant. Finally come those companies which fit into the 'turnaround' quadrant. These are businesses where IT was relatively low-profile in the past but where it is becoming critical to future operations.

Three forces drive companies round the grid: the match between the potential of IT and the strategy of the business; the strategic choices made by boards about IT, and lastly, the pressures exerted by the marketplace.

Despite the value of such frameworks to decision-making on how best to deploy information technology, fundamental problems persisted. Rising investment throughout the 1980s was not being rewarded with measurably greater returns for the majority of companies, regardless of whether they were information-intensive or not. Many boards came to see IT as a black hole into which money was poured, never to be recouped.

Several attempts have been made to address management

problems in appraising technology investment, but some of the most innovative work on value-for-money issues has been done by Paul Strassmann, a former Xerox vice-president and Director of Defense Information for the US Department of Defense under President George Bush. His research has shown conclusively that there is no correlation between investment levels in IT and business success. These findings led him to develop a quantifiable method of evaluating the contribution of IT to corporate results and for assessing the value of future investments.

His argument is that traditional accounting methods, such as return on investment or assets, are inadequate for measuring the impact of computers applied to managerial work. Beyond that, he makes the more fundamental case that businesses should be assessed in terms of their management value-added. Now that capital itself has become a commodity, the key variable in the business equation is how organizations are run. 'The scarce resource of contemporary society is not capital or technology, but management,' says Strassmann in *The Business Value of Computers* (1990).

Strassmann's Return on Management theory involves stripping out all costs attributable to management, operations and purchasing, and adjusting for shareholders' value-added to end up with management value-added. His research found that average management costs were three times higher than shareholder value-added; in service businesses, as much as six times higher. 'Companies also may have *Management Value-added* that is less than *Management Costs*. In such cases the *Management Value-added* is negative and *R-O-M* will be less than zero. Companies with a negative *R-O-M* are paying for their management out of their shareholder equity. If that continues, the company must get better management or eventually go bankrupt.' (*The Business Value of Computers*: author's italics.)

It is only in the context of Return on Management, argues Strassmann, that the contribution of information technology can properly be assessed, because it is inextricably bound up with the very process of decision-making. This analytic technique has now been adopted internationally by the Ernst and Young management consultancy.

Measurement of company performance in Return on

Management terms confirmed Strassmann's earlier analysis, which had been based on publicly available data. Interestingly, the most successful businesses and most effective users of IT were rarely the big spenders. Closer study of those who have turned IT to their advantage revealed some telling conclusions.

'Successful users are not technology innovators,' says Strassmann. 'They do not spend significantly more money on office automation than their competitors. Strategic users cannot separately identify the contributions of computers from their innovative marketing methods, the way they improve production management and how they take better care of customers. To get superior productivity and strategic advantage, computers must support the capacity to compete. Spending more money and taking the most sophisticated technology does not increase revenues or market share without changing how the firm runs its business.' (*The Business Value of Computers.*)

In other words, adapting Alfred D. Chandler's famous dictum, technology follows strategy, not the other way round. The same principle is now painfully being learned in companies undergoing business process redesign, having been lured into believing that 'systems' would do it all. The first essential of re-engineering, it is now realized, is to take a blank sheet of paper and think through the business before plunging into costly hardware and software.

On the very first page of *The Business Value of Computers*, Strassmann lays it on the line: 'Measuring managerial productivity is the key to knowing how to invest in information technologies. Improve management before you systemize or automate. Make management more productive, by electronic means, if you know where, when and how. Automate success, not failure.'

KEY TEXTS

PAUL A. STRASSMANN
From *The Business Value of Computers* (1990).

Information technology has the potential of delivering

more complete control, at a lower cost and with fewer risks, than any other managerial method.

The early alliance between computer technologists and financial controllers explains the first twenty years of business computing better than any study of electronics or computer science. The designations have changed from machine accounting to data processing and then to management information systems. Nevertheless, using computers for asserting control over increased business complexity continues to be the underlying rationale behind all hard-to-justify systems proposals. . . .

Information systems are used primarily to address a company's internal management and coordination needs. Delivering customer value-added is not where most of the money is spent, especially in manufacturing industries. If that is so, how do you measure and then justify your controller's need for more computing? How much is an Executive Information System worth? How do you explain the costs of a research data-base? What indicators will guide your acquisitions of computing resources, without which your enterprise could degrade into chaos?

The most controversial aspect of budgeting computers concerns internal communications that are of no concern to paying customers.

Computerworld and *Information Week* confirm the observation first published in 1985 that there's no simple correlation between the money spent on computers and a company's financial results. Correlations do not show up because information technology is not an independent variable. It is an arbitrary percentage of a company's revenues used to purchase what's affordable. Computers are not a direct cause of profitability, but a contributor. They may be an essential but surely not a sufficient ingredient of success.

What then differentiates between superior and inferior results in the use of information technology? Factors such as overhead, market share, pricing, taxation, capital intensity and overhead costs are far more decisive. The influences of computers on organizational behavior and financial performance involve more aspects of a firm's well-being than any other technology, but that effect is indirect and subtle.

Opinions or simple profit ratios comprised of only a few variables do not yield useful insights into how to manage information technology resources for greater profitability. Financial analysts' attempts to evaluate and control computer expenditure by means of a few simple ratios cannot succeed.

Return-on-Management is a more suitable measure than *ROI* or *ROA* when evaluating investments in management information systems because it focuses on the productivity of management, the principal user of computers. . . .
The research findings suggest a few useful lessons:

- Do not compare your operating results with industry-wide averages. It makes a difference whether your firm is average or superior. When you compare your firm against firms in a radically different performance range your evaluations will be misleading. I dislike comparisons that suggest that you imitate American Airlines, Citibank and American Hospital Supply in how they approach computers. Peer-group comparisons are more realistic. They will give you credible improvement targets.
- If your firm is under-achieving your approach to information technology investments should differ from firms where *R-O-M* exceeds 100 per cent. *Underachiever* information technology strategies are painful. You must self-finance overhead cost-reductions, innovate sparingly – with little investment – and deliver results in a hurry, without any margin for error.
- *Over-achiever* strategy options are challenging. *Over-achievers* rarely can sustain their elevated profitability positions. Invariably they gravitate toward the average. To sustain abnormally favorable results calls for a steady stream of innovations so that you hit a few that produce spectacular results. Extraordinary achievements are possible only by taking large but calculated

risks. The *Over-achiever* winning strategy is to invest in adventurous applications while plowing back technology profits into a steady stream of rapid cost reductions. *Over-achievers* know how to cut losses ruthlessly and without delay.

Knowing where you are leads to improvement. An uncompromising diagnosis of your firm's management productivity – which requires a reliable diagnostic database – is the prerequisite to finding whether information technology can work for you.

Whether or not computers improve societal productivity relates to the growth of bureaucratic workloads that increasingly depend on computers. Automating bureaucratic activities may be an efficient application of information technologies, but unless deployed wisely may not contribute to delivering *Value-added*. Performing unnecessary work faster does not increase the living standards of a country.

A computer is worth only what it can fetch in an auction. It has value only if surrounded by appropriate policy, strategy, methods for monitoring results, project control, talented and committed people, sound relationships and well-designed information systems.

The business value of a computer is its *Management*. The productivity of management is the decisive element that makes the difference of whether a computer hurts or helps.

You may question whether organizations require policies and analyses to govern their information resources. Do rules restrict the freedom of managers to act according to their best judgment?

The paramount issue of information management concerns the preservation of individual freedoms, personal creativity and the capacity to add value to society. To achieve these goals is the challenge to everyone who tries to apply information technology.

NOW READ ON . . .

MacFarlan, Warren, and McKenney, J.L., *Corporate Information Systems Management*, New York: Dow Jones Irwin (1983)
Porter, Michael E. and Millar, Victor E., 'How Information Gives You Competitive Advantage': *Harvard Business Review*, July–August 1985
Strassmann, Paul A., *The Business Value of Computers*, New Canaan, Connecticut: The Information Economics Press (1990)

Chapter 18

Global Management

'Globalization' as a business strategy is nothing new, although it scarcely figured in management literature until the late 1980s. As two leading authorities on transnational corporations point out, an early form of global management was being practised in the first years of the century by Singer, which built a mass-production plant in Scotland to serve European markets and export sewing machines to Asia. In automobiles, another early global product, Henry Ford commanded the world market for low-priced cars by exporting them from a central, highly mechanized plant at Highland Park, Detroit. This strategy of exporting from a high-tech base was to be successfully adopted by Japanese companies fifty years later. (C. Bartlett and S. Ghoshal, *Managing Across Borders*, 1989.)

Two world wars and the waves of protectionism they unleashed, along with the slowness of sea transportation and communications, delayed the advent of true globalization until the 1960s, when GATT inaugurated a more open trading environment, freight costs were revolutionized by containers and new technologies made economies of scale possible on a much wider geographic basis. By this time, leading US companies were well placed in marketing and brand development to extend their sights worldwide. Other factors propelling globalization were the rise of mass tourism and the gradual homogenization of tastes for global products such as Coca-Cola and Levi Strauss denims.

The prophet of globalization in the late 1980s was Kenichi Ohmae, head of McKinsey's in Tokyo, whose *Triad Power*

(1985) argued that companies must establish a presence in all three major trading areas – Europe, North America and Japan – or risk being overtaken by those who did. In *The Borderless World* (1990) he took this argument further: a key message in the book came from Japanese global successes like Honda, which treated all customers, overseas or domestic, as equally important; effectively, as though they were 'equidistant' from head office.

Ohmae now believes that a global strategy is 'almost a matter of survival' because competition is increasingly global in most areas of business, and customers can choose among products and services from many sources. 'Sovereignty is moving from states to consumers' is one of his favourite sayings. In seminars and video presentations, Ohmae argues that globalization is not exclusively for the big corporation; any company with a strong domestic market and equally strong export orientation can pursue the globalizing process.

This, in his teaching, has five stages:

1. An export-oriented company with a strong product concept.
2. Overseas branches set up to handle sales and marketing locally.
3. Manufacturing and production relocated to key local markets.
4. 'Insiderization' – i.e., when stage 3 develops into a clone of the parent company in key markets, complete with its own R&D, engineering, finance, personnel and other headquarters functions. This enables products to be tailored to local markets, and builds strong local management.
5. The complete 'global company', in which some core functions such as R&D and brand management may revert to the centre to build 'common shared values' while still maintaining dedicated local operations.

An example of stage 1 and 2 cited by Ohmae in his video seminar is Mulberry, the upmarket leather-goods company based in Somerset with a strongly branded chain of international outlets. Stage 3 is exemplified by Levi Strauss, which manufactures in 32 locations worldwide but retains marketing decisions in San Francisco. Stage 4 companies are Glaxo and Motorola, which are perceived as truly local companies wherever they operate, developing locally tailored products. Stage 5, the true global company, is typified by Sony, which maintains a unified culture while devolving most decision-making down to local level.

Global companies, say Bartlett and Ghoshal in *Managing Across Borders*, are defined in three ways: the multinational, such as Unilever, which operates as a decentralized federation, emphasizing responsiveness to national markets; the international, such as ITT, also a federation but more coordinated at the centre, with emphasis on developing expertise and knowledge on a worldwide scale; and the global organization such as Matsushita, which trades from a central hub and emphasizes global efficiency.

Bartlett and Ghoshal, respectively professors from Harvard Business School and INSEAD in France, found structural management weaknesses in all three models, especially the multinational based on a matrix principle, which they considered not flexible enough to meet the demands of responsiveness, efficiency and fully developed expertise. Their solution was the transnational company, an integrated network or 'set of organizational capabilities'. This requires different management processes, depending ultimately on 'a matrix in the mind of the manager'. The two professors admit that the model is 'an idealized organization type'.

Henry Wendt, former chairman of the pharmaceutical giant SmithKline Beecham, sees the structural solution for transnational companies as 'modified, matrix-based, multifunctional teams'. Flexible teams of managers, representing different functions, disciplines and cultures, can be deployed across organizational and national boundaries 'to deal with opportunities or issues that are strategically important. . . . one may call it flexible matrix management.' (H. Wendt: *Global Embrace*, 1993.)

'The essential load-bearing elements of the organizational structure,' he continues, 'are strong local management teams with the prime responsibility for customer-focused functions, including sales, marketing, and, where appropriate, the design of products and management. Meanwhile, global efficiencies are pursued at the corporate level by functional groups, such as manufacturing, information technologies, and research and development of new products, with world-wide responsibility.'

In the future, he suggests, 'more and more companies, especially transnationals, will adopt multidisciplinary, and increasingly multicultural, teams as the primary instrument of their organizational structures.' These will form the real centre of the new-style corporation, 'not at some head-quarters at the centre of a map, but conceptually at a point equidistant from all other points on the globe, no matter where a particular team is actually located.'

This chimes both with Ohmae's vision of equidistant customers and with Bartlett and Ghoshal's 'matrix in the mind of the manager'. It is not easy to translate into practice, but there is already an admired role model in Asea Brown Boveri (ABB), the vast Swedish–Swiss industrial and engineering group, in which Henry Wendt detects all the key elements of a true transnational.

In ABB's finely tuned global matrix, fifty worldwide business groups intersect with national companies serving their familiar local markets. Leaders of the business groups globally coordinate functions such as quality, performance, export markets and economies of scale. The national companies have local subsidiaries, all of which are responsible for their own profits, and whose heads report both to their national company president and to the leader of the appropriate global business group.

The system is the personification of 'think globally, act locally' and runs under a corporate headquarters staff numbering about a hundred. ABB is led by an executive committee of eight, each of whom is responsible for one of eight segments into which the fifty business groups are divided.

'We are not a global business,' ABB president Percy Barnevik maintains. 'We are a collection of local businesses with intense global coordination.'

ABB's matrix provides the best way of managing its diverse markets and products, some of which are global, such as gas turbines and power transmission systems, and some local, like electrical installations. The system also demonstrates that a cross-cultural, cross-national mix of managers and executives can work successfully. So impressive has been its performance, says Wendt, that IBM based its own massive reorganization of the early 1990s on a similar matrix.

Kenichi Ohmae's belief that size is no bar to globalization finds an ally in John Naisbitt's latest vision of the future. The author of *Megatrends*, a best-selling predictive work of the 1980s, argues in *Global Paradox* (1994) that 'the bigger the world economy, the more powerful its smallest players'. He cites the way that many big corporations are decentralizing and reconstituting themselves in smaller units as 'networks of entrepreneurs' to seize local niche opportunities. Already, he claims, half of the US exports come from companies with a workforce of nineteen or fewer; only 7 per cent from those with 500 or more employees.

Naisbitt sees all companies headed in the direction of Microsoft, 'essentially a peer network of software programmers who communicate directly with CEO Bill Gates. . . . Information is, indeed, power, and as more and more information becomes available to the individual through telecommunications systems, individuals will be empowered as never before.'

Increasingly, strategic alliances are seen as a way into global markets, with telecommunications and automobile companies leading the trend. These are usually defined as agreements committing companies to work together towards a shared strategic objective, often in a technological area such as semiconductors. If successful, the partnership may then develop into joint ventures or other long-term, close collaborations.

'Strategic alliances,' writes Henry Wendt in *Global Embrace*, 'can also pool resources to open new markets, spread risk and combine manufacturing techniques or plant capacity.' But he points out that their disadvantages lie in the very qualities that make them attractive: low risk also means that one or both parties can afford to fail, while the tentative, experimental approach 'makes it easy to back out if conditions change. And conditions usually change.'

Wendt is marked out from the academics or consultants writing on this subject by the fact that he has been at the sharp end of transnational business and knows the hard work needed to translate conceptual theories into practical, successful, cross-border structures. His book and Ohmae's *Borderless World* are the most readable and useful for the practising manager.

KEY TEXTS

CHRISTOPHER A. BARTLETT AND SUMANTRA GHOSHAL
From *Managing Across Borders* (1989).

Most companies also have a powerful *organizational psychology* – a set of explicit or implicit shared values and beliefs – that can be developed and managed just as effectively as the organizational anatomy and physiology. For companies operating in an international environment, this is a particularly important organizational attribute, for several reasons. When employees come from a variety of national backgrounds, management cannot assume that all will share common values and relate to common norms. Furthermore, when managers are separated by distance and time barriers, shared management understanding is often a much more powerful coordinating tool than either structure or systems. Yet managers attempting to guide organizational change tend to reach for the more familiar tools of structural reorganization and system redesign.

Our review of transnational organizations highlighted three techniques that seem particularly important in shaping an organization's psychology. The first is a clear, shared understanding of the company's mission and objectives. . . .

The second tool is the visible behavior and public actions of senior management. Particularly in a transnational organization, where other signals may be diluted or distorted by the sheer volume of information sent to foreign outposts, top management's actions have a powerful influence on the company's culture. When Sony's founder and chief executive, Akio Morita, relocated to New York to build the company's US operations, he sent the most convincing possible message about Sony's commitment to its overseas businesses.

The third and most commonly used set of tools for modifying organizational psychology are those of the company's personnel policies. To develop a multidimensional and flexible organization process, human resource systems must encourage appropriate kinds of people and behaviors. . . . Unilever used its personnel policies not only to develop human resources, but also to shape the organization's decision processes and to influence corporate values. Its selection policies emphasized the need for team players rather than soloists; its management development process moved high-potential managers across product lines, between countries, and from national companies to corporate headquarters, thereby broadening their perspectives while developing their skills and knowledge; its education and training programs reinforced corporate values and provided numerous opportunities to foster informal personal contacts across organizational lines; and its performance evaluation process considered not only measurable output, but also cooperation with colleagues and adherence to organizational values.

KENICHI OHMAE
From *The Borderless World* (1990).

Today, the pressure for globalization is driven not so much by diversification or competition as by the needs and preferences of customers. Their needs have globalized, and the fixed costs of meeting them have soared. That is why we must globalize.

Managing effectively in this new borderless environment does not mean building pyramids of cash flow by focusing on the discovery of new places to invest. Nor does it mean tracking your competitors to their lair and preemptively undercutting them in their own home market. Nor does it mean blindly trying to replicate

home-country business systems in new colonial territories. Instead, it means paying central attention to
delivering value to customers – and to developing an equidistant view of who they are and what they want. Before
everything else comes the need to see your customers
clearly. Only they can provide legitimate reasons for
thinking globally.

Decomposing the corporate center into several regional
headquarters is becoming an essential part of almost every
successful company's transition to global competitor
status. It is a trend that is consistent with recent developments in Europe as it moves toward economic union in
1992, in North America as it moves toward 1999 (the US-
Canada free trade agreement), and in Asia, where the economies of the newly industrialized countries are rapidly
integrating with Japan's. This move toward regional headquarters is also consistent with companies' growing need
to hedge exposure to currency fluctuations through sound
operating decisions and not simply through shrewd use of
financial instruments.

By becoming, in effect, an insider in key markets, a
global corporation can make its costs independent of
home-country currency – that is, at a par with those of
domestic competitors in each of its markets. But it can also
pull the trick of using cheaper sources of inputs from elsewhere in the world, something local players cannot easily
duplicate. The strength of a global corporation derives in
no small measure from its ability, as a full-fledged insider,
to understand local customers' needs. At the same time, it
can deploy human, financial, and technological resources
on a global scale.

Maintaining a corporate identity in a global environment
is different. Formal systems and organizational structures
can help, but only to the extent that they nurture and support intangible ties. Training programs, career-path
planning, job rotation, companywide accounting, evaluation systems that are equitable across national borders, and
electronic data-processing systems become more important as globalization proceeds. The most important,

however, is a system of values that all employees in all countries and regions unquestionably accept. A global company must be prepared to pull out of a region where its core values cannot be implemented. . . .

A global corporation today is fundamentally different from the colonial-style multinationals of the 1960s and 1970s. It serves its customers in all key markets with equal dedication. It does not shade things with one group to benefit another. It does not enter individual markets for the sole purpose of exploiting their profit potential. Its value system is universal, not dominated by home-country dogma, and it applies everywhere. In an informa-tion–linked world where consumers, no matter where they live, know which products are the best and cheapest, the power to choose or refuse lies in their hands, not in the back pockets of sleepy, privileged monopolies like the earlier multinationals.

HENRY WENDT
From *Global Embrace* (1993).

Asea Brown Boveri's enviable position, achieved in a rela-tively short time, demonstrates the power of the transnational concept when all its elements are brought to-gether. In sum, the key elements include the following:

- The pursuit and creation of broad equity ownership and market penetration – through mergers, aggressive acquisitions, or organic growth – in major markets around the world.
- The definition and development of core competencies that give the company a competitive advantage in skills. Developed over time, core competencies deserve com-plete organizational support and become a precious heritage that is passed from one generation of employees to the next.
- The relentless pursuit of global-*scale* advantages to achieve low-cost positions and leadership in vital busi-ness functions while considerable authority is delegated to the local level for implementing the strategy and

tailoring the presentation of products and services to customers in their own cultural terms.

- Movement toward a global *scope*, in which the allocation of assets and the sources of sales are roughly the same as the proportions of the world market for the business in which the firm is engaged.
- The development of a corporate culture of mutual trust and a pattern of flexible organizational behavior in which managers continually act to improve productivity, to learn and communicate across functions and national borders, and to respond sensitively to customers.
- An organizational structure – usually a transnational flexible matrix – that serves the global-local strategy and employs multidisciplinary and multicultural teams to integrate the organizational behavior with the strategic elements of skills, scale, and scope.
- Standards of behavior and commitment at all levels, particularly the local level, that earn insider status, winning for the company the same respect and admiration enjoyed by highly esteemed local competitors.
- Responsible corporate governance that is consistent with the concept of global ownership and global citizenship.

There is one additional element – people. The emergence of truly transnational companies will make great demands on future managers and employees. Essentially, these companies will recruit people who match the company's strategic and organizational requirements. Words and phrases like *global vision, cultural sensitivity, functional expertise, adaptable to change,* and *committed to continual improvement* become as descriptive of the people employed as of the way corporations conduct their business.

NOW READ ON . . .

Bartlett, Christopher A. and Ghoshal, Sumantra, *Managing Across Borders*, Boston, Massachusetts: Harvard Business School Press; London: Hutchinson Business Books (1989)

Ohmae, Kenichi, *The Borderless World*, London: William Collins Ltd. (1990)
Wendt, Henry, *Global Embrace*, New York and London: HarperCollins (1993)

Chapter 19

Re-engineering

'Re-engineering' as a fashionable management theory looks like stamping its brand as firmly on the first half of the 1990s as prescriptions for 'excellence' did a decade earlier. Whether it will prove to be more than a fad, or whether events will cause it to be superseded in the management literature, as largely happened to 'excellence' rubrics when a long period of stable business assumptions ended, remains to be seen.

Like excellence, re-engineering – also commonly known as business process redesign (BPR), although this tends to refer to parts of a business rather than the whole – has proved a gold mine for the production of books, conferences and seminars. Its life is likely to be longer than that of the excellence cult because its goals – the transformation or reinvention of a company for greater efficiency – are attuned to an age of recession and discontinuous change. It is all about reducing costs and waste and 'doing more with less'. It can also produce quantum leaps of improvement – in productivity, cycle times, quality management and cost reductions: figures of 70 and 80 per cent are common in the case studies, and hundredfold improvements have been registered in some areas.

Some management consultants are sceptical that the process is a genuine innovation. Geoff Elliott and Robin Holland of Computer Management Group (CMG) credit a work study researcher called Currie at ICI in the 1950s with techniques for determining added value and non-added value in business processes, and with introducing benchmarking and process cycle time reduction. 'One reason why Currie's work has been bypassed is that it was labelled "work study", which is often confused with "time and motion",' say Elliott and Holland. (Indeed, elements of re-engineering hark back to F.W. Taylor's fundamentals of first breaking down business activities into their component steps.)

Elliott and Holland believe that 'at the fundamental level, there is no difference between business process redesign, TQM, Change Management and Organizational Development. . . . All four approaches to change are supported by the same set of tools and techniques, for example process modelling, work flow analysis, competency modelling, failure mode analysis, etc. . . . There are some 100 or so creative problem-solving techniques which are consistently being used to underpin and support change within all four of the approaches.'

Despite their scepticism, Elliott and Holland concede that a 'single framework for change is emerging which draws on all the experience of the past 20 years.'

The framework started to coalesce at Massachusetts Institute of Technology (MIT) in the early 1980s in a programme of research into what would be required of 'the corporation of the 1990s'. One of the participants was an MIT mathematician called Michael Hammer. In 1990, Hammer pulled the concept out of the academic papers where it had been slumbering and published a seminal article in *Harvard Business Review* called 'Reengineering Work: Don't Automate, Obliterate', which coined a new, scientific-sounding term and aroused wide business interest. He has since established himself as a re-engineering guru in the same evangelistic style as Tom Peters. Among his more memorable lecture-hall sayings are: 'We're not talking about cutting the fat from an organization. We are talking about grinding it up and frying it out,' and 'If it ain't broke yet, you still have a chance to fix it.'

CSC Index, a Boston-based consultancy which also participated in the MIT programme, has since joined Hammer in the re-engineering crusade: its CEO, James Champy, co-authored Hammer's best-selling book *Reengineering the Corporation* and has filed a copyright claim to the term 'business reengineering'. (Hammer and Champy spell it without the hyphen.)

Hammer defines re-engineering as 'the fundamental re-thinking and radical redesign of business processes to achieve dramatic improvements in critical, contemporary measures of performance, such as cost, quality, service and speed.' The principles of re-engineering can be applied to any type or size of business, though it tends to be most effective used in medium-sized operations such as a business unit of a large multinational. Small companies usually don't need it, their management being close to the processes anyway, while large corporations are too unwieldy to re-engineer as a whole. In any re-engineering project, Hammer counsels against trying to re-engineer all the processes in a business at once.

Since its object is to organize the flow of work around processes rather than the tasks that make up those processes, and to perform those processes with as few people as possible, re-engineering does away with whole structures of supervisors and middle managers, replacing a hierarchy with multi-disciplinary, cross-functional teams. Hammer often describes the core concept as 'reversing the Industrial Revolution' because it up-ends Adam Smith's classic division of labour into tasks, thereby reducing or eliminating wasteful 'hand-offs' between departments, when paperwork is most liable to suffer delay or error.

'Every time there's a hand-off,' says Hammer, 'there's a major opportunity for error.' To illustrate the scale of delay that can be involved, he uses the equation $VT \div ET$ (value time, i.e., the time a core activity should take, stripped of hand-offs, divided by actual elapsed time): in one case, elapsed time totalled seventeen months against one hour of value time. It took Hallmark Cards, the US market leader, three years to bring a new card to the marketplace, but 'the VT was measured in nanoseconds'.

To put it as simply as Hammer does in his seminars, re-engineering means 'starting from scratch, with a clean sheet of paper'. Or, to quote Ed Arzt of Procter and Gamble: 'If P&G did not exist today, how would we create it?' Fred Missoni, managing director of Federal Mogul, the oil components company that re-engineered itself to become US market leader, expresses it differently: 'There is always a better way: it's our job to find it. We don't know what it is, or we'd be doing it.'

The basic discipline of re-engineering is thoroughly scrutinizing your business, understanding how it works through its processes, which means first of all identifying those processes. 'A process is a set of business activities that create a value,' says Hammer, and there are comparatively few even in a billion-dollar-turnover company, the average being around six or seven – for example, order fulfilment, which goes all the way from the customer's order through manufacturing to delivery and billing.

IBM Credit Control, one of the classic case studies in re-engineering, made several attempts to improve its turnround time on computer deals before coming up with the streamlined process that replaced four specialist staff (credit checker, pricing specialist, lawyer and administrator) with one generalist 'deal structurer'. Ninety-five in every 100 deals emanating from IBM's sales force in the field proved simple enough to be processed by the deal structurer alone; for the other five cases, the deal structurer now calls in the former specialists to work as an ad hoc team on the project.

The result, a powerful argument for re-engineering theory, has been that a previous six-day deal-completion cycle is now down to four hours, while the number of deals processed has been multiplied a hundredfold. Multiple hand-offs – essentially time spent with paper sitting in in-trays – had accounted for 90 per cent of the old cycle. Many other companies in the US and UK, across both manufacturing and service sectors, could furnish similar eye-opening statistics.

British case studies have involved businesses ranging from optronics to financial services. The historic Glasgow engineering firm of Barr and Stroud, sole supplier of periscopes to the Royal Navy since 1916, had 96 per cent of its optronics work dependent on defence contracts, and as contracts melted away with the end of the Cold War, the company plummeted in three years from record profits of £8.6m on sales of £85.3m to losses of around £10m. Within two years, after embarking on a ten-year re-engineering programme aimed at totally computer-integrated manufacture, it was back in profit, had soaked out £15m of stock and inventory costs, halved its lead times and improved its record of meeting delivery dates ninefold. Meanwhile, productivity had risen by 30 per cent and sales per employee increased from £25,000 to £79,000. Five of the previous nine management layers were stripped out – there will eventually be only one – and the workforce, though heavily unionized, was slashed from 2,500 to 740.

Redundancies are the dark side of re-engineering. Michael Hammer concedes that if the practice takes off on a large scale, as much as 75 per cent of existing management could be out of a job by the century's end. Many of these could effectively 're-engineer' their own careers into specialist or teamworking roles, but some will inevitably be thrown on the scrapheap.

The other downside of the theory is the high ratio of failures: UK consultants speak of up to 70 or 80 per cent. Hammer replies that what has happened historically is not necessarily a guide to the future, and stresses the need for committed leadership, with a number of key people such as a 'process owner' and a 'reengineering czar' involved in pushing the project through. Above all, the CEO has to be passionate about doing it, and has to understand exactly what it involves in human terms. Lucas, the giant Midlands-based automotive-aerospace-technology group, has grown its own re-engineering consultancy which begins every project with a two- or three-day workshop for senior management.

In selecting priorities among processes for treatment, Hammer suggests, look first for 'dreadfulness' – those with high costs or customer dissatisfaction; secondly for 'impact' – how much difference does it make to the customer? And thirdly, 'feasibility' – where are the opportunities for doing it fast? Most experts recommend a similar agenda.

The basic stages of a re-engineering, in the Hammer model, are:

- Diagnosis. Not to be confused with analysis, which bogs you in detail and 'ties you to history'. This part of the process should take six weeks and result in a document of around ten pages, 'mostly pictures'.
- Build laboratory prototype
- Implement pilot in the field

- Reap initial benefits as fast as possible. From diagnosis to first feedback on the redesigned process should take no longer than twelve months. Less is preferable.

Re-engineering is often a painful process, even for those who don't lose their turf or their jobs. It involves change in everything, from work units to values to the role of executives. Much of the first-wave work on re-engineering has been criticized, especially in Britain, for an overmechanistic approach, with too much reliance on IT systems and not enough care in winning hearts and minds. The second wave will need to focus much more on the human issues of change management.

That said, it could be the key to survival for many companies. Significantly, the concept is already gaining ground in fast-developing economies like Korea, Mexico and Singapore. 'This will be a new benchmark for everybody,' predicts Hammer.

KEY TEXTS

MICHAEL HAMMER AND JAMES CHAMPY
From *Reengineering the Corporation* (1993).

Some recurring themes or characteristics that we frequently encounter in reengineered business processes:
- Several jobs are combined into one
- Workers make decisions
- The steps in the process are performed in a natural order
- Processes have multiple versions
- Checks and controls are reduced
- Reconciliation is minimized
- A case manager provides a single point of contact
- Hybrid centralized/decentralized operations are prevalent

When a process is reengineered, jobs evolve from narrow and task-oriented to multidimensional. People who once did as they were instructed now make choices and decisions on their own instead. Assembly-line work disappears. Functional departments lose their reasons for being. Managers stop acting like supervisors and behave more like coaches. Workers focus more on the customers' needs and less on their bosses'. Attitudes and values change in response to new incentives. Practically every aspect of the organization is transformed, often beyond recognition. . . .

Changes that occur when a company reengineers its processes:

- Work units change – from functional departments to process teams
- Jobs change – from simple tasks to multidimensional work
- People's roles change – from controlled to empowered
- Job preparation changes – from training to education
- Focus of performance measures and compensation shifts – from activity to results
- Advancement criteria change – from performance to ability
- Values change – from protective to productive
- Managers change – from supervisors to coaches
- Organizational structures change – from hierarchical to flat
- Executives change – from scorekeepers to leaders

Managers in a reengineered company need strong interpersonal skills and have to take pride in the accomplishments of others. Such a manager is a mentor, who is there to provide resources, to answer questions and to look out for the long-term career development of the individual. This is a different role from the one most managers have traditionally played.

Companies don't reengineer processes; people do. Before we delve more deeply into the 'what' of the reengineering process, we need to attend to the 'who'. How companies select and organize the people who actually do the reengineering is the key to the success of the endeavor.

We have seen the following roles emerge, either distinctly or in various combinations, during our work with companies that are implementing reengineering:

- leader – a senior executive who authorizes and motivates the overall reengineering effort
- process owner – a manager with responsibility for a specific process and the reengineering effort focused on it
- reengineering teams – a group of individuals dedicated to the reengineering of a particular process, who diagnose the existing process and oversee its redesign and implementation
- steering committee – a policy-making body of senior managers who develop the organization's overall engineering strategy and monitor its progress.
- reengineering czar – an individual responsible for developing reengineering techniques and tools within the company and for achieving synergy across the company's separate reengineering projects.

Processes in a company correspond to natural business activities, but they are often fragmented and obscured by the organizational structures. Processes are invisible and unnamed because people think about the individual departments, not about the process with which all of them are involved. Processes also tend to be unmanaged, so that people are put in charge of the departments or work units, but no one is given the responsibility for getting the whole job – the process – done.

One way to get a better handle on the processes that make up a business is to give them names that express their beginning and end states. These names should imply all the work that gets done between their start and finish. Manufacturing, which sounds like a department name, is better called the procurement-to-shipment process. Some other recurring processes and their state-change names:

Product development: concept to prototype
Sales: prospect to order
Order fulfilment: order to payment
Service: inquiry to resolution.

No company can reengineer all its high-level processes simultaneously. Typically, organizations use three criteria to help them make their choices. The first is dysfunction: which processes are in the deepest trouble? The second is importance: which processes have the greatest impact on the company's customers? The third is feasibility: which of the company's processes are at the moment most susceptible to successful redesign?

Principle: As few people as possible should be involved in the performance of a process.

NOW READ ON ...

Hammer, Michael and Champy, James, *Reengineering the Corporation*, London: Nicholas Brealey Publishing (1993)

Chapter 20

Reading the Future

'The future,' as American baseball star Yogi Berra once famously lamented, 'ain't what it used to be.' Over the past twenty years, we and our businesses have all learned that, sometimes at painful cost, as discontinuous change has become the norm rather than the exception.

Peter Drucker, as ever the supreme pathfinder among social and economic observers, announced *The Age of Discontinuity* in his 1969 book of that title, prefiguring a post-industrial society and the rise of the 'knowledge economy' that would revolutionize ways of working and demands for labour.

Drucker's book, moreover, was published a full four years before the first great discontinuity arrived to shatter global economic assumptions. The oil price shock of 1973 and the energy crisis and rampant inflation that followed disrupted the future of decision-making in every industrialized country. The geo-political world, formerly remote except in times of war, had suddenly impacted on every business, large or small, and none would be immune from it again.

In 1989–90 that world took another unforeseen lurch, with the sudden collapse of Eastern Europe's Communist bloc, the subsequent end of the Cold War and the de-Sovietizing of Russia. Political change that used to take years now happens in days, confounding long-range planning. Even Hoechst, the West German chemical giant that operated actively in East Germany, was caught short in its strategic planning department when the Berlin Wall came down, almost literally overnight. The reunification of Germany was a future possibility on every German corporation's planning horizon, but no one imagined it would happen so quickly.

With history so liable to catch the best planners unawares, what techniques can managers use to gain insights into the future? The answer probably lies in scenarios, the drafting of alternative 'scripts' for how events will turn out. (Michael Porter, who recommends their use as a tool of competitive advantage, defines a scenario as 'an internally consistent view of what the future might turn out to be'.) The technique had been used by the USAAF in World War II to anticipate and prepare for possible enemy moves, and was adapted as a tool for business planning in the 1960s, notably by the futurist Herman Kahn.

One small cadre of scenario planners, for example, was not unprepared for the great OPEC upheaval of 1973. They were in the oil industry itself, working for Royal Dutch/Shell in a team headed by Pierre Wack, and by the early 1970s they had sketched out the possibility – even the probability – that Arab oil producers would decide on a huge collective price rise, ahead of the next round of oil price agreements due in 1975. Peter Schwartz, Wack's successor as head of Shell's group planning, has described how, when the energy crisis broke, Shell was the only one of the oil majors, the so-called 'Seven Sisters', to be 'prepared emotionally for the change'. Subsequently, the company rose from being one of the weaker 'sisters' to rank number two in size behind Exxon.

Wack discovered through experience that the only effective use of scenarios was to change the outlook and assumptions of senior management, the decision-makers. Without that, no amount of accurate forecasting would change anything. In the early 1980s, after retiring from Shell, Wack was one of a team drawing up alternative scenarios for South Africa's political future, both with and without apartheid. Their options, which included an apartheid-free future where whites were not threatened by the black majority (contrary to popular fears at the time), are said to have influenced President F.W. de Klerk in his decision to free Nelson Mandela.

Before leaving Shell, Wack had visited Stanford Research Institute, the Californian 'think-tank' now known as SRI

International, where he met and indirectly recruited Peter Schwartz as his successor. Schwartz's 1991 book *The Art of the Long View* is a lively distillation of what he learned at Shell's Group Planning and, from 1987, as head of his own futurist consultancy, Global Business Network. It is worth a place on every senior executive's bookshelf, and can be read for pleasure as well as for productive insights.

Some businesses have paid dearly for their reluctance to try the technique. In his introduction, Schwartz cites the fate that overtook many advertising agencies in the late 1980s as one that could have been avoided by the use of scenarios. Technological changes – cable TV, video, electronic mail – were always certain to change the industry radically, though the exact form those changes would take was still uncertain. Schwartz maintains that a set of scenarios to indicate the future for that industry could have been drawn up from looking carefully at important elements of the world in the early 1980s.

In 1987, the changes duly hit the agencies, profits declined and staff were laid off. The expected recovery did not materialize, yet managements were still not interested in taking part in scenario exercises about the effect of new technologies on media businesses, recalls Schwartz.

'Scenarios are not predictions,' he explains. 'Rather, scenarios are vehicles for helping people learn. . . . they present alternative images, they do not merely extrapolate the trends of the present. . . . Scenarios allow a manager to say, "I am prepared for whatever happens".'

Shell's scenario team also foresaw the likelihood of Soviet *perestroika*, or some similar liberalizing for economic reasons, and what such a movement would imply for the oil industry. They simply studied the sharply declining Soviet birthrate of the 1960s and 1970s and reasoned that the resulting labour shortage in the 1980s would drastically weaken the economy. Their scenario enabled Shell to make far-sighted and profitable decisions, such as not investing in costly oilfield developments when oil was $30 a barrel, as others were rushing to do, but waiting until the price fell to $15 a barrel.

'Scenarios gave them a huge long-term advantage and allowed them to think in long-term strategies,' writes

Schwartz. 'They could act with the confidence that comes from saying, "I have an understanding of how the world might change. I know how to recognize it when it is changing, and if it changes, I know what to do".'

Soon, he notes, scenario planners will be able to call on 'virtual reality' computer simulations, allowing even more convincing analyses of alternative futures, but successful practitioners will still need 'helicopter' minds, 'the ability to see the big picture and zoom down to focus on the key details simultaneously'.

Schwartz's book is a practical primer to building scenarios, which is essentially a team discipline, and it includes many pointers for the individual to develop the trained ability to spot emerging trends. Michael Porter's *Competitive Advantage* (1985) has a detailed and valuable section on constructing industry scenarios, crediting Shell's Pierre Wack and his team as the pioneers, but *The Art of the Long View* is the most accessible guide yet published to reading the future.

KEY TEXTS

MICHAEL E. PORTER
From *Competitive Advantage* (1985).

An industry scenario is an internally consistent view of an industry's future structure. It is based on a set of plausible assumptions about the important uncertainties that might influence industry structure, carried through to the implications for creating and sustaining competitive advantage. An industry scenario is *not a forecast* but one possible future structure. A set of industry scenarios is carefully chosen to reflect the range of possible (and credible) future industry structures with important implications for competition. The entire set of scenarios, rather than the most likely one, is then used to design a competitive strategy. The time period used in industry scenarios should reflect the time horizon of the most important investment decisions.

An industry typically faces many uncertainties about the

future. The important uncertainties are those that will influence industry structure, such as technological breakthroughs, entry of new competitors, and interest rate fluctuations. External factors such as macroeconomic conditions and government policy affect competition through, and not independently of, industry structure. Structural change almost always requires adjustments in strategy and creates the greatest opportunities for competitors to shift their relative positions.

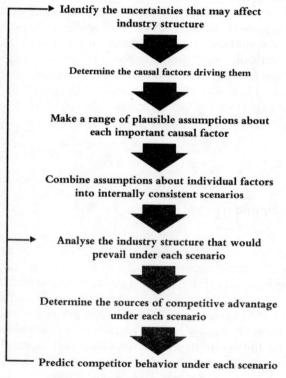

The Process of Constructing Industry Scenarios

Industry scenarios are best developed by business unit managers, with guidance and input from others in the firm as well as outsiders. This places the task of understanding the effects of uncertainty in the hands of those who must actually set competitive strategy, and ensures that scenarios are truly relevant to the business unit. Industry scenarios should be constructed well into the planning process, once basic industry, competitor, and value chain analysis has been done. Industry scenarios will be ineffective without a good base of knowledge, and probably should not be introduced into the planning systems of firms without good basic planning skills. Scenarios are best used to guide the choice of a strategy, rather than as a means of confirming one.

Scenarios are not needed every year for every business unit. They are necessary only when significant uncertainties are present in an industry. However, constructing industry scenarios irregularly runs the risk that managers will overlook key uncertainties in their industries. Scenarios force a creative search for possible structural changes. How often scenarios are constructed must depend in part on the confidence of top management in the objectivity and vision of business unit managers.

PETER SCHWARTZ
From *The Art of the Long View* (1991).

STEPS TO DEVELOPING SCENARIOS

Step One: Identify Focal Issue or Decision

When developing scenarios, it's a good idea to begin 'from the inside out' rather than 'from the outside in'. That is, begin with a specific decision or issue, then build out toward the environment. What will decision-makers in your company be thinking hard about in the near future? What are the decisions that have to be made that will have a long-term influence on the fortunes of the company? . . .

Step Two: Key Forces in the Local Environment

If the identification of a focal issue or decision is the first step, then listing the key factors influencing the success or failure of that decision is the second step – facts about customers, suppliers, competitors, etc. What will decision-makers want to know when making key choices?

What will be seen as success or failure? What are the considerations that will shape those outcomes?

Step Three: Driving Forces

Once the key factors have been listed, the third step involves listing driving trends in the macro-environment that influence the key factors identified earlier. In addition to a checklist of social, economic, political, environmental and technological forces, another route to the relevant aspects of the macro-environment is the question: What are the forces *behind* the micro-environmental forces identified in Step Two? Some of these forces are predetermined (e.g., often demographics) and some are highly uncertain (e.g., public opinion). It is very useful to know what is inevitable and necessary and what is unpredictable and still a matter of choice. . . .

That is the most research-intensive step in the process. In order to adequately define the driving forces research is usually required. Research may cover markets, new technology, political factors, economic forces, and so on. One is searching for the major trends and the trend breaks. The latter are the most difficult to find; novelty is difficult to anticipate.

Step Four: Rank by Importance and Uncertainty

Next comes the ranking of key factors and driving trends on the basis of two criteria: first, the degree of importance for the success of the focal issue or decision identified in step one; second, the degree of uncertainty surrounding those factors and trends. The point is to identify the two or three factors or trends that are most important *and* most uncertain.

Scenarios cannot differ over predetermined elements like the inevitable aging of the baby boomers, because predetermined elements are bound to be the same in all scenarios.

Step Five: Selecting Scenario Logics

The results of this ranking exercise are, in effect, the axes along which the eventual scenarios will differ. Determining these axes is among the most important steps in the entire scenario-generating process. The goal is to end up with just a few scenarios whose differences make a difference to decision-makers. If the scenarios are to function as useful learning tools, the lessons they teach must be based on issues basic to the success of the focal decision. And those fundamental differences – or 'scenario drivers' – must be few in number in order to avoid a proliferation of different scenarios around every possible uncertainty. Many things can happen, but only a few scenarios can be developed in detail, or the process dissipates. . . .

The logic of a given scenario will be characterized by its location in the matrix of most significant scenario drivers. For example, if an automobile company determines that fuel prices and protectionism are two of the most important scenario drivers, there will be four basic scenario logics: (1) high fuel prices in a protectionist environment – where domestic suppliers of small cars will have an advantage; (2) high fuel prices in a global economy – where fuel-efficient imports may capture the low end of the market; (3) low fuel prices in a protectionist environment – where American gas guzzlers will have a good market at home but not abroad; (4) low fuel prices in a global economy – where there will be intense global competition for fuel-efficient models, but larger cars may enjoy strong foreign markets. . . .

Step Six: Fleshing Out the Scenarios

While the most important forces determine the logics that distinguish the scenarios, fleshing out the skeletal scenarios can be accomplished by returning to the lists of key factors and trends identified in steps two and three.

Each key factor and trend should be given some attention in each scenario. Sometimes it is immediately apparent which side of an uncertainty should be located in which scenario, sometimes not. If two scenarios differ over protectionist or nonprotectionist policies, then it probably makes sense to put a higher inflation rate in the protectionist scenario and a lower inflation rate in the non-protectionist scenario. It is just such connections and mutual implications that scenarios should be designed to reveal.

Then weave the pieces together in the form of a narrative. How would the world get from here to there? What events might be necessary to make the end point of the scenario plausible? . . .

Step Seven: Implications

Once the scenarios have been developed in some detail, then it is time to return to the focal issue or decision identified in step one to rehearse the future. How does the decision look in each scenario? What vulnerabilities have been revealed? Is the decision or strategy robust across all scenarios, or does it look good in only one or two of the scenarios? If a decision looks good in only one of several scenarios, then it qualifies as a high-risk gamble – a bet-the-company strategy – especially if the company has little control over the likelihood of the required scenario coming to pass. How could that strategy be adapted to make it more robust if the desired scenario shows signs of not happening?

Step Eight: Selection of Leading Indicators and Signposts

. . . If the scenarios have been built according to the previous steps, then the scenarios will be able to translate movements of a few key indicators into an orderly set of industry-specific implications. The logical coherence that was *built into* the scenarios will allow logical implications of leading indicators to be *drawn out* of the scenarios.

NOW READ ON . . .

Porter, Michael E., *Competitive Advantage*, New York: The Free Press (1985)
Schwartz, Peter, *The Art of the Long View*, New York: Doubleday (1991); London: Century Business (1992)

INDEX